Global Enterprise and Private Profits

Javier Ortega and David Shapiro

Global Enterprise and Private Profits

How the Citizens and the Public Interest Are Being Shortchanged

PETER LANG
Lausanne • Berlin • Brussels • Chennai • New York • Oxford

Library of Congress Cataloging-in-Publication Control Number: 2023017971

Bibliographic information published by the **Deutsche Nationalbibliothek.**
The German National Library lists this publication in the German
National Bibliography; detailed bibliographic data is available
on the Internet at http://dnb.d-nb.de.

Cover design by Peter Lang Group AG

ISBN 9781636671802 (paperback)
ISBN 9781636671819 (ebook)
ISBN 9781636671826 (epub)
DOI 10.3726/b20913

Published by Peter Lang Publishing Inc., New York, USA
info@peterlang.com - www.peterlang.com

This publication has been peer reviewed.

To Lourdes and Mariana

To Susan, Emily Rose, and Ari

Contents

List of figures

List of tables

About the authors

Javier Ortega is an Argentinean lawyer, professor of Criminal Law and Public Policies Law at the Universidad Nacional de Avellaneda and the Universidad Nacional de Lanús. He has a master's degree in Latin American Economic Development, a doctorate in Public Law and Government Economics, and another doctorate in Political Science. Javier Ortega has extensive experience as a private attorney in the public sector, directing his practice on the legal regulation of the economy. As a writer, he has published "External Debt and the Restoration of the Rule of Law," a study of the legal regime applicable to the indebtedness of Latin American countries, as well as the effects of transgressions therein. He has also written "El SegomontoTardío" and "Lithiumland," novels in which he uses the cover of fiction to expose the institutional dynamics of plundering of the rights and privileges of citizenship. From Tucumán, he lives in Buenos Aires, and this is his first book published in English.

David Shapiro is a professor at the John Jay College of Criminal Justice, a senior college within the City University of New York. He has a master's degree in business administration and a Juris Doctor degree in law. David Shapiro has experience in the public and private sectors, focusing on fraud examination, financial forensics, and inspection and oversight. He has written two books: "The Gig Mafia: How Small Networks and High-Speed Digital Funds Transfers Have Changed the Face of Organized Crime" and "Applications of Accounting Information Systems." Specifically, his experience is comprised of work as a public prosecutor, criminal and corporate investigator, public accountant, and management consultant. In brief, his career has been a long journey of exposing the reality hidden in the words. He lives in the New York City metropolitan area.

Acknowledgments

My thanks to all my UNDAV's students for their enthusiasm in this learning that asks for more of Law. To Gabriel Delgado, Luciano Zarich and their team, for having chosen me to defend the Argentine State. To Carlos Cheppi, Omar de Leon, Antonio Palazuelos, and José Déniz for guiding me throughout the years. To Aldo Casella, Sergio Arelovich, Carloncho Zamboni, Sebastián Spiller, Irene Gandolla, and Peky Monzón, the six musketeers who fought with me in Reconquista city. To Father Paco for blessing us in difficult times. To Edgardo Ruibal, Andrés Devoto, and Fabian Musso, for their indispensable contributions from Corporate Law, Criminal Procedural Law, and Criminal Law. To Claudio Casparrino, Nestor Leone, José Slimobich, and Mario Bianchi, who taught me that economy, politics, psychology, and psychiatry are a single complex. To my colleagues from INTA who explained the intricacies of agricultural industry. To Raúl Zaffaroni, magnanimous teacher for those of us who believe in Social Justice as something inseparable from the Rule of Law. And finally, to David Shapiro, for his generosity in inviting me as a co-author of this work, for teaching me

Anglo-Saxon Law, and opening the doors of John Jay Criminal College, whose staff I also thank for the hospitality they have shown me.

I, David Shapiro, extend unlimited gratitude to Javier Ortega for his intellectual courage and dedication to real justice. The examination of VICENTÍN provides the world with an understanding of what's going on: who is benefiting and who is not. I give a shout-out to family (humans Susan, Emily Rose, and Ari, as well as felines Otos and Ephialtes). This project would not have been possible without the explicit and implicit support of so many professionals, academics, and colleagues with whom I have been fortunate to work and from whom to learn. Seeing the world for what it is is worth the effort: live, learn, and commit to justice!

Preface

These lines are written at a time characterized by material contradictory data. Regarding COVID-19, while the World Bank speaks of the worst economic crisis in the last 80 years, with a decline in Global GDP[1] of 3.4 percent and with an uncertain and potentially uneven recovery, the ten richest people on the planet doubled their fortunes—making profits at the rate $15,000 per second during the pandemic (Ahmed, 2022). Some fortunes have grown more during the COVID-19 pandemic than in the last 14 years prior to COVID-19. How can it be possible that in a world that is producing less there is a comparatively slim minority that gets richer?

The apparent contradiction in this panorama may be understood if we take the theoretical framework of inequality in the market economy addressed by, among other authors, Thomas Piketty. After an effort to review and reconcile statistical information from several countries, the French author concluded that what characterized the 21st century is the rate of return (earnings in relation to invested capital) greater than

1 Gross Domestic Product.

the growth of production; i.e., earnings growth exceeds productivity. Specific enterprise profit is not directly and invariably contingent on broadly measured growth in the political economy: some parts bulge; some parts stay more or less the same; some parts shrink considerably.

Inequality, as well as the unsustainability of the underlying ideological regime in the long-term,is to be explained by the so-called rise of patrimonial capitalism, under which the economy is dominated by the wealth accumulated in the past and transmitted hereditarily according to rule of law. Under this regime, the enhancement of preexisting wealth is a dominant priority in the political economy. Innovation, productivity, and the creation of new goods and services that may improve the quality of life in general, if they do not serve the dominant priority, are given secondary consideration where considered at all. This prioritization shares conceptual relevance with what some Marxist authors call "rentier capitalism," which focuses on obtaining benefits through, among other practices, the imposition of interest payable (cf. usury) on debt and rent for use of land (a natural fixed resource). These and similar extractive practices limit industrial production of goods and services, as well as impair the general welfare, through the extraction and distribution of wealth from producers not arising directly from the production of goods and services. This is a form of private (rentier) taxation benefiting the capitalist (extractive) class—those owning and controlling the means necessary to produce goods and services—at the expense of the productive class (e.g., laborers). This evidences a regime with features of idleness and parasitism. (Harvey, 2014)

We posit that finance and financial managerialism has become in material respects less a function of neutral intermediation and support for the facilitation of the exchange of goods and services and more a function that extracts profits (presently generated and future earnings) realized in the political economy through production and work. Every time the merchants of finance absorb more than what the real economy materially produced or is capable of producing tomorrow, crisis and potential insolvency ensue. Debt overhang strangles the real economy. (Locke & Spencer, 2011).

Financial managerialism has peculiarities, methods, and cycles in its practice that, when considered alongside traditional modes of capital accumulation known as original accumulation and accumulation by reproduction, suggest a revised modern process of capital concentration should be added: accumulation of capital by financial, legal, and contractual extraction independent of the production of necessary goods and services. The tail is wagging the dog.

The objective of this work is not the specific study of the concentration and centralization of capital through finance. Nevertheless, it does offer an overview of how the regime of obtaining profits without useful, commensurate material production creates its own institutionalism, formal and informal, to reproduce itself and enhance its own dominant position in the political economy at the expense of real production of goods and services. The practice and role of financial managerialism in the biased and self-serving allocation of capital to the capitalists are examined.

Accumulation, centralization, and prioritization of capital without real production does not contravene the established legal order. Following Guy Standing (2017), the rule of law developed within and enforced through the State may protect and strengthen the dominant position of financial capital. Indeed, they do so. Individual liberties and the State's law enforcement, regulatory, and criminal justice systems are all affected by the dominance of finance capital in the political economy. These effects are not neutral but biased in favor of capital at the expense of the opportunities available to the undercapitalized for mature development (e.g., available and affordable health care, higher education, and shelter).

We analyze one of those cases, one that was chosen for the following reasons: its importance for the economy of a country; the problems it poses for the public policy of its government; its international implications, and the special access to information that we have had as academics and professionals intimate with the details and evidence.

One of the authors of this book resides in Argentina, the end of the world according to Pope Francis, and the material epicenter where the events of the case occur, which justifies its centrality in the subject matter of this book. The other author resides in the New York City metropolitan area. Far away geographically, but when one goes through the judicial files of the Argentine cities of Reconquista, Rosario, and

Buenos Aires, Wall Street financial entities appear everywhere as the nodes through which financial flows passed, as well as invoking the legal regime (the jurisdiction of the U.S. and the venue of New York City) in support of finance capital. The inspirations of the American author were born in the essential consultations that his Argentine colleague had to make to him—a set of facts, practices, and patterns that, while especially inimical to the general welfare of Argentineans, are not unique to Argentina.

This manuscript aspires to articulate and expose this exploitative and extractive fact pattern. Consciousness of the fact pattern is necessary to understand the legal and financial cross-border phenomena in which borders only matter to the extent they serve business owners in pursuit of capital through financing arrangements. Ihering taught us that law is a conflict and struggle. He never said that it should be limited to just one country as this would bias the scales of justice. The proper lens of interpretation of the material adverse effects of financial managerialism and modern finance capital is global—cross-border and inclusive (i.e., the interested parties are not limited to the profit and gainextractors but are extended to the alienated society at large that must live with capital flight and offshore hoarding of capital).

Chapter 1

The power of finance

Finance creates the possibility to control what others own and sell what is not yet in existence.

Keywords: financialization, value capture, extravagant earnings, unlogical fictions

1.1. Synthesis

The question we all ask ourselves: How does finance create value and what kind of value is it? In brief, the value is monetary and represented by accounting entries arising from exchange and non-exchange transactions (e.g., underwriting the sale and purchase of goods or services for cash; supporting the imposition and collection of cash due to governmental tax liabilities). Monetary value—the bread and butter of finance—is represented as symbols memorialized in writings (e.g., journals, ledgers), primarily created by and transmitted through electronic pulses (e.g., automated clearing house transfers). The symbols are numerical data, standing for the valuation of rights / obligations to receive from or transfer to counterparties a sum expressed in monetary value. Importantly, symbols such as numerical data are materially different from commodities and services such as potable water and repair and maintenance of heating, ventilation, and air-conditioning systems. Trading and speculating in contracts of fixed / contingent monetary values are materially different activities from harvesting grain and maintaining water pipelines: the former are possible in contemporary society, but the latter are necessary historically and currently to human civilizations.

In this chapter, we will try to explain that finance can create value, but it does not directly, invariably, and immediately create useful goods to satisfy human needs. Hence, we must distinguish between the use value and the exchange value. Use value is the ability of a good to satisfy the needs of the human person. The exchange value is the power of a good to be exchanged for other goods. These functions may overlap. The key point is that finance mediates (cf. brokering the relationship) between buyers and sellers and taxing authorities and taxpayers.

When capitalists produce, they are interested in exchange value. The use value is something that they must consider so that others will desire the goods they produce and want to give something in exchange for it. But if they could dispense with the productive efforts involved in endowing production with use value, the capitalists would do so, assuming a satisfactory level of profitability and gain (cf. casinos). In some cases, finance gives them that opportunity. They can (if they have power) produce assets that would not be facilitators for final material production (as finance should ideally be if focused on benefiting society). These assets have no use value, but through symbolic manipulation, they may be sold profitably. For example, finance can support a market in financial instruments such as derivatives that are separate and apart from the goods represented by the derivatives (e.g., futures contracts requiring the exchange of a commodity such as coffee on a future date). The instrument allows for profitability and gain without requiring the actual production of the commodity such as coffee.

Finance allows the generation of legal instruments (e.g., financial instruments such as derivatives) that independently have exchange value. These legal instruments establish an obligation to give or do something and, due to their legal nature, require counterparties, whether actual or alter ego. However, it may happen that none of these are the ones that must directly produce the underlying commodity and its income stream that will be needed in the long-term to satisfy the commodity-based obligation. Finance may create and trade in artificial instruments that bear no necessary relationship to the production of goods and services; in this sense, finance is imaginary and symbolic and not natural and tangible.

The issuance of a company's equity interests does not represent its materiality. It is a legal instrument that contingently commits the payment of future dividends that have not been earned (or return of past earnings retained in the company). On the one hand, there is the issuer of the equity interest, which may receive economic benefits immediately once the buyer pays for the company's products and services. Those who must produce the goods and services allowing for the dividend in the future are at economic risk in the short- and long-terms. The workers and administrators of the company have their specific material tasks, however, these workers' and administrators' interests and objectives may diverge from the issuer and its controlling persons: the former are dependent on wages and salaries; the latter are made wealthier through capital gains, dividends, and appreciating stock options.

The initial issuance of equity (i.e., an IPO) or the incurrence of bank debt and bond proceeds as a means of finance allows the issuer / debtor to obtain financial resources that may contribute to the issuer's growth (e.g., additional investment in income-producing assets such as equipment) or the cash proceeds may be used for goals divorced from issuer growth (e.g., equity share buybacks). Finance is at first look neutral, but the use of financial resources is biased according to the controlling persons (e.g., officers and directors).

Finance manages the expectations that there will be sufficient material production in the future to structure and sell a financial instrument in the present that promises to obtain those material benefits that do not exist today. It sells today things that may exist tomorrow. When there is an abuse of this game, overloading the future to satisfy a material production that it will not be able to satisfy, crisis induced by, among other conditions, unsustainable debt over hang ensues. For example, debt overhang will eventually strangle a company that cannot grow quicker and greater than the compounding of interest on unpaid principal.

Obtaining gain (economic benefit) in the financial world is faster, more profitable, and less uncertain than awaiting the profits from agricultural or industrial production. Many capitalists, even when they work in the aforementioned areas, if they can, will venture into the financial world. The uncertainty of the future contributes to prioritizing short-term benefit; something that happened to the VICENTÍN company.

1.2. The financial institutionalism and the obtaining of profits without producing

How are exorbitant material benefits obtained by symbolic / abstract financial transactions? It is a difficult problem to understand in part because academia and social communicators neutralize and naturalize transactions focused on financial assets and liabilities (e.g., transactions speculating in the rise / fall of interest rates) rather than explain in a non-biased manner these phenomena.

Non-heterodox Western academia present and analyze in a neo-classical approach, forgetting and partitioning the contributions of the classical economists. Communicators propagate ideas and public policies supported by principles and models (i.e., the dominant ideological regime) that, while superficially mathematically elegant to the lay person, are deficient in explanatory power and truth-value when applied to practice and effects in the real economy. The map is not the territory.

Ideas and policy prescriptions such as legal certainty, lower taxes on capital, and globalizing labor cost reduction opportunities are represented as essential to producing more goods and services for the individuals, households, businesses, and governments served by / serving the market. Metaphors are created and disseminated that conceal more than they reveal about the relationship between speculative finance and the real economy of goods and services to support society at large. For example, reference to speculative finance as a "great global casino" where fortunes are made by gambling is dissemblance. Nothing is less like a casino than speculative finance, unless the financier is seen as the owner of the casino but also a player that has all of the dice loaded and cards marked. The unexamined purpose and effect of the casino metaphor is to misunderstand speculative finance, presenting it as a game characterized by a level playing field with equal opportunity for all to become financially secure and thrive. In fact, opportunities are limited by one's credit line and disposable income, as well as one's social network (e.g., persons with political / bureaucratic / economic power and influence) and material infrastructure (e.g., high-speed computers) specifically and exclusively available to the well-capitalized speculator. Moreover, speculators and traders are terms composed in reality of commingled investors that are misleadingly presented as a monolithic-aggregated class (e.g., speculators in derivative instruments such as credit default swaps have financial interests that may significantly differ from investors with long equity positions saving for retirement).

In a capitalist society, material human needs are satisfied through the production and exchange of commodities (e.g., food, water, shelter) and services (e.g., health care, higher education). With higher productivity and better distribution of goods and necessary services, the standard of living of people (i.e., their general welfare) is theoretically expected to improve.

The exchange transaction as one of the bases of social organization in capitalism depersonalizes social relations. Men and women do not interact directly with each other, except under the rules of the exchange transaction. For example, the baker who produces the piece of bread on the table is paid for it with money received from the purchaser's vocation (e.g., selling smartphones). The relationship is impersonal generally and mediated by money generally.

A commodity can be a material thing, or it can be the hours of work that a person sells (i.e., blood, sweat, and tears). The exchange between commodities (be it objects or hours of work) is the predominant method of social relations in capitalism. In this regime, there are inequalities and subordinations of some individuals in relation to others. These inequalities and subordinations are structured, reproduced, and deepened through the exchanges of goods and services. A smartphone is more expensive than a piece of bread. Whoever produces one will have an advantage over the one who produces the other; the inequality will be reflected in the exchange. The exchange values of commodities and labor vary intra and inter groups, resulting in rankings and hierarchies that elevate or impair one's position.

An underappreciated fact of capitalism: it may be more profitable (e.g., lower costs of distribution) to sell a large quantity of one item (e.g., gallons of fresh water) to one buyer (e.g., an individual that can afford to hoard) than to sell this same quantity to many individuals, many of whom may urgently need this commodity for survival. This profit-seeking fact of manufacture and distribution results in material inequality, as well as higher costs to the buyers that cannot afford to hoard and whose existences may depend on the affordability of the commodity, e.g., real estate.

Evaluation of capitalism and its effects on society at large and the general welfare through macroeconomic measures as GDP presents a misleading assessment as capitalists themselves evaluate their efforts according to measures such as gain and profitability, which are generally based on the legal reporting entity's (e.g., corporation's) results of operations. Lower labor costs imply higher profits. As these results are self-reported by the entities, with some independent checks on performance exist (e.g., external auditors), accuracy of measurement is subject to bias.

1.3. The value of things and people inequality

To carry out the exchange of goods, we need to establish equivalences between them. Why is a smartphone quantitatively more valuable than a piece of bread? Why do I need so many pieces of bread to offset the value of a smartphone? How was that value formulated?

We define value as the power of a good or service to be exchanged for another good or service (e.g., barter transactions) or financial resources (e.g., cash / money). This power is created by and originates from a set of unequal dynamic relationships among people that will later crystallize in the form of a monetary value. The commodity has value that is determined and defined in terms of money,which is an abstract symbol with no direct and inherent material utility (i.e., use value) but is interchangeable for other goods and services in a market-based economy (i.e., exchange value).

The classicists Adam Smith and David Ricardo began to solve the problem of the origin of value. They agreed that the value was in the work applied in the good. The labor added to produce the good was what imparted value. A smartphone requires more work and costly inputs than a piece of bread. But this is not enough to explain the origin of capitalists' profit. In an essential sense, the capitalist is different from the worker who assembled the phone: the capitalists strive to maximize profitability, which is in its simplest form sales revenues less the costs of sales, however the worker presents to the capitalist a necessary (though the development of forms of artificial intelligence makes many workers less necessary) input whose value (e.g., wages, salary) needs to be minimized to maximize profitability. The capitalist and workers' goals diverge structurally and materially.

Marx, the third important classical author discussed in this manuscript, provided a continuation of many theories of Smith and Ricardo, solving the question of where the profit of the capitalist came from. The expenditure of human energy, both physical and intellectual, is work, and this work is what creates value. From the sophisticated coordination of knowledge and skill to transform a complex of materials to produce a smartphone to the simpler tasks of handling flour and water to produce a piece of bread—these indicate transformations of material inputs of production (e.g., sheets of steel, grains) into outputs of value per Marx's analyses. He concludes that work is embedded in the form of exchangeable / marketable commodities. (Marx, 2017).

Work is hours of activity that are bought and sold in the market. The worker sells his labor force as a commodity, so that the labor force in turn produces more commodities derived from and dependent upon the labor. The labor commodity in turn reproduces material commodities. The labor power sold, taking the form of commodity, is separated from the worker as individual. In effect, it is alienated from the worker and processed into the outputs. The worker "sells" his physical and intellectual strength in exchange for a salary. (Dobb, 1938)

Following Ricardo, value originates in work. However, Marx goes one step further and adds a new entity: value originates in work, but this value is reified in another entity that is a commodity. Value is then the reification of labor in a commodity. Value is constituted by work, but it is represented in the production of commodities. The commodity is the resultant form of value (Macias, 2017). Workers make machine tools, which make machines, which make goods, which facilitate the provision of services, and so on. This is the cycle of reproduction and transformation.

The capitalist accumulates value in his/her exchange with labor. The capitalist buys the "labor hour" commodity (sold by the worker) to produce another commodity such as a smartphone. When the employee produces that commodity, the capitalist sells it and gets money, which is yet another commodity but abstract and without inherent / use value, serving as a medium of exchange and store of value. There is another part that the capitalist retains to satisfy his own survival needs—what is left over (the residual value) will be to be used for saving or investment (accumulation of surplus capital). With the accumulated capital, he/she will restart the production process of more telephones, thus gradually increasing the capital he accumulates, so long as the capitalist is profitable. Meanwhile, the employee's salary, if it is low, barely allows him to subsist, not being able to save or invest. Thus, through the exchange of goods, unequal relations are created and hardened.

Karl Marx in *Capital* begins his work by addressing what a commodity is and distinguishing its use value from its exchange value. The commodity has use value if it satisfies a human need and has an exchange value (if it can be swapped for a certain number of other commodities). Additionally, the cycle of production and sale of commodities and services offer the capitalist the opportunity to hoard value (e.g., profits not reinvested in the operations but distributed separately to the capitalist for personal accumulation or spending).

The capitalist does not always care to produce something useful; the capitalist cares about producing something with exchange value. He is not necessarily interested in the qualitative characteristic of the commodity (e.g., whether it satisfies to a material need). He/she is interested in the quantitative characteristic of this commodity (e.g., levels of profitability and gain), which comprises its value in exchange for other commodities. If the capitalist could produce something with exchange value yet without use value and reduce production cost and increase profit, he/she will do so; this happens in the case of financial assets (e.g., financial instruments such as derivatives purchased and sold by financial speculators) exchanged for other financial assets (e.g., cash). In brief, the potential profit drives the cycle of production and not the intrinsic / use value of the product (e.g., cigarettes over bread and butter).

1.4. Finance creating or taking value?

Finance is the branch of the economy that is responsible for the management of symbolic instruments that represent material assets. Primarily, it is money management, including abstract financial assets and financial liabilities such as bonds, securities or stocks (equity instruments), and derivative financial instruments.

Money is a commodity the role of which is to be a general equivalent—a medium of exchange. It works as a mediator of exchange, quantifier, and store of value. It has no intrinsic / use value (i.e., it cannot be directly consumed in satisfaction of human needs and wants). It has only exchange value.[1]

> Money is a commodityand therefore, an embodiment of value. But money differs from all other commodities in that it is equivalent to all of them; that is, the commodity that expresses the value of all of the others. That it has become such is the result of all the processes of change(Hilferding, 1963: 22).

Money represents or stands in for the value of other things, facilitating exchange and non-exchange transactions (e.g., purchase of goods and services and satisfaction of tax liabilities, respectively).

If seen in a superficial way, each symbolic asset of the world of finance would only be a representation of amaterial asset of the real economy to which it is linked. This vision would limit finance to be a mere tool of the exchanges of material goods. Thus, finance should

1 Money is the financial asset that people agree to use as an equivalent measure of value, a means of payment for exchanges between different goods, unit of account, and reserve of value. The national States are those that impose money as legal tender in the exercise of their sovereignty; i.e., what will be the money that will be mandatory legal tender to carry out the transactions of assets within the territory where the respective State exercises jurisdiction. The power of that money will be given by the size and diversification of the national economy that accepts it as a means of payment, and in the strength of the State that designates it as a means of payment for the contributions that in its power of empire fixes as taxes.

be that branch of the economy that deals with the administration of capital, and whose task would be to direct it to the activities that are most effective and efficient in the production of material goods (Stiglitz, 2000); evidence does not show this to be true.

Finance is not only a reference to the value and abstract titles that facilitate the exchange of tangible material goods. Where value originated in the material commodities of the real economy, finances facilitate trading in it. However, experience shows that finance has become a means and an end entirely in itself.

Finance became independent from the real economy to which it referred. Financial instruments are swapped and traded independent of any material goods. If not, we could not explain how by 2020 world debt is 256 percent of Gross World Product. Lenders are lending two-and-a-half times the total value of goods and services that exist in the world (Gaspar, 2021). It seems that someone is lending something that they do not actually possess. Financial derivatives[2] are around tentimes the value of the Gross World Product. Someone is linking many things that do not exist to a few things that, in reality, do.

The distinctions of the types of finance may be simplified as follows: finance that directly supports the production of goods and services would be comprised of additions of cash to the investee-producer (accounting debits to assets) and its concomitant obligation to the investor (accounting credits for debt / equity). Finance that supports speculation for profit implicates accounting debits (financial assets) and accounting credits (financial liabilities) to and from institutions / counterparties that trade these rights and obligations without producing the necessities of life (e.g., food, water, shelter). They are more like wagers than investments.

2 A financial derivative is an abstract instrument whose value is tied to the price of another asset. The asset on which the financial derivative depends is called the underlying asset. The underlying asset can be a commodity such as gold, and the derivative will increase based on the price of the metal. Or the derivative can in turn be tied to another abstract asset. A CEDEAR (Argentine Certificates of Deposit) links its price to the quotation of a share (another abstract instrument) of a company in the United States.

A commodity can have a material utility and an exchange value. That it has a material utility is almost "a necessary evil" for the capitalist, since his/her purpose when he/she produces something is not to solve a material problem but rather to sell the product to accumulate exchange value (Macias, 2017). In a sense, capitalism is the private ordering of economic activities that need not be ranked according to their contribution to the general welfare: what is highly profitable may be acceptable notwithstanding its adverse effects on the general welfare (e.g., expensive private health care, private jet travel).

To understand capitalism, we must understand that the production of wealth in the form of useful things that improve people's lives is a secondary effect (if not lower) of the dominant social relationships through which value is generated. These social relations of production are unequal relations, since they are made up by capitalist owners of the means of production and crammed down on workers who have only their blood, sweat, and tears to sell. There is a hierarchical ranking: those who dominate, and others who are dominated. From this relational inequality, a material object is produced. The fact that it has utility is something that does not matter to the dominant person who owns the capital. He just wants to sell it. He is interested only in its exchange value (i.e., what it will bring the capitalist in return—the cycle of production for profit does not imply production supportive of material welfare). We insist with the clarity of Alfredo Macias's concept that the utility of the good is "a necessary evil." The value is not inherent in the thing. The value is in the exchange (i.e., what it brings in return). Value is in the relationship of one thing to another. In capitalism, relationships between people are operationalized through the intermediation of goods and services: relationships are transactional. Like any relationship, there is power and direction in it.

1.5. Capitalism: An immaterial kingdom

Power is not owned. Power is exercised. Power is dynamic and moves in the relationships of one person with another. It is not inside the person himself. It is in the relational bond of that person with the other.

As in any relationship, there is always one person who exercises power and another who resists it (Foucault, 1991).

In this way, we arrive at the concept that capital is not matter. Capital is something abstract. Capital is a relationship between one person and another, mediated, and objectified in a commodity. If the commodity is a thing, the capitalist will be the owner. If the goods are hours of labor, the capitalist will be the boss. Capital is a concept summarizing the monetary value of what one owns and controls against the remainder of the world. It is exclusionary in nature.

This relationship, which is capital, puts the capitalist in a position to demand behavior from another as the lender demands payments from the debtor, or the employer demands work from the employee. However, capital is neither the "commodity credit" nor the "commodity hour of labor." Capital is the power that enables the capitalist to direct others to meet his/her objective. Let others do what he says to do. Capital is the possibility of imposing will. We must then read capital as both a relation and an abstract thing.

Capitalism hides behind and within objects, concretizing the social relations of domination. Capital is an abstract relation and expression of domination reified in a material thing.

To understand capital as a set of goods or services that are useful to satisfy human needs, such as activities or material things that help the survival or well-being of people, is to glean only a part of how financial capitalism generates value: exchanges of intangible assets memorialized in writings such as bonds, stocks, currencies, or derivatives are an entirely different domain for financial capitalism's growth. The writings may be in the form of paper (e.g., bearer bonds); they may be digital such as electronic impulses that carry symbolic information through a virtual network.

How can financial capitalism generate value between abstract and symbolic exchanges that do not satisfy needs for nutrition, shelter, and habitat?

Value is nothing more than a social relationship crystallized (for a period) in a good or service that is traded in the market (commodity). The commodity does not contain the value itself. The value is in the social relationships that constituted that commodity. Value is dynamic, not static like the matter that makes up the commodity. Value relations continue operating on this commodity after its production. The value is variable and manipulable. It changes as the social relations that constitute it fluctuate and transform it.

Relationships that happen between subjects are not equal where there is a subject that dominates and another that is dominated. In capitalism that domination is not direct like that of the lord and his servant in feudalism. In capitalism, this domination is mediated impersonally through commodities. In a sense, one's place and rank is commensurate with what one can buy and the amount of financial credit that one can command.

Finance realizes the dream of the capitalist as an empowering subject over objects.The power to give orders despite of producing nothing. Finance can create value that does not have to be reified into a material good or service. It is value as a product of unequal social relations in its pure state. Finance as elevated by rule of law and priority of public policies comprises a web in which subservience is imposed on many without their invariable receipt of sufficient consideration and stability in return (e.g., a missed payment may obligate the debtor to leave his/her premises notwithstanding decades of compliance with the terms of the debt instrument). The rights and obligations of creditors and debtors are not equal, balanced, and fairly reciprocal. Who owns and controls the capital in a capitalist regime significantly influences the rule and implementation of law and public policy.

1.6. Travel through space-time

Everything we saw above collides with our common sense, in which we have been raised, trained, and educated throughout our lives. We grew up as three-dimensional beings. And one fine day, we confront the fourth dimension: the fourth dimension is time. Time flows differently, depending on the situation and the speed of the observer.

Something similar happens with finances. While for the real economy, everything happens in three dimensions and seems to be limited to present goods and services of a three-dimensional world, finance moves through four-dimensional time. And it can operate in the present with assets that are not there today but that (perhaps) will exist in the future. Time flows differently in finance (e.g., the compounding of interest payable on debt).

Let's look at two concrete examples of how finance does not refer to the three-dimensional material world but moves independently of it.

Classical economic theory holds that interest is a part of the increase in profit that the capitalist obtained when he invested the money he received from a moneylender, increasing his production thanks to the loan. That is, the businessman bought more equipment, with which he manufactured more and better articles that he sold, obtaining greater profits. Part of earnings will be sent, as interest, to the lender who allowed him to make the investment. This explains where the surplus that is paid to the lender came from.

But transactions with a sovereign (e.g., underwriting a bond for the ostensible benefit of the sovereign) are different from for-profit ventures common in the private sector. Governments do not look for profits. Their goal is the well-being of its citizens. When a person buys a sovereign bond from the government (a method that the government uses to finance itself, to borrow money), the government does not use the amount to increase its productivity. Even if it did so, for example, by investing in schools to improve the population's preparation and achieve greater technical capacities, it would be an investment that would only begin to increase the community's productivity after decades.

Generally, the debts that the government assumes are used to remediate fiscal deficit problems (Macias, 2017). Or in countries like Argentina to obtain foreign currency to import things. Or sustaining luxury consumption and tourism abroad. Or servicing debt. Or financing capital flight from individuals (Basualdo, 2018). Nothing that improves productivity.

Sovereign bonds are not a loan that directly generates an increase in production from which the surplus will come out to pay interest. Payments will come from taxes to be paid by the citizens of the country that issued the bond. (Hilferding, 1963). Productivity runs separately from financial management.

In the case of companies that make a public offering of their shares, something similar happens. The symbolic capital of the shares runs in parallel with the tangible assets that make up the firm. It is practically independent. Otherwise, we could not explain how the share capital of Amazon, a mega-messenger that applies a technology that can be understood by any computer science student, is worth six times than automaker Toyota. What a thing, what an enterprise, what an asset is worth—these questions are not necessarily related to the general survival value of the goods and services produced. Value is contingent on financial managerialism (e.g., earnings management).

The share of a company does not represent its materiality as its infrastructure and technology. The stock only embodies the contingent rights to obtain a fraction of the dividends that the firm is expected to produce in the future (Hilferding, 1963). A contingent right to cash drawn against expected future earnings (or the prospect of capital gains from the secondary market, including subsequent stock buyouts by the issuer).

Finance allows the capitalist to generate value without producing. As the future is open-ended and subject to many influences, corrupt and/or well-meaning, it serves as an intangible, unrealized venue in which one can imagine accretions to value that are chimerical and fraudulent.

1.7. Generating value from value-less production

The capitalist can, through commodification (i.e., creating and exploiting markets for goods and services characterized by unequal relationships), exercise his/her power to demand that other subjects carry out certain behaviors that he will use. In a society with onerous exchanges and a sophisticated division of labor, the well-capitalized are at the top of the social pyramid. They are the ones who have the power to demand that others do things for them by requiring the financing and paying of money for necessary material resources.

The influential capitalist manufacturer of fashion cosmetics is not powerful because of the importance of cosmetics to satisfy vital needs of the human being. He/she is powerful for the exchange value of his production, which allows him/her to demand that others carry out certain behaviors for his benefit. Cosmetics are not terribly important, but the capitalist uses these goods to obtain the exchange value that allows him/her to buy the behaviors that he uses (e.g., others' labor).

Finance allows the capitalist to jump one stage: the capitalist can produce things that have only exchange value. It is not a fictitious value, since the value originates in a series of unequal social relations of subordination, especially command-and-control vis-à-vis the cycle of production that characterizes market economies. Only these relationships no longer necessarily created a commodity with use value (e.g., food and water). They now often create a commodity that has only exchange value (e.g., financial instruments). There is an uneven pathway from the production of useful goods and services that directly support society such as health care to the production of frivolous goods and services such as cosmetics to the production of financial assets and liabilities such as mortgages and derivatives that result in an informal (social position) and formal (legal) hierarchy of creditors and debtors.

The pinnacle of the capitalist's aspirations is financial assets. A vehicle that creates value without manufacturer's costs (materials, time, and wages). A financial asset is a symbol that can be expressed in a title, a byte or a record in a database (e.g., intellectual property such as copyrights). It gives its owner the right to demand a benefit from another person within a specified period of time. It is pure abstraction. It is a legal fiction organizing how legal benefits (e.g., the creditor's right to receive cash) and legal detriments (e.g., the debtor's obligation to pay cash) are allocated among members of society, ultimately resulting in divisions of members into who can afford to thrive in the long-term and who can barely afford to live in the short-term.

The owner of a private financial asset can ask another person for a specific behavior.That other person is the counterparty that appears in that financial asset, which can be a promissory note, a stock, a sovereign bond. The holder is to be able to demand compliance with the legally prescribed conduct (e.g., the payment of principal, interest, dividends, royalties, license fees, and so on).

Financial instruments are nothing other than contractual forms that regulate rights and obligations between the issuer and the borrower. It will also regulate behaviors of third parties that have nothing to do with the contract. There are main effects on the contracting parties and spillover effects on society at large (e.g., what gets financed is not neutrally determined by society—these decisions are dominated by financial gain seekers in a diseased web of profit contagion). In a sense, globalization of markets is the functional equivalent of a pandemic of profitcontagion (a key concept and theory more fully developed in Chapter 2 of this monograph, however it signifies not merely the overarching quest for profits characteristic of for-profit entities but the obsession with efficiency and cost / expense reduction observable in not-for-profit entities, including public sector agencies).

With these instruments, finance can create value without it being tied to an immediate material anchor in the present. An anchor made up of a thing that has some use to satisfy a need. Liberated of all material ballast, finances are more versatile, agile, and faster. They move in four dimensions, managing time, while the real economy, tied to the present, is anchored in three. That is why, for us three-dimensional beings, it seems that finance creates things out of nothing; they create profit out of nothing itself with the manipulation of values unrealized in the present. They transfer the unrealized consequences of current profit-taking to the future. Consequences that may burden societies with debt overhang and distorted priorities and preferences. See the figure below.

The concreteness of the present is weighted down and constricted by the artificiality and legal enforceability of financial assets and liabilities that have been developed by profit-seekers to command and control in the present and the future under a regime of capitalists' rights bearing down on debtors' obligations. The overwhelming majority of society's members have their degrees of freedom (and associated opportunity to develop) constrained by debt overhang.

When financial activity is carried out uncontrollably, it commits the future to a productivity that it may not be able to materially satisfy. To demonstrate, we use the algebraic equation F = P / T, where "F"

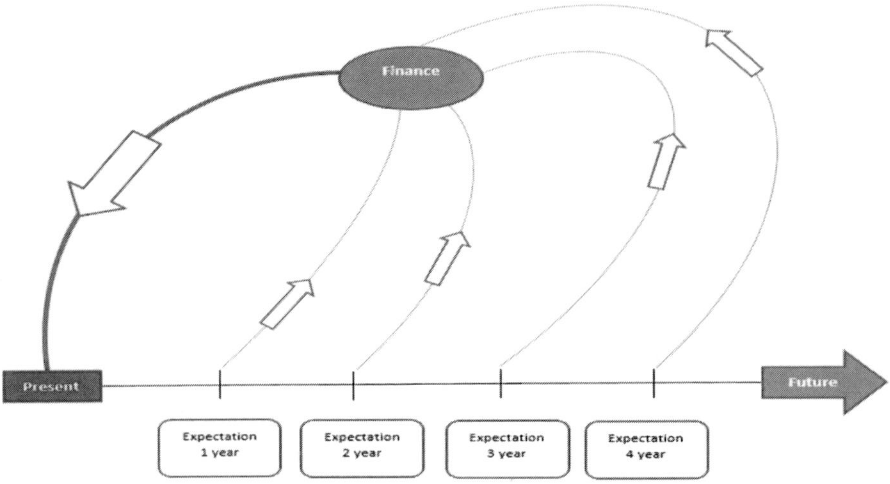

Figure 1.1: Playing with the time.
Prepared by the author

is financial utility, "P" is material productiveness, and "T" is the time demanded by this productivity.

If F < P / T, we can conclude that with more trade, the economy would grow more quickly. But is F>P /T, it means that material goods have not been produced with sufficient speed to support financial gains. There will be a crisis.

Financial activity can create a financial product. For example, Bond "A" stipulates that in the future (within 1, 2, 3, 4, or more years), it will pay interest. That is the expectation for the future because this money today does not exist. See Figure 1.1. But the bond sells just the same with the promise. And what is more, since finance moves through the fourth dimension, the buyer of the bond does have to wait 4 years to make money from that issue. This is because he can sell it (at the same time) in the secondary market to another person. He can sell this Bond A and get money in the present. Bond A is not mature yet, however is already giving profits by trading in expectations. However, profitability and gain through trading in financial instruments has real costs in the present that are not borne by the traders (i.e., they are externalized to society at large such as pollution, unsafe water, unaffordable health care, and so on). The conduct is driven by profit contagion and not human development generally (or even locally).

1.8. Big trees and fragile trunks

Finance has created value in the present without producing a material commodity that serves to satisfy current real needs. Depending on the power dynamics of the different social subjects in the game, the future bonus payment embedded in expectations may increase or decrease. According to these fluctuations (rational or manipulated), Bond A can be resold innumerable times in the secondary market at a higher or lower price. If it is higher, value is continued to be created in an immaterial way. It's not real, tangible, material value but speculative financial value (e.g., so-called paper gains).

In turn, from this Bond A, new financial products can be created. The bondholder can use Bond A as financial collateral,[3] and issue from this sub-series of bonds financial derivatives. Thus, it will be able to issue sub-Bond A.1, sub-Bond A.2, and sub-Bond A.3, all of which will have the original Bond A as backing and guarantee in the event that A.1, A.2, and A.3 do not pay. Value continues to be created without having to manufacture anything material that meets people's food, clothing, shelter, and health requirements.

For example, when someone happens to bet against Bond A and the possibilities that it pays or does not pay what is stipulated in the future—in this way another financial derivative is created, bought, and sold as insurance against cessation of payments (i.e., credit default swaps). This contract, which is an insurance-like financial instrument, is traded in the market / over the counter as if it were another security from which speculators seek profits and gains from the work and labor of others. One can speculate and trade these derivative instruments without having any insurable interest (e.g., naked default swaps). They

3 Collateral is a financial asset that is taken as security for a loan. When a subject takes a credit in money, he can grant the lender a mortgage, for example, which is a financial and legal interest in real estate as a guarantee that he will return what he borrowed.

are the equivalent of gamblers who bet for or against someone else's horse. Financial value continues to be created without anything material that is useful. Today's general health, welfare, and related materials' needs recognized at the level of society's members are sacrificed at the altar of possible future gain by those who can afford to speculate currently (a slim minority of individuals).

The sub-prime mortgage crisis in the United States took place on this logic. Based on the real activity of the construction and sale of homes for families, a series of financial instruments was structured without correlation with the materiality of the business. Mortgages first appeared to finance the housing, then guaranteed mortgage title insurance appeared, and loan titles were guaranteed with these mortgages (e.g., mortgage-backed securities). These titles were collateral for other papers and other financial loans; on these, default insurance was issued.

A heavy tree structure supported on the flimsy trunk of the reality. This reality is that the housing business did not have enough demand and profitability to sustain itself. Debts that cannot be repaid will not be repaid. The price of housing was inflated by the easiness of credit available to the creditors (e.g., quantitative easing policies of the U.S. central bank trickling down), facilitating the development of socially useless financial activities enabling short-term profits for speculators. However, these activities drove up the price of housing, exceeding what the wages of the debtors could support in the medium-term.

And this is how crises in the financial system happen. Recharging and overloading the future with profit expectations that reality cannot and will not provide (cf. the Minsky moment). At some point, the disconnection of the truth with the illusion induced by the financial capitalist bubble becomes self-evident, with reality takes revenge on fantasy, and debt overhang becoming the noose of strangulation for the undercapitalized.

According to specialists from the United States Federal Reserve, 10 years after the 2008 sub-prime crisis events, the capital loss for each American citizen that had a stake in the crisis ranged around $70,000. (in the aggregate, approximately $2.3 trillion) (Barnichon, 2018). An amount arguably seven times enough to implement the global zero hunger initiative by 2030 as outlined bythe United Nations Food Organization using calculations estimated by the International Food Policy Research Institute. (Fan, 2018)

1.9. Conclusions

Finance is an institutional framework of symbols that allows for trading in the present material assets that are expected to exist at some point in the future. Finance obligates actors in the real economy so they produce tomorrow to cover what the empowered actors of the financial economy enjoy today. In effect, public policy (e.g., bailouts of creditors!) is significantly influenced, if not materially controlled, by speculators that create markets for financial instruments divorced from the duty to support the general welfare. Resources are allocated according to the application of the rules of profit contagion, a game in which few can participate meaningfully.

A financial instrument is a legal product with the capacity to regulate the rights and obligations of those who enter into contract under its terms and conditions, as well as third parties unrelated to it; these third parties will have to produce in the future the material surplus symbolically traded currently between those parties of the agreement. Future rights and obligations of individuals unrelated to the financial instruments are expected to conform to the expectations and demands of individuals wagering on the profit and gain probabilities of speculators in the present. Of course, these probabilities are the subject of disagreement for these speculators. They take positions that have spillover effects.

Financial instruments (on some occasions) function as mere extractors of the value produced by third parties. The hierarchy of creditor rights creates a structure supporting the extraction of resources from the legally imposed subservience of debtors through their obligations to creditors, immediate and removed. In effect, an overwhelming majority of society's members are controlled through debt overhang.

When a government issues a sovereign bond, the taxpaying citizens of the issuing State will fund through future taxes the amount of payment for the benefit of the creditor. When a company increases its share capital, it will be its workers who must produce to pay the future dividends promised in the new shares issued. When real production does not support the hyper-demand to extract goods through the agreed-upon financial framework, the real economy experiences a crisis. The government may come to the rescue by bearing the costs (e.g., a bailout of the creditors and/or debtors, with the former, as more influential actors in the political economy, usually receiving priority in the remedial public policies and support systems). Ultimately, the losses are foisted on the taxpayers. (This is a more likely possibility where the government does not have control over its own currency through political incompetence or lack of political will or the debts incurred are denominated in a reserve currency such as U.S. dollars not under the control of the government.)

To make compliance with these extractive finance rules compulsory, the State's power of empire is essential. When neoliberalism calls for less State gravitation, the resulting policies are in essence reductive of protection to the weakest sectors. The strongest (i.e., the well-capitalized) absolutely need the State to sustain such rules of preference and priority. This is only possible with the monopoly of legitimate violence (Weber, 2002), an option that belongs only to the State. Currently, neoliberalism and market economies tend to enact and enforce public policies that are supportive of influential creditors' rights at the expense of debtors and the taxpayers at large. Power in such a political economy is vested in those with the currency and credit to shape and direct it.

Finance allows banks to lend the funds deposited by their clients; to create investment funds; to sell what does not yet exist in futures markets; to create capital from wishful thinking (e.g., initial public offerings of equity); to make a profit by managing something that will generate losses (e.g., short positions in the stock market); to insure against a loss something that is not owned (e.g., derivatives of insurance against default of third-party debts); to market a universal resource without an owner (e.g., quoting water in the futures market); to dominate something which one does not own (e.g., anonymous companies managed by shareholders without possessing a majority of the capital), and so on—a political economy with financialization at its core.

The political economy as a system is rationally developed and executed to meet the demands and expectations of the influential creditor class. This is not to suggest that the creditor class is monolithic (as parties and counterparties, even influential, stand to gain or lose). However, the real priorities are less general welfare than private profitability and economic gain (i.e., profit contagion). The creditors seek the largest gains with the smallest efforts and risk; this is efficiency and effectiveness operationalized for the disproportionate benefit of an oligarchic (and plutocratic) elite.

The rule of law does not embrace the inequitableness of this phenomenon. The norms are individual liberty to do with one's property as one wishes, generally. This legitimizes practices functional for and subservient to real power (Cárcova, 2012; Foucault, 1991). The rule of law is designed and operated like a tool without self-knowledge and reflective capacity. It compartmentalizes rights and obligations based on the influence of a few, without due recognition of the biases and adverse effects of its own making. It is a non-neutral process masquerading as a logical and rational system affecting all equally: to paraphrase Anatole France (1894)—the law forbids the rich as well as the poor from sleeping under bridges and stealing loaves of bread.

Where the rule of law does not intervene with its regulations to avoid economic abuses, which are easy to perpetrate from the manipulable financial system; if the authorities that must apply the rule of law do not operate to prevent the plundering of the work of others, the results would be the promotion of the consolidation, organization, and protection of an unfair status quo.

Discussion and analysis in the last part of this work implicates a professional of financial tricks known in its corporate form as GLENCORE, which, using devices like leverage buyoutsand taking advantage of distressed debtors, took over one of the world's most important processors in soy-crushing—RENOVA, which had formed an essential part of VICENTIN's property.

References

BARNICHON, R., MATTHES, C., and ZIEGENBEIN, A. (2018). *The Financial Crisis at 10: Will We Ever Recover?* Federal Reserve Bank of San Francisco.

BASUALDO, E. -Director- (2018). Endeudar y fugar, Buenos Aires, Siglo XXI.

CÁRCOVA, C., et al. (2012). "Análisis funcional del Derecho", Las Teorías Jurídicas Post Positivistas, Buenos Aires, Abeledo-Perrot.

DOBB, M. (1938). Introducción a la Economía, México. FCE.

FOUCAULT, M. (1991). Microfísica del poder, Madrid, Ediciones de La Piqueta.

FRANCE, A. (2002). "The Law, in Its Majestic Equality, Forbids All Men to Sleep Under Bridges." *Journal of public health policy* 23, no. 4: 501.

GASPAR, V., et al. (2021). Global Debt Reaches a Record $226 Trillion, December 15, 2021, 15 https://blogs.imf.org/2021/12/15/global-debt-reaches-a-record-226-trillion/, Accessed January 5, 2020.

HILFERDING, R. (1963). El Capital Financiero, Madrid, Tecnos.

HOFFMAN, J. (2002). "The State." *Politics review* 12, no. 2: 13–13.

International Food Policy Research Institute. (2018). 2018 Global food policy report. Washington, DC, International Food Policy Research Institute. https://doi.org/10.2499/9780896292970

LOCKE, ROBERT R., and SPENCER, J.-C. (2011). Confronting Managerialism: How the Business Elite and Their Schools Threw Our Lives Out of Balance. 1st ed. London u.a, Zed Books.

MARX, K. (2017). El Capital, Madrid, Siglo XXI.

MACÍAS, A. (2017). El colapso del capitalismo tecnológico, Madrid, Escolar y Mayo.

STIGLITZ, J. E. (2000). "Capital Market Liberalization, Economic Growth, and Instability." *World development* 28, no. 6: 1075–1086.

STIGLITZ, J. (2002). El malestar en la globalización, Buenos Aires, Santillana-Taurus.

Chapter 2

Capital and the puppeteers' strings

In order to subjugate people, Western civilization advanced by substituting the rule of capital for coercion through chains.

Keywords: capital power, managerialism, profit contagion, abusive earnings, impaired welfare

2.1. Synthesis

To some, the idea that the undercapitalized experience the impairment and constriction of their opportunities to develop (e.g., access to high-quality health care, higher education, and an adequate general welfare safety net to mitigate risks such as those pursuant to involuntary unemployment) resulting from a capital-influenced / dominated legal and financial system may seem obvious. To others, the condition of impairment of opportunity may seem an unfortunate but fair result of the system's purported meritocracy—however ill-defined in theory and poorly constructed in practice—(Sandel, 2021). Still others may be uncertain or have other ideas (e.g., salvation through God).

This chapter explores the meaning and application of the term "capital," a concept that is used and interpreted differently in economics (e.g., factors of production) and accounting (e.g., equity in a commercial entity, net asset reserve to absorb losses). In a sense, economists discuss and analyze capital as the productive capacity of the political economy, whereas accountants discuss and analyze capital as a financial interest in a for-profit enterprise (e.g., debt or equity). For the accountant, the productive capacity inherent in capital assets (e.g., property, plant, and equipment) are summarily reported as debits in the permanent accounts of the statement of financial position (i.e., assets on the balance sheet), but the financial interests to which the reporting entity is beholden are disclosed as credits in the permanent accounts of the statement of financial position (i.e., debt as liabilities and capital as equity). In brief, those holding debt and equity interests may directly or indirectly control or significantly influence the productive capacity reflected by the assets.

Capital is a proxy for measurement of control over the entity's policies, procedures, and practices (e.g., a debt holder may exercise more actual control than a holder of an equity interest). Essentially, capital offers current and future material benefit and service potential; i.e., a resource of monetary value. It is memorialized and evidenced in an informational writing (e.g., electronic records, bearer instruments) that allows the controlling person(s) to possess and enjoy it, while also potentially excluding others from exercising dominion and control over it according to the rules of law. Capital is the medium of power in the neoliberal political economy. Generally, it is an object of financial transactions.

Capital is also a proxy for one's ability to obtain credit from lenders, influence over political campaigns, and opportunity in the political economy. In a sense, money (capital) talks and walks: it allows a person to obtain financial resources from his/her own capital investments (e.g., interest receivable, dividends, capital gains) over and above one's value in the workforce (e.g., wages as a physician, attorney, or accountant). Capital allows for unearned income (i.e., income produced by others).

Capital is recognized, disclosed, and measured in the general purpose financial reports of for-profit entities; this is the accountants' / auditors' interpretation of capital. Principles of accounting (e.g., Financial Accounting Standards Board and generally accepted accounting principles – GAAP) and standards of auditing (e.g., Public Company Accounting Oversight Board and generally accepted auditing standards – GAAS) apply. The accountants contribute importantly to the assessment of capital at the entitylevel; the economists contribute importantly to the assessment of capital at the countrylevel (e.g., gross domestic product).

However, at the individual level, capital is monetary value by which to measure by proxy the individual's degrees of freedom (e.g., in which neighborhood and home to reside; at which, if any, institution of higher learning to attend; the extent, if any, of health care to receive, and so on). Essentially, capital is a commonly applied factor to evaluate a given country's competitiveness; an entity's line of credit—marginal capital—with a lender; and an individual's quality of life, depending on the availability of affordable public goods (e.g., subsidized health care, higher education, and social welfare). In brief, the undercapitalized cannot realistically compete with the well-capitalized for any prolonged period (e.g., any one may win one wager, but the casino wins in the long-term).

As a practical matter, capital is monetized (i.e., characterized by having a monetary use and/or exchange value to obtain necessities and luxuries). This chapter comprises a focus on an accountant's perspective of capital. Capital is recognized and measured by agreement among parties (e.g., market values based on sales activities) and/or by assessment of individuals (e.g., specialty appraisers, models based on assumptions and estimates). In the case of sales activity, the value is realized (e.g., a share of equity in a publicly listed corporation is sold for $10,000); in the case of expertized valuations, the value is unrealized (e.g., the model marks the value of a share of equity in a privately held corporation for $10,000). Its monetary value is not fixed but variable under social and commercial processes that may appear rational such as model-based evaluations or appear irrational such as speculative frenzies and asset bubbles.

In the short-term, differentiating between rational and irrational processes of valuation may not matter much (e.g., exchange for money and run); in the medium- and long-terms, it does (e.g., retirement savings and purchasing power may deflate significantly in value). Essentially, capital is monetarily valuable so long as it can obtain goods and services necessary and desirable for living well (or at all). Its use and exchange values merge, and it should not be examined independently of the social context referred to herein as the political economy (i.e., collectively, the public and private sectors). An individual's store or share of capital ranges widely as follows (though with a few well-capitalized and most under- or barely capitalized):

- From having a deficit (i.e., in the position of a net debtor after accounting for all of one's assets and liabilities – the undercapitalized);
- To having none (i.e., in the position in which the valuation of one's liabilities is approximately equivalent to the value of one's assets – the barely capitalized);
- To having a surplus of capital (i.e., in the position of a net creditor, the surplus of which may vary greatly – from having savings to having millions and millions).

In practice, the story of capital is a long, complex set of events composed of debtors and creditors under rule of law (or caprice / chaos / rule of might, in the absence of law). The field of conflict resolution is unequal (e.g., superior access to participants, such as powerful lawyers, essential in the administration of the rule of law is an opportunity for the well-capitalized; ability to influence lawmakers and law-enforcers is significantly more of an opportunity for the well-capitalized than the undercapitalized). Unsurprisingly, the creation of the rules of law and outcomes thereunder are also biased in favor of the well-capitalized.

Capital is a proxy for whom controls or significantly influences the course of conduct of modern society. It is a relationship between persons (natural and artificial) and their things (tangible and intangible property), recognized, measured, and disclosed (if at all in the case of tax havens and secrecy jurisdictions) in monetary values. However, these relationships are not consistently transparent. For instance, the well-capitalized may act as undisclosed principal for the shadow actors (e.g., legislators, lobbyists).

In its simplest accounting terms: capital is a monetarily valued credit against a monetarily valued asset. For example, the purchase of a 10,000 shares of equity capital for $10,000 is recorded as follows by the entity:

- Debit cash received in the amount of $10,000, and
- Credit paid-in capital in the amount of $10,000.

Herein, the power of having the legal capacity and privilege to issue and create currency may be considered. For example, a commercial bank would record the following journal entries upon loaning $10,000 to a customer:

- Debit loan receivable – customer A in the amount of $10,000, and
- Credit depositor liability – customer A in the amount of $10,000.

Thus, debt capital is held by the customer, whose net assets (total asset value less total liability value) have not increased. But for the fees and charges levied against the customer, the bank's net assets would not have increased. In reality, the customer would pay fees, which would lower its net assets, and the bank would receive fee income, which would increase its net assets.

An overview of the interaction of types of financial capital with the world is noted below in Table 2.1.

Table 2.1: An outline of the role of financial capital in the political economy.

Financial Capital	Debt	Equities	Derivatives
Well-capitalized persons	Opportunities to save & invest globally	Opportunities to save & invest globally	Opportunities to speculate globally
Public sector	Borrow at the risk of creating debt overhang in society	Unavailability (except indirectly in public–private partnership)	Opportunities to hedge against financial risk
Private sector	Principal means of obtaining shelter & transportation (e.g., loans)	Opportunities primarily limited to institutional investors (e.g., mutual funds)	Risk of loss ordinarily prohibitive for all but well-capitalized (only low-risk, low-return investments available)

Prepared by the author

Thus, capital is largely a specialized instrumentality for use as an asset by the well-capitalized to influence the undercapitalized, for whom it is primarily a liability. The well-capitalized invest; the undercapitalized finance. For most, capital is a liability without which public and private goods and services (e.g., public projects and programs administered by the public sector as well as developmental opportunities such as higher education and necessities such as medical care available to the private sector) could not be enjoyed. In a sense, the well-capitalized finance (where they elect to do so at all) on a for-profit basis the development of most of the remainder of the public and private sectors. The result is an investor-centered and influenced society and political economy.

2.2. Obtaining and accumulating capital

As capital is in all material respects (especially, under jurisdictions that do not require by rule of law or otherwise a sufficient level of public goods as noted above), a primary factor affecting one's capacity to thrive; live; or, if lacking, perish (i.e., capital's effects are long-term; medium-term; and short-term), obtaining sufficient or even adequate capital is a preeminent focus of individuals (e.g., getting a job to get money to pay the rent).

Some persons have significant amounts of capital (e.g., savings in banks, investments in equity portfolios). Others have only their labor to offer to obtain capital. Initially, having significant capital is the surest way to accumulate capital as the costs of living (e.g., health, education, shelter, food, and other necessary expenses in support of one's welfare) exceed the wages of most, requiring the incurrence of debt (e.g., car loans, mortgages, student loans) to raise one's labor value in the workforce (e.g., becoming a professional). Being capitalized under a system characterized by unequally distributed surplus value is having the use and exchange values of an excess of assets, especially money. Colloquially, being capitalized is functionally equivalent to being wealthy and/or receiving a comparatively high income. It is indeed a state of being separate, apart, and above the state of the undercapitalized noted above.

One may become transformed from being capitalized to being undercapitalized through many courses of conduct and circumstances. For instance, one may speculate in financial instruments well beyond one's means—obtaining margin credit to borrow exorbitantly—and lose. Assuming the lack of a public sector bailout, the person becomes undercapitalized. Alternatively, public sector taxation progressive taxation schemes may redistribute the well-capitalized surplus. This indicates why influence over the legislation and enforcement of laws, regulations, and rules is essential for the well-capitalized preservation of his/her position. No one wants to be undercapitalized.

While capital is an abstraction, it is nonetheless real. It empowers the individual and his/her legal fictions (e.g., corporations, trusts, donor-advised funds, private foundations) to obtain material goods and services essential for survival (or luxurious lifestyle). While capital may appear to be created out of thin air in some cases (e.g., bank loans), it may also be generally obtained through the following activities:

- From operations (e.g., the exchange of goods or services, including employees and agents' wages);
- From investments (e.g., the profit, gain, or other accounting return from other's commercial ventures, including speculative activities);
- From finance (e.g., the proceeds of loans from banks, proceeds from initial public offerings of equity);
- From inheritance and/or gift (e.g., non-exchange transactions characterized by one-way transfers of capital).

Capital may accrue through exchange transactions (e.g., selling high and buying low; buying low and selling high). It may accrue through non-exchange transactions (e.g., rich Uncle Peter's bequest). Importantly, capital is an accrual or accretion of value. It is not merely cash or currency; it is monetary value imparted without a corresponding liability of equal value incurred by the capital holder.

Capital is created and preserved by rule of law (e.g., a bank's legal right to lend and pay interest on deposits, the permission to conduct lawful business). Also, capital is transferred and protected by rule of law (e.g., through the laws of inheritance). However, capital may have a considerable cost for some recipients (e.g., interest payable on debt capital, transaction fees for the issuance of equity capital), while almost no cost for others (e.g., receiving gifts and inheritances).

Additionally, some capital is less risky than other capital: realized gains on cleared and settled transactions with bona fide, solvent, and liquid counterparties are more certain with respect to the value of capital received than unrealized gains in which the investment may be marked up to a current valuation consistent with generally accepted accounting principles but not result in the corresponding receipt of capital proceeds (i.e., historical cost of an investment may be eclipsed by its current reported valuation). In a sense, unrealized capital gains are like legal fictions.

In the case of public sector sources of capital, the public sector contributes to obtaining and accumulating capital in the following ways:

- The rule of law, including taxation and direct and indirect enforcement of protection of property rights, which affects the valuation of capital (e.g., the overall higher taxation on wages, including in the U.S. Social Security and Medicare programs' taxes levied on wages, compared against the overall lower rates of taxation on long-term capital gains). The public sector through its law-making and law-enforcing regime gives preference and priority to some forms of obtaining and accumulating capital over other forms.
- Development and redevelopment of venues, including construction of roads, schools, and other public benefits, that directly and indirectly increase the valuation of private sector enterprises and individuals with interests benefiting from such improvements (e.g., a landowner may charge higher rents to his/her tenants resulting from the publicly subsidized enhancements to the surrounding land such as new schools). The public sector increases the value of accumulated capital through some projects while neglecting other programs (e.g., building a highway to a workplace empowers some, and not covering health and welfare benefits disables others).

The public sector may promote the obtaining and accumulating capital through its schemes of taxation and development. It may absorb private sector capital via taxation of income and/or inheritance and estate taxes, and it may redirect and redistribute these proceeds through its projects and transfer payments (e.g., publicly supported activities for their public and private benefits, including health, education, and the general welfare). Importantly, public policies implicate priorities (e.g., government contracts in support of wars do not have effects on capital similar to government bailouts of banks). In many material respects, public policies and laws implementing these policies significantly influence, if not control, the course of (re)development of the private sector by promoting growth of capital for some and not others (e.g., low-wage earners may subsist at best; ultra-high net worth / income individuals and families may save and thrive for generations under dynast trusts, family offices, donor-advised funds, and private foundations).

In many material respects, the creation and accumulation of capital is an activity largely under the control and influence of the sovereign. For instance, the public sector at the federal level in the U.S. may operate with significant fiscal deficits (i.e., routinely spending more capital than it receives) due to its control and influence over the federal appropriations and funding legal processes. As of September 30, 2021, the U.S. Government had accumulated a net deficit of approximately $30 trillion over the preceding years (United States Government, 2022). In effect, this capital was created and transferred to the private sector in the form of cash payments (e.g., wages, capital projects, prosecution of wars) expended on behalf of the U.S. Government. The nature of this capital was debt (e.g., treasury securities, including bonds payable). Thus, the federal government financed its operations from private sector and foreign governments' investments, promising to repay these lenders in principal and interest payments in future years. Federal deficit spending may create a superabundance of capital in the private sector.

Importantly, the U.S. federal government need not constitutionally support deficit spending with taxation and borrowing activities. Its congress has coinage power. Constitution Annotated n.d. Using taxes and/or debt to fund programs and projects is a policy preference of the U.S. Congress and the executive branch—not a constitutional necessity.

The U.S. Congress in fulfilling its spending power obligations, which include providing for the general welfare (Legal Information Institute n.d.), has policy options. Some policy options are conceived as preserving the value of money (e.g., taxation, debt under interest payable), and some are not (e.g., congressional coinage and/or debt jubilee). Obviously, the well-capitalized and creditor class benefit more under one set of policy options, and the undercapitalized and debtor class would benefit more under another set of policy options.

The federal government in its sovereign capacity may create private sector capital as observable from the following journal entries (simplified for explanatory purposes):

- Debit expenditures – John Q. Public in the amount of $10,000, and
- Credit capital contribution for the general welfare in the amount of $10,000.

Commonly, governments create debt (e.g., issue U.S. Treasury securities in the amount of $10,000) to fund John Q. Public's receipt of cash capital. Additionally, the government may claim tax revenues as a source of funding (e.g., credit revenues from tax collections for $10,000). However, these are not necessary relationships; they are contingent on custom and rule of law in effect in the issuing sovereign. As noted above in the case of the U.S. Government, the amount of deficit spending may be increased greatly without hardship. In fact, there may be little practical difference in absolute terms between issuing enormous values of debt allowed to grow uncontrolled year-over-year and issuing capital contributions for the general welfare. In comparative terms, the distribution of federal largesse matters enormously under any scheme.

Presently, the U.S. Government in its capacity as sovereign and owing debt issued in its own currency can in effect capitalize this debt without impairment to the general welfare (cf. debt jubilee). Instead, the U.S. Government finances its operations through debt issuance (which normally entails paying interest to creditors) and taxation (which overly burdens labor, inclusive of Social Security and Medicare program levies).

The problem of inflation will not be a topic considered in this chapter. However, inflation is a complex phenomenon requiring not so much deprivation of the general welfare as recapitalization of the debtor and adjustment of the debtor–creditor relationship. Inflation is relevant as it is commonly deployed as an excuse or justification to suppress deficit spending by the sovereign. Whether the measurement of capital would resulting an overstatement or inflated value such as that which occurs in the bubbling of asset prices specifically or in the unaffordability of necessary goods and services generally is commonly considered the essential concern. Investments in cryptocurrency that skyrocket irrationally may be a concern for a few, but the unaffordability of other goods and services such as energy, housing, health care, and higher education may have root causes not materially related to the absolute value of sovereign deficit spending. In fact and potentiality, sovereign deficit spending may comprise the most effective and efficient remedy to remediate such essential unavailability and unaffordability. The devil is in the details (i.e., the allocation of the spending). For instance, inflation may be asserted as a problem for low- and mid-level wage earners that does not affect corporate profitability or C-suite compensation (Johnson, 2022).

In many material respects, the creation and preservation of capital, which may be referred to commonly as net assets, net worth, net position, and changes therein, forms the subtext of the rule of law vis-à-vis federal expenditures and property rights. Whatever the nomenclature and particular circumstances, a key characteristic of capital is that it is a proxy for degrees of freedom. The more capital one controls and influences the more likely he/she can obtain necessary and desirable goods and services. Capital highly influences quality of life for oneself, one's family, and one's heirs under the applicable rule of law in jurisdictions such as the U.S. where levels of capital impact greatly one's health, education, and welfare.

The accumulation of capital is a process, legal (e.g., authorized commercial activity) and illegal (e.g., unlawful money laundering), by which persons obtain a monetarily valued reserve against future necessities, luxuries, and calamities. Theoretically, one may never have sufficient capital due to the inherent uncertainty of the future. Accumulation of capital serves as a form of insurance against financial crisis. Where social safety nets are materially incomplete and tenuous, the need for accumulation of capital is amplified. Thus, there is an inverse relationship between the availability and affordability of public goods and services and the hazards of disease and discomfort from profit contagion generating habitual pursuit of accumulation of capital. The adverse effects of profit contagion aided and abetted by neoliberalism are indicative of a social and individual disease, widespread and severe, chronic and acute, especially for the undercapitalized (Parramore, 2022). To be clear, profit contagion reflects the physical and emotional conditions of living inside hyper-capitalized environments under which the private (and public) profitmaximization strategy imposed by employers significantly affects and often impairs the opportunities for development of employees and agents within these environments. Insecurity is the resultant norm for most.

The theory and practice of profit contagion as a material component of how capital is obtained and accumulated should not be underestimated. As much of the capital for entities comes from persons already possessing significant stores of capital (e.g., investors in initial public offerings of publicly traded corporations), the flow of capital is often more an allocation and redistribution than an origination of a novel source. Money goes to money. In respect of profit contagion, the capital is redistributed in the effort to obtain and accumulate even more capital. This has, among other effects, the result of driving down labor costs, which comprise both a material impairment of profitability and a primary factor in driving profitability. (One may readily observe how slave-holding states and entities were able to generate enormous profits—low cost and high productivity of the forced labor.) Capital suppresses wage growth notwithstanding productivity. (U.S. Department of the Treasury, 2022).

While capital is an artificial constraint (e.g., a government controlling the conditions and issuance of its own currency may create a landscape on which health, education, and general welfare are assured independently of private capital), it has real effects. It may be implicitly allowed, if not explicitly encouraged, by law and custom to control and significantly influence society. Its accumulation supports a hierarchy of social influence.

A discussion and analysis of the alleged reasons explaining the differing capacities of persons to obtain and accumulate capital will not be addressed in this chapter. For example, the argument that in a meritocracy, the definition of which may be key to this argument, those with heightened abilities tend to receive more capital as their expected and actual contributions to the society are greater than others, may be countered both historically and morally. Those from wealthier families do tend to obtain and accumulate more capital, but the root causes of this condition demand an impartial examination—not a self-serving explanation propounded by those benefiting from such accidents of birth. Moreover, thereis no moral force justifying the allocation of capital according to one's abilities and capacities—the disabled are no less deserving of opportunities to obtain and accumulate capital than the fastest runners. A careful analysis that distinguishes between excuses and rationalizations disguised as justifications and factual soundness is necessary.

2.3. Using and transferring capital

Financial capital such as debt and equity may be specifically stored as cash reserves in a bank. Alternatively, it may be used to purchase economic resources (e.g., property, plant, and equipment), investments (e.g., equity in other entities), and political influence (e.g., campaign contributions, contributions to political action committees). Capital may be used and transferred in accord with the holder's liberty and property rights under the rule of law. In fact, the rule of law may not present a serious impairment of the well-capitalized in their quest to pursue schemes of alpha (higher than normal) profitability and gain (Goldstein and Enrich, 2022). The rule of law enables the use and transfer of capital.

Capital is used to trade and speculate, including the manipulation of capital markets. Capital is transferred offshore (e.g., tax havens or secrecy jurisdictions such as Jersey and Cyprus to be concealed from creditors, including government taxation authorities). The rules of law, including those operative in the U.S., do not demand that private capital be used and transferred for any public benefit. Materially, it is a privatized power to do things. This creates the conceptual foundation for profit contagion—conduct that seeks to maximize the growth of capital independently of any public good or service or even of the employees and agents contributing to the growth of private enterprise capital. For example, wages are driven down, while work demands for productivity are driven up to obtain higher levels of profitability for the stewards of capital (usually, directors, officers, and influential shareholders / debt holders). (Harvey, 2014)

While titans of industry may deem themselves job creators, in an important sense, they are closer to job minimizers under profit contagion. Goals such as efficiency and economy serve to suppress input values such as labor costs while leveraging these inputs to produce higher levels of output value: the workforce does more for less. This discrepancy between expenses and revenues results in increased profits, as well as discretionary and surplus funds available for the controlling persons such as directors and officers to lever up their own remuneration. Capital used and transferred in for-profit operations is not distributed equally across employees and agents. Moreover, capital may be used and transferred in related party transactions, often a biased allocation of capital.

Capital used and transferred under not-for-profit entities (e.g., charitable organizations) does not conform to the technical language of profit contagion in that these entities are not legally empowered to obtain and accumulate profits. However, they do strive to maintain a levels of net assets (i.e., assets less liabilities) and changes in net assets (i.e., revenues in excess of expenses) that operate analogously as the functional equivalent of profit contagion. The entity does not seek to become insolvent through an excess of expenses, including labor costs. Indeed, the allocation of capital under not-for-profit entities materially follows the command and controls of the *de facto* controlling persons (e.g., executive directors, funders).

Some not-for-profit entities obtain and accumulate a superabundance of capital only to legally save / hoard it. For example, the net asset value of Harvard University's endowment fund as of June 30, 2021, including funds with and without donor restrictions, exceeded $53 billion (Harvard, 2021a). With tuition charges approximating $52,000 for the academic year 2020–2021 (Harvard, 2021b), more than one-million students could have attended tuition-free for this academic year. Harvard's value of net assets increased by approximately $13 billion for the academic year 2020–2021, representing an approximately 26 percent increase over beginning net asset value for this year. *Qui bono* from this education? Arguably, if the public policies emanating from institutions such as Harvard were characterized by contributing importantly to the public benefit and general welfare, such private hoarding of financial capital could be justifiable or even excusable. Historically, Harvard's (and other elites') outsized role in the development and implementation of public policy may not support such a favorable inference. For instances, see Cohen (2016) specifically, and see Maximino (2014) generally.

Capital is used and transferred by private sector actors (e.g., investments, bequests) and public sector actors (e.g., expenditures of public funds). These movements of capital are not natural like the revolution of the earth around the sun but the results of intention, policy, and law, reflecting the interests and preferences of the influential in the political economy. There is no necessary invisible hand that sculpts the improvement of society and the general welfare; instead, the planners' hands are often opaque and concealed as undisclosed principals.

Capital is moved contingent on its holders' will and the applicable and enforced rule of law. Capital may be accumulated and transferred within a family dynasty over generations; alternatively, it may be used to establish institutions of higher education, public hospitals, and similar ventures benefiting society broadly. Capital is neutral in appearance but intentional in action.

Theories and concepts rationalizing and systematizing persons' property rights (e.g., liberalism, neoliberalism), while disregarding the effects of the exercise of these rights on society at large, characterize some current regimes (e.g., the U.S.). The individual may be allowed to prosper and prepare his/her immediate family and future generations for specific lives with an abundance of capital notwithstanding the state of affairs broadly. Thus, the vertical relationship of capital vis-a-vis an individual and heirs is distinct from the horizontal relationship of capital vis-a-vis an individual and society. This structure is foundational for conflicts, actual and potential, between the often-unacknowledged sets of the have so much capital and they have so little capital. The right to do what one wants with one's property, including capital, without any material balancing relationship composed of one's obligation to society (other than avoiding and evading the tax authorities) leads to a narcissistic ruling class / parties. The "we" of society bows to the "I" of capital.

Moreover, the diagonal effect of capital controlled vertically by dynasty and inheritance (i.e., cross-generational capacity to impair current and future states of society due to the legal protections afforded to the current generation of capital holders) enormously benefits those that did not contribute either to the obtaining or accumulating of capital. These third-party beneficiaries (the future donees / inheriting class) experience opportunities the less well-endowed will not. Both current and future generations are impaired. Their developmental opportunities are artificially constrained by rule of law to promote both the interests of present holders of capital andtheir heirs in a plutocratic, oligarchic, patrimonial system that is and will likely be anything other than a real meritocracy, notwithstanding the self-serving rationalizations of the ruling elites and professional managerial classes (Press, 2019).

However, impairment of development policies, procedures, and practices is not necessary. They are, again, contingent on the customs and rule of law of the sovereign, which may approach capital as a limiting resource (e.g., to be created by private sector banks and/or public sector expenditures funded exclusively by taxes and public debt) or a liberating resource, allowing society and the general welfare to develop notwithstanding the initial state of the members of society (e.g., children do not experience a paucity of opportunity due to the comparative impoverishment of their parents). Limitations on using and transferring capital are artificial, directed by the influential in the political economy.

In brief, capital may be created, used, and transferred for purposes supportive of the general health, education, and welfare. Alternatively, capital may be so created but accumulated within family dynasties for the particularized health, education, and welfare (and, of course, luxury items) for these few persons. The rule of law in effect (not merely the design but the implementation thereof) guides the intensity, flow, and directionality of capital. It may be a vector for the public benefit or a boon for private exploitation and hoarding.

The sovereign may be viewed like a private sector corporation beholden to a few, or it may be understood as a generative source and store of capital to be properly directed for the use and enjoyment of the citizens there under. Transfers of cash from the sovereign to its citizens for use as capital may be interpreted as transactions with unrelated parties; alternatively, they may be interpreted as redistributions and allocations of the principal (i.e., the sovereign or government) to its employees, agents, and beneficiaries. In a sense, the government like the corporation is a legal fiction. Its reason for existence is to maintain proper relations between it and the governed, generally according to rule of law. Capital is an instrumentality for public good and private benefit. How it is used and transferred is directly related to whether and how it is protected under the rule of law and/or tyrants, plutocrats, and oligarchs.

We note that rules of law created properly for the benefit of the general health, education, and welfare are likely materially different from rules of law created through plutocratic and oligarchic influences that are less directed for the general welfare than biased in favor of private income and wealth development across generations. The undercapitalized are not really focused on or concerned with generation-skipping / dynasty trusts, donor-advised funds, or private foundation's allocation of capital they don't and will highly likely never have, to particular infants and the unborn of the well-capitalized. Intentionally, capital flows into and out of the well-capitalized under growth strategies for the well-capitalized class.

Moreover, rules of law are not entirely effective in controlling the flows of capital into and out of legally disfavored jurisdictions. The use and abuse of shell companies and other legal fictions may act as proxies to circumvent rules of law.

> According to the documents and Western officials, the clandestine banking system works like this: Iranian banks that serve companies barred by U.S. sanctions from exporting or importing engage affiliate firms in Iran to manage sanctioned trade on their behalf. Those firms establish companies outside of Iran's borders to serve as proxies for the Iranian traders. The proxies trade with foreign purchasers of Iranian oil and other commodities, or sellers of goods for import into Iran, in dollars, euros or other foreign currencies, through accounts set up in foreign banks. (Talley, 2022).

Thus, the secrecy of actual and beneficial ownership structures and the legal technicalities in the rule of law allow ready circumventing by those with adequate capital to deploy the necessary company formation agents, attorneys, accountants, and other facilitators to thwart stated public policies and reported objectives. Intransparency and legal fictions help the well-capitalized, independent of value judgments such as levels of integrity, fairness, and justice. Capital is driven by the influential, deserving or not.

2.4. Protecting capital

The monetary value of capital corresponds directly to financial net worth. It is a monetary value that may be consumed or liquidated in satisfaction of debts to creditors, including taxation authorities such as the Internal Revenue Service (IRS) of the U.S. Its use to meet financial obligations and exchange value in pursuit of profitable economic opportunities should not be underestimated.

As capital is abstract yet socially real, its protection is derived principally from the following sources:

- Wide acceptance among persons for completing exchange (e.g., commercial purchases and sales) and non-exchange (e.g., payment of tax liabilities to governmental authorities) transactions;
- Widely held confidence in the sovereign responsible for issuing and otherwise controlling the supply of money (e.g., to suppress inflation risk lest the currency symbolizing the capital become devalued), and

- Reliable and predictable rules of law on which holders of capital can exclude others, including creditors, taxation authorities, and others such as investigative journalists, from knowing the identities, amounts, and instruments representing their capital.

Capital has no inherent use value, so it is without value unless its exchange value is protected and preserved. The mechanisms for such protection are grounded in the rule of law and confidence of market participants, large and small. At core, the general acceptance of capital in its variable forms (e.g., financial instruments such as equities and bonds, bearer instruments such as currency, hard assets such titles to real estate, vessels, aircraft, and vehicles) arises from the legal and financial systems in place and in effect both domestically and internationally.

Sometimes, capital needs to flee, if necessary, due to changes in the relevant political economy (e.g., nationalization of an industry rendering equity in the affected companies potentially less valuable), as well as smaller scale changes (e.g., imposition of financial penalties, fines, and schemes of restitution in criminal, civil, and administrative proceedings). Also, it needs to be stationary (e.g., to be a store and reserve of value in a particular financial institution used to complete exchange and non-exchange transactions), as well as to accumulate capital such as cash reserves. Capital is held in accounts for use and transfer, as well as symbolized by documentation of ownership / control in legal repositories (e.g., land title offices of the state or county).

To be protected, capital needs to be made legally, financially, and socially real through documentation. In a sense, capital is made empirical in outward appearance yet concealable as to ultimate ownership and control to satisfy the potentially conflicting demands of excluding the rest of the world from exercising dominion over the specific form of capital and including the rest of the world as potential transferees to satisfy debts and obligations of the holder of capital. Capital, while intangible, is evidenced by writings, electronic, and/or hard copy. This evidentiary support functions as its justification to invoke legal protections, as well as its vulnerability in that ownership / control of capital cannot remain entirely opaque. The reality of who controls it is ultimately accessible, given the appropriate permissions in the given legal and financial context. As X must prove X owns Y through writings, X cannot completely exclude Z from discovery of the relationship between X and Y through following the audit trail of writings.

Capital is transparent (e.g., X owns this real property and may exclude non-X); capital is also intransparent (e.g., X, a legal fiction owned by Y, another legal fiction or straw owner, owns bank account Z from which financial transactions may be initiated and authorized). Capital is both real (i.e., it materially and empirically affects decision-making and actions in the political economy) and unreal (e.g., it may exist in unrealized, unearned gains to capital reported as an asset such as with equities held at fair market value).

Capital as accounting energy underlies the dynamics of initiating, authorizing, recording, processing, and reporting of transactions through which public sector projects and programs and private sector exchanges of goods and services are recognized, measured, and disclosed in the world (e.g., the project costs \$XXX; the article is worth \$YYY). However, it is still a contingent condition of society that creates, supports, and protects its usefulness as property excludable from others (i.e., it is not necessary that all societies be founded on capital conditioned on property rights). Its monetary value is allocated among projects, programs, goods, and services—sometimes according to the market and sometimes according to other means such as historical cost—together which form the generally accepted valuation and measurement process of accounting for capital. As its value can be used and transferred in support of the holder's desires, necessities, and luxuries, capital needs protection under the rule of law and/or the rule of might (e.g., military power). These levers of protection include the following (a non-exhaustive list of factors):

- Laws of inheritance, empowering accumulations of capital to remain in dynastic trusts (and private foundations) for generations, resulting in abusive capital hoarding (cf. donor-advised funds) (U.S. Internal Revenue Service, 2022);
- Laws of money creation, empowering the privileged few (e.g., bankers) to determine how much capital can be allocated and to

whom, independent of the health, education, and general welfare of most;

- Laws of intellectual (intangible) property, empowering controllers of technology (commonly referred to as Silicon Valley) through government-protected rights (e.g., patents, copyrights) that create a highly influential and intrusive oligarchic / monopolistic force in the political economy, reducing many to the status of consumers and providers of data with little to no input in the public policies and specific laws impacting their lives;
- Laws of private tangible property, empowering controllers of land, buildings, aircraft, vessels, equipment, and so on to exclude the participation of others (e.g., price-based hurdles before one may use the property);
- Laws of public property, empowering the government units, and agencies to act like private corporations to exclude public participation (e.g., lawful uses to which public property may be extended);
- Laws of bankruptcy, empowering the courts to determine which creditors and stakeholders such as employees are made whole and whom are not;
- Laws of taxation, empowering those with sufficient capital to contest government action, leaving most without any practical remedy;
- Laws of public finance, empowering those leading, benefiting from, and supporting favored projects and programs, often at the expense of the health, education, and general welfare of most.

Broadly, law is the generally accepted mechanism to control the rights and obligations of capital. Specifically, capital is supported by a three-legged stool of executive, legislative, and judicial instrumentalities that create and exercise the powers enumerated above. Liberal (including neoliberal) jurisdictions evince a bias and sensitivity that favor the holders and controllers of significant stores of capital, not only preserving but expanding the roles of material component units of the status quo (e.g., efforts in the U.S. to reform the health care delivery system embedded more deeply and pervasively the role of private health insurance corporations, effectively impairing individual policyholders and elevating the preferences of corporations).

While there are no laws expressly prohibiting those who are undercapitalized from becoming well-capitalized, there are policies, procedures, and practices that protect the already well-capitalized from the undercapitalized (e.g., stores and reserves of capital largely undiscoverable that are lawfully isolated in domestic and foreign tax havens and secrecy jurisdictions—like Delaware and Nevada in the domestic case and like Jersey and Cyprus in the foreign case) (Tax Justice Network, 2021). The implicit operating principle is that capital can protect itself from those without, using the financial and legal systems to exclude, secrete, hoard, protect, and pass on capital to future generations.

The value of capital, in the foreground as a monetization of human capacity and talents and in the background as a reason to make private- and publicpolicy decisions, is something from which to conceal from creditors and others entirely, as well as something to protect in the effort to limit one's liability to creditors (e.g., forming bankruptcy remote corporations; holding assets in tax havens and secrecy jurisdictions) (Segal, 2016: 55). The rules of the game of avoiding, evading, or otherwise defeating creditors are global in nature, pitting one jurisdiction against another in a race to the regulatory bottom. In reality, jurisdictions may care more about fees generated from financial and legal services protecting capital than about creditors and aggrieved others in remote and foreign jurisdictions. This occurs within the legal and financial systems (i.e., internal / domestic asset protection schemes) and beyond the domestic legal and financial systems (e.g., use of shell corporations in offshore jurisdictions).

2.5. Conclusions

An accountant's capital is reflected by the residual monetary value of total asset value less total liability value. These values are recognized, measured, and disclosed in accounts. However, capital is not necessarily included in any particular account; it may be freestanding (e.g., X owns the real property in X's individual name yet not subsumed in any formal account controlled by X). Capital may be contained within accounts; it may transcend accounts. However, both natural person's and artificial person's capital may theoretically be recognized, measured, and disclosed in their statement of financial position; this is not generally accepted practice in most jurisdictions (e.g., U.S) (Ganos, 2019) (ICO Services, 2017). Generally, the rule of law protects the attribution and measurement of capital under privacy rights.

Capital, however incompletely recognized, measured, and disclosed, empowers those who have a comparative abundance of it. This advantage may be described as deserving, unfair, or otherwise, but it undeniably affects one's capacity and likelihood of development in innumerable essential ways. To be born into wealth and to thrive under conditions of high-income results in the skewing of opportunity and successful development in favor of the wealthy and high net income persons and families. Under a jurisdiction with sufficiently broad and deep leveling mechanisms (e.g., highly progressive, rigorously enforced, and largely unavoidable taxation schemes to finance publicly the availability of affordable and necessary opportunities to others such as health care, education, and shelter), the skewing, while advantageous to some, would not seriously and adversely impact the development of others.

However, increased taxation of the wealthy and/or high net income recipients is neither necessary nor sufficient. Public policy priorities and rules of law would need to account for and finance support for the general welfare in so many of its particulars (e.g., health care, education, retirement). For example, jurisdictions that were to fund public goods, services, and benefits with the same mechanisms used to fund other priorities (e.g., national security and defense in the U.S. under conditions of tolerance of large fiscal deficits) would not necessarily experience conditions of extreme inequality in the availability and distribution of opportunities in the political economy. An underappreciated effect of the failure to level opportunity and benefit is answerable in the question: *qui bono*? Capital limitations result in a deficit of full and fair competition; the undercapitalized are outgunned. The well-capitalized may accrue influential positions in the political economy independently of ethics or integrity or even fairly and rigorously defined conditions of merit; this is the power of capital. To place oneself and to move others.

A society dominated by those with capital oppresses those without (Glyn, 2006). Capital is not especially sensitive to ethics, rule of law, integrity, and similar imperatives where these specifically conflict with profit contagion. Collective action in support of such noble virtues may be thwarted by the influence of capital on the executive, legislative, and judicial functions of both domestic and foreign governments. Nightmarish scenarios of polluted environments, volatile responses in the climate, and related so-called externalities (the practice of offloading costs and effects of production such as impairment of the environment through water and air pollution and the impairment of general welfare through underfunding of necessary health, education, and related concerns by transferring profits and gains to low- or no-tax jurisdictions) threaten many societies (Pike, 2022). A society under capitalism and conditions of profit contagion is not merely figurative.

A society dominated by capital like the U.S. is subservient to corporate interests, which are infected with profit contagion, including hegemony over higher education—the foundation of a society's future growth, intellectually and otherwise(Neem, 2022). While liberal democracy seems a noble concept in theory, its practice under conditions of profit contagion includes the following attributes and their effect on development of the undercapitalized:

- Accounting and economic profit and capital gain drive the decision-making of influential members in the political economy (e.g., corporate and political leaders), inducing a short-termism elevating the bottom line (i.e., the increase in value of net assets, net position, and/or net worth) above the material conditions of the undercapitalized. Accounting classifications such as wages and salaries for common labor are expenses and costs to be minimized such that profits and equity prices of the public corporation are increased. The well-capitalized, including directors and officers endowed with appreciating stock options and equities, benefit at the expense of so many other employees and agents performing the work. Moreover, conditions of oppressed wages spread under profit contagion such that one major employer's race to the bottom affects others similarly.

- The creation of tax havens and secrecy jurisdictions, offshore and domestic, under which capital may accumulate and be concealed from the legitimate interests of others such as creditors and tax authorities, resulting in underfunding of public projects and programs that do not offer adequate opportunities to increase the bottom line of the well-capitalized (cf. The finance and prosecution of war implicating jurisdictions and venues containing valuable commodities and raw materials needed by well-capitalized producers against the finance and delivery of health care and higher education with debt to the undercapitalized).

The demonstrated ability and willingness of the well-capitalized to increase their lot and influence in the political economy is perhaps too obvious to belabor. Their demonstrated ability and willingness to transfer and use capital under anonymized and protected shell companies, donor-advised funds, and trusts for self-aggrandizement is also nothing new to the well informed. However, the most astonishing aspect of capital's scheming and succeeding is in its fraud and dissemblance: the well-capitalized not only need the rule of law to protect its interests; they also need the undercapitalized to misunderstand the role of capital. It is not neutral and not driven by physical laws like gravity. It is a role nurtured by public sector legislators, executives in the public and private sectors; it is enforced under the commands of public sector judges. It is not a necessary role but one contingent on the power of the few behind the shadows.Importantly, capital benefits not necessarily the deserving or moral or public spirited; it benefits the well born. In brief, see Table 2.2 below.

Thus, capital is directly related to one's ability to absorb loss (e.g., chronic / acute medical care where privatized and inadequately regulated); one's ability to improve one's development (e.g., high costs of higher education where privatized and inadequately regulated); one's ability to care for one's family (e.g., high costs of shelter / rents; inadequate coverage afforded by public transportation). Capital does not level the availability of opportunities for personal and familial development

Table 2.2: Summary of dynamics of capital under regimes of deficient public funding.

Effects in Society	Obtaining & Accumulating Capital	Using & Transferring Capital	Protecting Capital
Well-capitalized persons	Global opportunities, including favorable credit terms	Global opportunities, including worldwide financial system	Specialized onshore & offshore jurisdictions
Public sector	Principal reliance on issuance of debt and taxation	Principal reliance on executive & legislative commands	Acquiescence to regulatory races to the bottom
Private sector	Principal reliance on debt capital for most	Cost of necessities for living consume most	Not relevant issue for most due to cost of necessities

Prepared by the author

in the political economy; it allocates these in an auction-like manner to those who can afford them. The good life is for sale, affordable for some but creating hazardous debt overhang for most.

In sum, capital is the monetary value credited to persons in a hierarchical exchange-and-transaction-based political economy. Figuratively, it comprises the rungs of the ladders of dominion and control in the system, rationalizing the valuation and allocation of opportunities of development within it.

References

COHEN, A. (2016). "Harvard'seugenics era."Harvard Magazine, March-April 2016. https://www.harvardmagazine.com/2016/03/harvards-eugenics-era, Accessed March 27, 2022.

GANOS, T. (2019). "World's best tax haven: the United States."Forbes, September 19, 2019. https://www.forbes.com/sites/toddganos/2019/09/19/worlds-best-tax-haven-the-united-states/?sh=55b7ceac4049, Accessed March 21, 2022.

GLYN, A. (2006). "Marx's reserve army of labour is about to go global."Guardian, April 4, 2006. https://www.theguardian.com/commentisfree/2006/apr/05/comment.businesscomment, Accessed March 21, 2022.

GOLDSTEIN, M. and ENRICH, D. (2022). "How one oligarch used shell companies and Wall Street ties to invest in the U.S."New York Times, March 21, 2022. https://www.nytimes.com/2022/03/21/business/russia-roman-abramovich-concord.html, Accessed March 22, 2022.

HARVARD UNIVERSITY. (2021a). "Financial report fiscal year 2021."https://finance.harvard.edu/files/fad/files/fy21_harvard_financial_report.pdf, Accessed March 15, 2022.

HARVARD UNIVERSITY. (2021b). "Tuition charges."https://registrar.gse.harvard.edu/files/gse-registrar/files/tuition_rates_2020-2021.pdf, Accessed March 15, 2022.

HARVEY, D. (2014). Seventeen contradictions and the end of capitalism. London: Profile Books.

ICO SERVICES. (2017). "USA: the strongest tax haven in the world."ICO Services, July 11, 2017. https://medium.com/@icoservices/usa-the-strongest-tax-haven-in-the-world-6d7cef7ccedb, Accessed March 21, 2022.

JOHNSON, J. (2022). "'Their inflation strategy is working': corporate profits surged to record high in 2021."Common Dreams, March 31, 2022. https://www.commondreams.org/news/2022/03/31/their-inflation-strategy-working-corporate-profits-soared-record-high-2021, Accessed March 31, 2022.

MAXIMINO, M. (2014). "The influence of elites, interest groups and average voters on American politics."Journalist's Resource, November 14, 2014. https://journalistsresource.org/politics-and-government/the-influence-of-elites-interest-groups-and-average-voters-on-american-politics/, Accessed March 27, 2022.

PARRAMORE, L. (2022). "Our economic system is making us mentally ill."Institute for New Economic Thinking, March 18, 2022. https://www.ineteconomics.org/perspectives/blog/our-economic-system-is-making-us-mentally-ill, Accessed March 19, 2022.

PRESS, A. (2019). "On the origins of the professional-managerial class: an interview with Barbara Ehrenreich."Dissent, October 22, 2019. https://www.dissentmagazine.org/online_articles/on-the-origins-of-the-professional-managerial-class-an-interview-with-barbara-ehrenreich/, Accessed March 27, 2022.

SANDEL, MICHAEL J. (2021). "Toppling the myth of meritocracy."The Harvard Gazette, January 5, 2021. https://news.harvard.edu/gazette/story/2021/01/the-myth-of-meritocracy-according-to-michael-sandel/, Accessed March 20, 2022.

TALLEY, I. (2022). "Clandestine finance system helped Iran withstand sanctions crash, documents show."Wall Street Journal, March 18, 2022.

TAX JUSTICE NETWORK. (2021). "The state of tax justice 2021."Tax Justice Network, November 16, 2021. https://taxjustice.net/reports/the-state-of-tax-justice-2021/, Accessed March 20, 2022.

U.S. DEPARTMENT OF THE TREASURY. (2022). "The state of labor market competition."U.S. Department of the Treasury, March 7, 2022.

U.S. INTERNAL REVENUE SERVICE. (2022). "Donor-advised funds."Internal Revenue Service, January 21, 2022. https://www.irs.gov/charities-non-profits/charitable-organizations/donor-advised-funds, Accessed March 28, 2022.

UNITED STATES GOVERNMENT. (2022). "Financial report of the United States government."https://fiscal.treasury.gov/reports-statements/financial-report/current-report.html, Accessed March 15, 2022.

Chapter 3

The new Olympus: Corporations (and other fictitious entities)

The unity that the working class did not achieve with the communist manifesto was achieved by capital's ruling elite through its corporations.

Keywords: capitalists' organization, capital centralization, stock corporations, impunity and privileges bylaw

3.1. Synthesis

Stock corporations are the legal configuration in which many of the most powerful and richest companies in the global order are organized. In this chapter, we will analyze the reasons for this structure. They are not neutral.

Stock companies are considered by law as different persons from the partners that control, influence, and operate them. From the legal sciences, the joint-stock company is studied focusing on the limitation of the liability of its members (individuals) for the acts of the company (the legal person). Moreover, the members become agents of the company as principals. This results in an imaginary *alter ego* (a legal fiction) with great potential for absorbing legal effects of bad conduct and adverse externalities of high managerial agents (e.g., officers and directors of the company). The individuals are isolated and protected; the legal fiction is exposed.

The property of equity interest acquires peculiarities in the stock company itself. Stock companies constitute an effective element to collect dispersed capitals and unify them under a single direction and will like a vector in the political economy, a means of alliance of capital enviable by any union of workers. Most frequently, it is a group of owners of shares that may not constitute a majority in the company but can nevertheless manage the destinies of the entire society. Minority equity interest in a public corporation can confer power, vertical in the corporation and horizontal across society. Through the construction of corporate networks, where a company is in turn "partner" of another company and so on (including interlocking corporate directorships), rhizomatic structures are formed (Arelovich, 2020). It is often impossible to establish the civil and criminal responsibilities of the individuals who operate behind them. The company controls private policy vertically from within and significantly influences public policy horizontally among business partners and political leaders by extension of its network. The corporation is an actor with limited liability manipulated by its controlling persons such as directors, officers, and significant shareholders.

The characteristics mentioned in the previous paragraph are used by capital management companies (corporate banks, hedge funds, investment funds) which, by acquiring shares in different corporations, end up forming a true spider's web that controls or significantly influences much of the corporate world. Of interest is the management of the logics of fictitious capital. This is precisely the expertise of capital management companies ultimately deciding issues of agricultural, industrial, and service production that are foreign to them. Access to and allocation of large pools of capital to maximize profit do not logically or practically confer integrity or knowledge / skill in contributing to the general welfare upon these influential stewards of financial resources. Power and leverage do not require talent, integrity, or a sense of justice.

The expansion produced by the combination of stock companies with the management of financial instruments results in capital management companies ending up dominating multiple companies—companies that in turn trade and provide services to one another. In this way,central interest is from both sides of the economic operation. It conceals material reality, substituting its own belief and value system.

Judges tend to dogmatically apply the principle that companies are entities different from their partners, reaching a fetishism of legal personality, which exacerbates the strong protection that the law already grants to corporations. Where legal fictions are acceptable and treated as if they were as objective and independent as the trees growing (or not) in the forest, reality is inverted. A religious order—the magic of capitalism—is created.

The board of VICENTÍN set up a rhizomatic structure of companies under whose structure they operated, being swallowed up in these matters by another network of companies managed by a much more powerful transnational actor: GLENCORE. Corporations layered among corporations—related and affiliated horizontally and vertically—yet without due process, effective legal liability, and personal responsibility checking the conduct of controlling persons, as well as lower level employees and agents, against a just standard.

The internal (vertical) and external (horizontal) growth and expansion of a company such as VICENTIN could not result in such socially harmful consequences extending well beyond the individuals directing its policies and decisions without the implicit / explicit support of the rule of law applied to the financial system and its actors. Under (neo) liberalism, the property owner can largely do what he/she wishes with their property, including contributing to a network of highly influential and ultra-high net worth individuals' dominance of public policy. Essential material goods and services such as the availability and affordability of shelter, education, health care, and so on do not receive due preference under these plutocratic, oligarchic, and kleptocratic schemes empowered at the core by profit contagion.

3.2. Fictions

The explosion of the information technology communication revolution (telecommunications, internet, algorithms, and smart telephony) opens two opposing possibilities in the field of law: 1) advancement of the handling and processing of information to serve effectively to control transgressions of the law, or 2) an avalanche of gigabytes acting as a blanket that covers responsibilities and conceals accountability. The last option can occur when symbols take on a life of their own, becoming independent of what they symbolize and represent.

In the Borge's tale *Tlön, Uqbar, Orbis Tertius*, the author fantasizes about a secret, inter-generational society that produces an encyclopedia. In it, the existence of an imaginary world is fictionalized in detail, describing its peoples, languages, cultures, regions, etc. At the end of the story, the apocryphal encyclopedia (which was lost), is found. "Almost immediately, reality gave way on more than one point. The truth is that he longed to give in." The fictional accounts of the found "First Encyclopaedia of Tlön" begin to replace reality, and Borges predicts that even their imaginary languages will replace English, French, and Spanish over time.

The Argentine wrote a text that anticipates what we know today as hyper-reality or post-truth composed of those statements that are not consistent with the materiality of things or can be explained through cause-effect relationships. Nevertheless, they are held as existing and truthful by people. Much of this happens within the corporate world: a displacement of reality that is neither empirical nor rational, resulting in a financial system unsupported by common sense.

The substitution of the language of law for the language of facts supported by evidence has grave consequences, especially where the law supports a fictionalized version of real events. Legal fictions such as corporations are not materially real; they are not empirically detectable; they are not substantively independent of their controlling persons. The legislators and enforcers of the rule of law can lawfully sponsor and direct obedience to that which is unreal.

3.3. Legal status and joint-stock companies

Law is a way of institutionalizing social practices imposed through power relations. The person of ideal or legal existence such as legal entities (treated as a subject to rules of law like men and women) is a fictional tool created to facilitate commercial transactions, to group assets, and provide protection for the risk assumed by the investor limiting his/her liability only to the investment made. Thus, legal responsibility and accountability are only partially capitalized by the company's assets.

The joint-stock company appears in the 17th century with the so-called Dutch Company of the Indies.Like the current one, the capital was represented by tradable shares. The liability of the partners was limited, dividends were distributed every 2 years, and careful accounting had to be kept. The reason for the birth of this vehicle was to avoid risk. Organizing commercial expeditions from Holland to Africa, Asia, and the other continents of the globe was too costly an undertaking. If bad weather or other circumstances such as piracy caused the ships to be lost with their cargo (which ranged from precious metals, pepper, and ivory and, at times, human beings trafficked as slaves), the large investment made was not recovered and the ruin of the ship would impair the investor. To raise the necessary funds and to set up a tool that limits the investor's liability to the capital integrated in the company, the structure of the public limited company appears. A structure that is the daughter of mercantile and internationalized capitalism. What else was the Dutch India Company but a transnational with the power to set the agenda for a state like the Netherlands?

With the economic and legal tool that was the joint-stock company in use, the philosophy of law explanation followed, creating a specific political framework. A characteristic of legal discourse (as of all other discourses) is to validate actuality resulting from the power of decision-makers that present laws to appear neutral and strictly rational. The rule of law is intended to apply not only to the property in motion and transaction but also to the property's relationship with others near and remote from the origination of the rule of law. The law seeks to generalize the rules protecting property domestically and internationally.

The joint-stock company is a species within the genre of legal entity. Legal entities are organizations of people, an ideal entity, to which the rule of law gives the ability to act in the legal world as if it were a real, physical being. In an important sense, individuals subject to this regime of rule of law are lawfully coerced to act as if the imaginary and artificial is an independent thing worthy of obedience.

The legal entity would be a creation of the rule of law that ideally synthesizes individual persons (inter-subjective human behavior), organized with a certain purpose (values) to build a unitary center of normative reference. Rights and duties (legal norms) will be attributed to this center (Sánchez Morales, 2013). Individuals' conduct is directed, controlled, and managed by this lawful but unreal core.

The commercial legal entity is an instance of institutionalization to organize a group of subjects (men and womenholders of capital) to relate to the rest of society. Society is compelled not so much to negotiate with these men and women of fleshandblood but to deal with the protective shell of the corporation. This creation of the rule of law may be explained and viewed from different concepts.

- One of these concepts is that the legal entity is fiction. The law gives birth to a new abstract being. That is, it is an artificial creation constituting the norm, which delimits a set of goods. The handling of these goods by a group of human beings will be treated as if it were (in fiction) another subject of law other than those human beings. This is based on reasons of convenience within the framework of a market economy. The legal fiction gives and takes—not the controlling, directing, and managing persons.
- Another concept is that the legal entity is a real entity. It is the reality theory. Among other authors of this school, Otto Von Gierke maintained that the legal person was a real entity since it exists, has a life and a will of its own like physical persons. The rule of law does nothing more than recognize this preexisting situation (like the human person) but it does not create it; it only records it. The legal entity already existed before this recognition (Junyent Bas, 2009). We could call this thesis that of the

fetishism of a concept or abstraction. What would happen to us in the case of a law such as 26,994 in Argentina (modifying the General Law of Companies 19,550) that authorizes the creation of a sole proprietorship limited company? When was that legal person born? When was the human person having a coffee during which it occurred to him/her to constitute it? How does his own will work differently from the sole proprietorship? Is the human person a schizophrenic with a double-will, one physical and the other a legal fiction/entity? And even if it was not a sole proprietorship, if it has its own will who are those ladies and gentlemen who sit in the shareholders' meeting to vote? And what are dividend distributions? Donations from whom or what?

- A third concept is that the legal person acquires the entity of a subject of law because the State recognizes it as such. The legal person is then a reference, a repository in which the State grants certain rights and obligations. It would be a legal category, which, though recognized in the law, does not acquire corporality or spirituality: it is a legal situation, a status (Rodríguez Rodríguez, 1977). The aforementioned doctrine suffers from the problem that it ignores the political-economic realities that produced such recognition. Who are the subjects, the human persons who can operate this recognition and create another subject different from them? Can everyone do it? Fictional maybe, but in practice? What sociocultural and patrimonial requirements must be met by those who want to create another subject of law (legal person) different from themselves?

From Juan Dobson regarding legal status:

> An advantage is granted that is denied to the rest of the population, namely: the right to respond to debts with only a sector of their assets, while the rest must respond for debts arising from their activity with all their assets. (Dobson,1991:64)

Ricardo Nissen adheres to the doctrine of fiction. For the author, legal status is a practical solution devised by the legislator to unify, in a single estate, the effects of the actions of a group of people who have a common lawful purpose. He understands that fiction is the thesis adhered to by Vélez Sarsfield (author of the old Argentine Civil Code) following Savigny, Laurent, Aubry, and Rau. Despite of its antiquity, Nissen considers the thesis of current fiction since, citing Borda, he understands that when the law treats a natural individual as a person, it is not conferring personality on it. Rather, it only confirms a preexisting personality. With the legal person, when the rule of law grants capacity to this entity that has no thought or will, everything is a fiction createddue to economic and social interest. This will not imply denying the existence of legal persons as a different subject from the human persons that constitute them. However, considering legal persons a reality in themselves entails serious problems (Nissen, 2010). These problems arise when certain theoretical constructs are empowered that, being apparently aseptic, constitute a "Trojan horse" that sets traps and operates privileges.

For our part, we believe that it is necessary to have a transdisciplinary vision to understand the reason for the existence of the institutionalization of the legal entity. It is a legal artifice that does not arise from the free abstract intellect of some jurist, or from something immanent that comes from the depths of time, as was intended in theories and concepts of natural law. It is simply an institutional channel to consolidate a given power situation within the framework of the market economy where there are winners and losers. In this context, legal status emerges as a legal shield to cover the assets of certain subjects (human persons) who hold capital. To collect, centralize, and organize capital to leverage the power of the organized capitalist. Therefore, it serves the capitalist more than anyone else, while impairing those injured or damaged by the corporation to an artificially but lawfully shrunken net asset pool that may be greatly diminished and gravely inadequate to remedy the wrong.

If commercial companies with legal personality are only a way of protecting assets, they would have positive effects to the extent that they are a means of breaking down investor reluctance. Thus, it would stimulate the circulation of capital. However, this is not always what happens. Often, the corporate shell is used as a protective layer and tool to circumvent the law and as a smokescreen to cover up its real authors, the human beings / controlling persons. The rule of law may protect some assets (e.g., capital management company's) at the expense of others' assets (e.g., domestic producers, their employees, society at large). The rule of law exists to prioritize relationships to assets and capital (e.g., debtors are subservient to creditors independent of the goods and services produced so long as these are lawful and not contraband like narcotics). The rule of law institutionalizes preferences of some (e.g., the well-capitalized) and disregards the needs of many (e.g., the undercapitalized victim of corporate wrongdoing and injustice).

3.4. Stock corporations

Stock companies are a subject of law; that is, they have legal personality. The law regulates them in a flexible manner, underestimating, in our opinion, very essential issues that make up their very nature. First, its enormous capacity to multiply, direct, and extend the power of the great capitalist. Second, its ductility to generate utility from nothing. And third, its ability to cover up the real protagonists of commercial operations and detach them from the consequences that their actions produce. The corporation is the capitalists' armor.

3.4.1. Multiplying and extending the power of the elite capitalist

The union that the proletarians did not achieve with the proclamation of the Communist Manifesto the capitalists achieved with the stock company. Stock companies are a formidable tool for recruiting dispersed capital and placing it under a single management that is strengthened and grows with that levy. At the same time, it dilutes the owner's bond with his/her property.

Acquisitioning shares of a company, the small capitalists that were dispersed join in capital accumulation of the company which shares they buy. This increase mainly benefits the majority capitalist who, in fact, ordinarily controls such a company. Contrary to what one might think, the process of multiple small capitalists that join the company through the acquisition of shares does not have any hint of democratization of the company. This is because the small acquiring capitalist will be excluded, in practice, from the governance of the company. In fact, such governance will continue to be exercised by the largest shareholder capitalist, who ordinarily manage increased capital thanks to the absorption of the other small capital shares.

Thus begins one of the paradoxes about the concept of property that we currently have: corporations invigorated by the management of what belongs to others. A capitalist owner of 51 percent of the share package will be able to dominate the company and manage the other 49 percent of foreign capital of the other small shareholders. This derives from the assumption that there is only one class of stock with all stockholders having rights to vote proportionate to their holdings; in the case, for example, of a hierarchical class structure of voting stock (i.e., dual-share classes), one or more classes of equity holders may be given more voting rights and power per unit of stock owned, resulting in a situation where minority stockholders control the majority of the vote. The majority capitalist enhances the operability and gravitation of his capital. The question deepens when, in compliance with what Hilferding pointed out, we verify that for a capitalist to predominate in the management of joint-stock companies, it is not necessary for him to

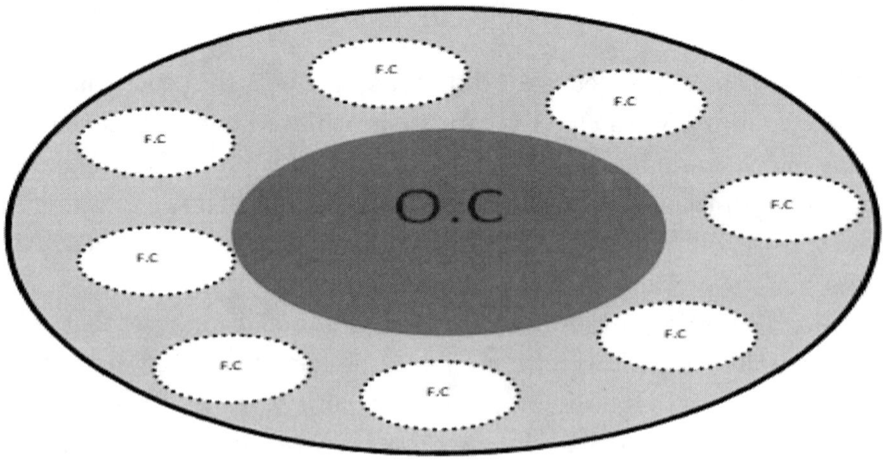

Figure 3.1: Gravitation of big capital.
Prepared by the author.

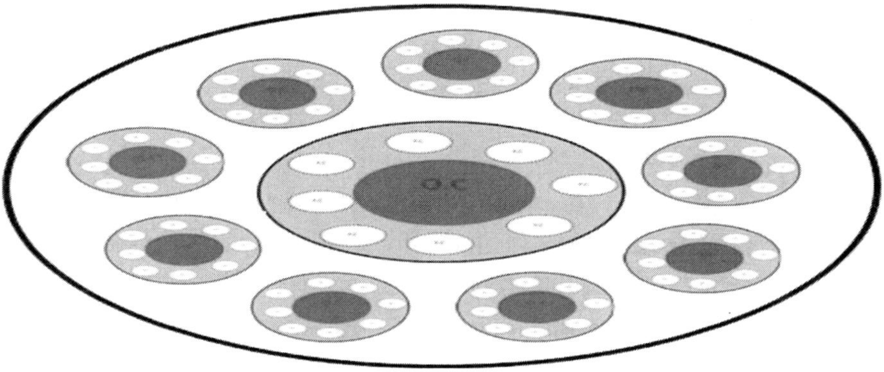

Figure 3.2: Gravitational system of big capital.
Prepared by the author.

have the majority. It is possible with just a third (or less) of his shares (Hilferding, 1963). See Figure 3.1.

The figure shows how the big capitalist's own capital (OC) has been enhanced with the incorporation of foreign capital (FC) to the mass that he manages. The large capital of its own attracts the small capital of others, and without losing control enhances its volume by incorporating it through the jointshareholder company, gaining power.

In turn, with that fattened capital, it can reproduce the process by subsequently acquiring shares in other companies. The great capitalist thereby achieves control of a network composed of numerable companies. Cf. Figure 3.2.

BlackRock is an asset management company that owns shares in more than 5,000 companies. Their shareholdings in most of these companies do not exceed 9 percent.[1] However, with that arithmetic minority in each one, it has the power to set the broad political and governance guidelines of the companies in which it participates (Pawliczek,2021). The practice of having a portion of the ownership capital as investment assets in multiple stock companies has leveraged the power of BlackRock and extended its influence globally.

1 Data according to the Stockzoa database, consulted on January 14, 2022, website https://stockzoa.com/fund/blackrock/

John Maynard Keynes taught that the economic agent preferred liquidity; that is, having cash. While the classicists argued that the actors preferred money for practicality and liquidity, for the British, an additional reason was the ability to speculate (Keynes, 2001). However, liquidity is not limited to cash; it is holding any short-term asset (e.g., marketable securities) that may be quickly sold for cash without significant risk to its monetary value. Illogically, cash is an asset readily convertible to cash within 90 days.

Speculation is the action of buying a good without the intention of benefiting from its use or transforming it. The purchase is made only with the expectation of reselling it in the future, taking advantage of a rise in its price. This, of course, is only one strategy; i.e., of buy low then sell high; there are other strategies to obtain capital gains such as short-selling (i.e., selling high, then buying low). These stratagems make a profit and capital gain without producing anything new. To take advantage of the opportunities that arise in this field, it is necessary to have a significant store of quick (uncommitted) money available.

The industrial entrepreneur or farmer is tied to the property that he operates with, and for him is the means of production with which he will make his profit. But with the shares of a company, the logic is different. Although these share titles entail a property relationship with the company, here the financial owner can dispose of that property very quickly and use the money to speculate. This instant sale is accomplished on the stock exchange where the shares are listed. Owning such public shares puts one in a position of liquidity. With equity-based ownership management, it is easy to move quickly from a losing position to a winning one. The speculator is less committed to material productivity with respect to his/her companies than the manipulability of the price of their equity (and/or debt) positions.

Of relevance is the difference between concentration and centralization of capital: concentration of capital is the process of accumulating and increasing capital through the cycle of reinvestment of the profits that reproduce it. It is the businessman who, after having obtained profits by selling an industrial article that he manufactured, reinvests part of them in acquiring more raw materials, contracting with workers, improving production technology to manufacture larger and better quantities of things, restarting and strengthening the cycle, and so on. It entails the power and opportunity of the large capitalist, who, having a larger capital size, can gradually defeat its smaller competitors by taking advantage of economies of scale (greater marginal productivity per material resource-input or worker employed) or by monopolistic and abusive behavior inherent in a dominating position. For example, selling below cost will render its competitors without customers but may be a viable (if practicably lawful) strategy for a monopolistic producer. In any case with the concentration of capital, new capital is being created by increasing production.

On the contrary, nothing new is created in the centralization of capital. The capital of an entrepreneur increases because it absorbs other existing capital. For example, when an entrepreneur takes over another company already in operation, there is not necessarily any new production. This happens in mergers and acquisitions, where one company consolidates another. By uniting two preexisting sets of capital, though nothing new is being created, an increase in the volume of capital ensues immediately.

Share companies are an efficient means for the concentration of capital and extremely efficient for its centralization. As we have pointed out, a larger capital can gradually recruit smaller capitals through the issuance of shares. The small capitalists that subscribe to them will be subsumed in the larger capital, which is the one that will continue to dictate the direction of the now fattened company. Another possibility is hostile acquisitions, where a company can directly take control of another, surreptitiously or openly, through strategic purchases of its shares over time.

Shares as vehicle to transfer ownership strengthen the strongest players in the market. It can function as a fishing net to ensnare small, scattered capitals little by little, or as a harpoon to quickly capture other concentrated capital.

Equity interests in companies allows the leveraging of more powerful and wealthier companies into global enterprises. A comparatively small socially and economically networked core of individuals organize through their controlled and significantly influenced entities (e.g., interlocking corporate directorships and business partners) to create an enterprise like an octopus with tentacles reaching into venues and jurisdictions across the world. Thus, profit contagion spreads, with the private priority of profitability and economic gain reducing the influence of the public at large to bring about material improvements in the general welfare. Local power becomes global (and remote) power, and its influence and plans are not neutral but focused on self-interest and self-aggrandizement. In a word, profit contagion is amoral. Under the direction and significant influence of a comparatively small group of ultra-high net worth individuals and families organized under insulating corporate and trust form, it is hazardous and adversely biased against the general welfare in its concentration and centralization of capital, diminishing its availability for others (where governments do not correct the collective conduct of capitalists via public policies countering such hoovering up of essential capital).

3.4.2. Generating profits from illusions

We wonder how stocks like Uber, Lyft, Pinterest, Slack, or Beyond Meat can rise in value while the companies they represent are losing money. In the period from 2019 to 2021, Uber invariably had losses, but the value of its shares went from $40 to $60/share. The web-based trading company Alibaba has a share capital that is four times the value of the oil company Shell. The online payment firm PayPal is twice the market valuation of carmaker Volkswagen. The logic of share value is something different from the materiality and technology of the company. The market value of equity interests may not be grounded in the goods and services sold; this is both irrational and unstable.

Once the share is issued, it is dissociated from the material capital of the company it represents. The centralization of capital and the speculation that the action allows is a much faster method of value creation than reproduction through the accumulation of material capital. The circulation of shares, which represents the transfer of ownership, by favoring centralization or by speculation (born in manipulated expectations) makes this financial share capital independent of the material company that it should represent. And the financial gains are faster, so it is tempting to operate there, avoiding being tied to the lethargy and drudgery of producing material goods.

Uber's stock is value based on future growth or profitability expectations and not the material reality of its losses. The dream of a bright tomorrow sustains the dark present. It should not be surprising that legal fictions allow the marketing of unrealized capital gains. This disconnection from reality to make quick profits without producing starts from the moment that the company is constituted as a joint-stock company. It is manifested by the profit-seeking of the founder(s).

Founder's profit is the value of the first-time offer of issued shares (i.e., an IPO or initial public offering). The founder's profit is equal to the difference between price of all the shares sold relative to the sum of the material capital invested in the company. With each new share issue, the process can be repeated. Article 188 of the General Law of Companies of Argentina allows capital to be increased through issuance of new shares of up to five times the initial value of the company.

In the joint-stock company, the logical order of things that we know is reversed. In an ordinary business, the owner must first accumulate the capital to set it up and sustain it, making and selling goods and/or services to increase the overall value of his/her assets and capital. In the joint-stock company, the organizer starts at the end. It begins by selling its property with the issuance of shares, to constitute it, thus accumulating capital.

Creating profit by issuing a title resembles the right of seigniorage of the State when it mints currency. But in the joint-stock company, this power belongs to a private person. An individual or small group of individuals organize to create privately a legally approved currency (i.e., equity interests in their corporation) that may be transferred to others in exchange for state-sanctioned currency (e.g., monetary valued embodied in U.S. dollars) or may be held to rise in monetary value through artifice and manipulation (e.g., pump-and-dump fraudulent promotional schemes) or other means (e.g., influential positioning in the political economy such as with favored government contractors) without a cause-and-effect relationship to the production of valuable goods and services. The measurement of valuation of shares of stock is inflated by exaggeration and hype divorced from material reality. It is chimerical.

3.5. The abuse of legal personality: Removal of the corporate veil

The legal personality of companies can be used to hide behind it the economic reality of commercial operations. In Argentina, given the abuses of legal personality that had been pointed out by the jurisprudence,[2] the General Act of Companies in its article 54 and the Civil and Commercial Code of the Nation (CCyCN) in its article 144 provide solutions for these abusive cases (Nissen, 2010). In such abusive situations, the corporate veil will be removed, and the separate legal status will become unenforceable.

The enactment of the doctrine limiting the lawful protections ordinarily available under the corporate veil advocates that the legal entity cannot be used for illicit purposes, or to cover them up. When used in this sense, it is ineffective. Therefore, the corporate veil (legal status) must be removed to see what human beings operate behind it. In Comparative Law, it is the doctrine of "Levée du voile corporatif " (peering of the corporate veil in French Law, and *Quebecoise,* article 309 of its Civil Code) or "Disregard of legal entity " (seeing beyond the legal personality) of the ruling *Bank of the United States v. Deveaux.* In the latter, Justice John Marshall ruled that it should be penetrated through the corporate personality to bring to light who was part of the company, since the latter was an entity of ideal existence that should yield when it was used by its partners for the purpose of circumventing the law.

Argentine Acts (something that does not occur in all compared legislations) have incorporated the institute of the penetration of legal status. It is done by Article 144 of the Civil and Commercial Code of the

2 In the historic Swift-Deltec case, the Supreme Court of the Argentine Nation understood that different corporations that formally had the status of creditors and debtors separately were in economic reality a single group, with a single mass of assets under the same address. Thus, the bankruptcy was extended to all of the companies that made up said group. Fallos: 286:257.

Nation and the third paragraph of Article 54 of the LGS. The formal legal entity is not recognized when it is used to violate the law, public order, not bona fide, or to frustrate the rights of third parties.

However, experience shows that civil and commercial judges are reluctant to lift the corporate veil (Ilharrescondo, 2008). Moreover, when the overwhelming evidence of abuse of legal personality leaves them no choice but to do so, it is often too late. The damage to the victims resulting from this patrimonial capitalism as described by Piketty (functionally, a hereditary plutocracy) will have been consummated. For our part, we observe that the legal entity "fetish" prevails (in judicial hermeneutics).To date, little seems to move the judge in his fundamentalist conception of legal entity as a sacred thing, even where a rational interpretation suggests the legal entity circumvented the doctrine of economic reality. It is common to read rulings that go beyond the anthropomorphizing of corporations, granting them even greater protection than that which would have been given to a human person. This has its application even in criminal matters.

The sanctity of the corporation as a legal fiction providing protection to individuals operating under its shell is peculiarly a hallmark of modern human rule of law. Imagine attributing the movements of the tortoise to its hard covering and not its fleshy part. The corporation justifies exploitation (e.g., purportedly under the guise of enhancing shareholder value) and excuses shifting costs onto those outside the corporation (e.g., pollution). It is an ideology seemingly neutralized under the term "rule of law" that superficially seems to represent an equality among all, but in fact and upon examination, the "rule of law" is enforceable only to the extent that one can afford to do so, whether by influencing legislators in their creation of the law, influencing regulators and law enforcement agencies in their pursuits to remedy unlawful conduct, and/or influencing the decision-making of the judiciary through the means of high-powered lawyers. When stripped of its hype, rule of law is fundamentally an ordering of protected priorities via state-sanctioned process (a process in which the state has a monopoly on the legitimate use of force to effectuate its own rules). The rule of law is not neutral but biased in favor of well-heeled corporations and other legal fictions (e.g., trusts).

3.6. Corporate instruments as tools of criminality

Following Carolina Damha Najjar, corporate forms and corporate instruments are tools that can be used to break the law:

> What attributes do they have that facilitate the commission of crimes? The obvious answer is limitation of liability, of course. But to this, we must add that corporate vehicles are capable of disguising a wide range of facts, elements and events, including: the true partners, the decision-making mechanisms and with it the identity of the true orchestrator of the crime, the true business purposes or accounts, sources of income, anonymous financing, etc., and for this they use fictitious/ghost companies, complex structures, the use of intermediaries and figureheads, a situation that is accelerated and fostered in turn by the ease of transfer of shares. (Damha Najjar 2016:70)

The author adds that the ease provided through corporate instruments to open accounts abroad and disguise the origin of the income-produced that feeds them, as well as to create shell companies to intermediate in transactions that should be direct, contribute to global and transnational attributes extending their influence and ideology well beyond any one venue or jurisdiction.

The Organization for Economic Cooperation and Development (OECD) is an international organization made up of the richest countries that are part of market economy logic. Therefore, it is unsuspected of statism or interventionism. However, the OECD itself points out that most economic crimes are made through the abusive use of corporate entities. Thanks to commercial companies and other vehicles, the origin of illicit profits and transactions is disguised, bank accounts are opened under the name of shell companies, wealth is hidden in tax heavens and secrecy jurisdictions, simulated commercial operations are registered between entities that correspond to the same owner, evasions of the state treasury abound, defrauding of creditors, and so on—these are among some of the operations in which commercial companies are used as a tool to violate the law (OECD, 2021).

The phenomenon of fraud using corporate structures can generate a global network. This occurs when, according to the ORGANISATION FOR ECONOMIC COOPERATION AND DEVELOPMENT (OECD), "chains of corporate vehicles" are created to commit crimes. These chains appear when a company owns the shares of another company, and the latter also in turn owns the shares of another, and this one of another... and thus the chain is prolonged, hiding the true owner like the nested Russian doll (matryoshka) game. In this type of construction, it is typical that the real owner either appears registered with few shares, or directly does not have any with respect to the company that is controlled from the shadows (e.g., the use of straw man who seemingly hold the interest but in fact lack any real influence over the enterprise).

The correctness of what is pointed out by the OECD follows from the intuitive and from the empirical. In Argentina, maneuvers through corporate abuse (used to manipulate transfer prices) cause the treasury an annual loss of approximately 6 billion dollars(Zlotogwiazga, 2018). In the global order and according to Nicholas Shaxson, tax havens (where profits are hidden under shell company names) cost governments between $500 billion and $600 billion a year in lost tax revenue (Shaxson, 2013), equivalent to a sum more than the Argentinean GDP.

Faced with this reality, controls on corporate vehicles can be promoted. For authors such as Gabriel Zucman, it would be easy to track inter-company financial transactions, as well as how much they are taxed. True international cooperation would suffice, since we have the technological means to do so (Zucman, 2015). In Argentina, for example, there is no longer a computerized registry of shareholders to see whom the human persons are who hold the property of legal entities. Under the current system, in the case of corporations that do not make public offerings of shares, they can change ownership overnight. The State's lack of exercise of control along with the public's lack of a direct right to obtain knowledge of the actual controlling persons results in tardy discovery of what has occurred, if they find out at all.

Opacity and limitation of liability, which are essential in corporations, is combined with the weakness of state and interstate controls. This is not only because the corporate sector is too powerful but also because the imposition of a cultural ideology is in effect. The prestige of shareholder companies is promoted and sponsored as a religious ideology. The for-profit sector (cf. job creators v. job minimizers) is not disturbed as it purportedly is exclusively responsible for and controlling of job creation.

Moreover, if the corporate section was to become displeased, their investments would migrate to another venue and jurisdiction. This is constitutive of the current relations between the large transnationals and the Latin American countries. Ironically, corporations move their operations and assets across the world under the obsession of profit contagion anyway, notwithstanding the current mythology.

Notwithstanding the incredibility of some of the hype surrounding corporations and their controlling interests (e.g., they are not precisely "job creators" but rather job minimizers in their profit contagion), the mythology of corporations persists. Even its critics may conceive of the corporation as a necessary evil. This may in significant part be due to a paucity of imagination focused on alternative political economies and the lack of any accurate, complete, and timely accounting of the full effects of corporate conduct. Additionally, the effects of propaganda should not be underestimated (e.g., dissemination of materially misleading narratives through the corporate media).

3.7. Conclusions

This chapter's content was presented to stimulate debate concerning the different layers of economic and legal advantages that, in a commercial company through shares of equity ownership, overlap. Also, to highlight societal concerns about the inherent possibilities for natural persons to use them in an abusive manner.

Using current theories of manipulable legal personality, a human person in civil matters can create multiple subjects, *alter egos*, transferring to them the patrimonial consequences (good or bad). Commercially, it enables the human person to trade and contract with himself, as if he/she were with a third party. In tax matters, the legal personality may establish fiscal domicile where the tax burden is lighter (or does not even exist) regardless of where the economic activity has its epicenter. In criminal matters, the legal personality may establish an inextricable density that will make it extremely complex to be able to attribute the intellectual authorship of the punishable behavior with the human person who executed it. The corporation did it (without arms; legs; a brain; and so on).

Economically, it allows generating profit from nothing and centralizing capital without correlation to production. Like setting up a virtual feedlot that has not been built yet beginning to sell meat not produced because the cows do not exist. This is the state of selling financial interests such as equity or other financial instruments today under the hope that the unrealized future would be prosperous.

In the conscience of legal operators, these instruments, these symbolic and abstract vehicles that are joint-stock companies, take on a life of their own. They become independent (in perception) from the human persons who constituted and operate them. It is the fundamentalism of legal entity / personality. The ideal and symbolic subject ends up stronger than the common man and woman who must face social life without having the shield of legal entities / personalities to protect them. Even when the material and economic reality arises in all of its contrasting colors, disarming virtual corporate hydra, and exposing who operates behind it, a process that will take years of costly litigation, the endeavor hardly seems worth it. When economic reality is reached, it would surely be too late.

Like Borges´ tale, the virtual can engulf the real. In post-truth times and financial flows moving at the speed of light across the globe (and what is finance but a virtual world?), this occurs in broad daylight yet opaquely.

A transdisciplinary and holistic approach to mitigating the risks and actualities resulting from legal entity / personality is imperative. Goals such as justice and equity need to reassert their deserved place in the public order. Operators under the legal entity / personality are like the men in Plato's cave myth who, seeing those projected shadows, believe that the shadows are the ones that manipulate the world's wealth. It is human energy, talent, dedication, diligence, imagination, and the arc of justice that empowers the best of human beings in the operation of legal entities / personalities. The shadows are in effect not the essential material reality. Indeed, individuals benefiting from this induced confusion can and do mount actions injuring the general welfare and impairing the development of many while promoting an ideology / religion of the legal entity / personality.

The issue is who is to control / significantly influence the operations of for-profit and not-for-profit activities that necessarily impact, often adversely, the societies in which and for which these operations purportedly function. Are the structure and priorities of societies to be designed and implemented in a top-down, pyramidal apparatus with value, inflated or not, rising primarily to the sparsely inhabited top tier for its use and exchange; or are there alternative pathways of addressing and mitigating the risks of the human condition vis-à-vis the political economy? We have observed the effects of profit contagion on human dignity, the environment, and the lesser advantaged / lower positioned; is this the best / optimal state of affairs? The dogma arising from profit contagion should be reconsidered.

References

ARELOVICH, S. (2020). "Informe individual de auditoría" en la causa VICENTÍN S.A.I.C. S/ Concurso Preventivo, Juzgado Civil y Comercial Segunda Nominación, Reconquista.

DAMHA NAJJAR, C. (2016). El levantamiento del velo corporativo en delitos ejecutados a través de la implementación de estructuras societarias complejas, Tesis de Grado, San José, Universidad de Costa Rica.

DOBSON, J. (1991). El abuso de la personalidad jurídica, Buenos Aires, De Palma.

HILFERDING, R. (1963).El Capital Financiero, Madrid, Tecnos.

ILHARRESCONDO, J. (2008). Delitos Societarios, Buenos Aires, La Ley.

JUNYENT BAS, F. y RICHARD, E. (2009). "Acerca de la Persona Jurídica a propósito de los debates sobre su conceptualización y otros aspectos derivados de ello."V Congreso de Derecho Civil, Córdoba.

KEYNES, J. (2001). Teoría general de la ocupación el interés y el dinero, Buenos Aires, FCE.

NISSEN, A. (2010). Ley de sociedades comerciales, Buenos Aires, Astrea.

OECD (2021). Ending the Shell Game: Cracking down on the Professionals who enable Tax and White Collar Crimes, OECD, Paris. http://www.oecd.org/tax/crime/ending-the-shell-game-cracking-down-on-the-professionals-who-enable-tax-and-white-collarcrimes.htm

PAWLICZEK, A., et al. (2021). "A new take on voice: the influence of BlackRock's 'Dear CEO' letters." Rev Account Stud 26, 1088–1136. https://doi.org/10.1007/s11142-021-09603

RODRÍGUEZ RODRÍGUEZ, J. (1977). Tratado de Sociedades Mercantiles, Ciudad de México, Editorial Porrúa.

SÁNCHEZ MORALES, G. (2013). "Rasgando las vestiduras de la dama sociedad: la teoría del levantamiento el velo societario, presupuestos necesarios para su aplicación práctica"Centro de Estudios de Derecho Corporativo, Universidad San Martín de Pores., Santa Anita.

SHAXSON, N. (2013). Las Islas del Tesoro, México DF, FCE.

ZLOTOGWIAZDA, M. (2018). Estudios internacionales revelaron que hay mucho más delito económico que corrupción, Infobae, August 10, 2018. https://www.infobae.com/economia/2018/08/10/estudios-internacionales-revelaron-que-hay-mucho-mas-delito-economico-que-corrupcion/, Accessed June 13, 2023.

ZUCMAN, G. (2015). La riqueza Escondida de las Naciones, Madrid, Siglo Veintiuno Editores.

Chapter 4

Emigration of the surplus value (cui bono?)

The veins through which capital flows sometimes support a foreign heart.

Keywords: capital flight, territorial underdevelopment, economic dependence

4.1. Synthesis

In this chapter, we will see how a country with insufficient industrialization, is an importer of technological goods, and has debt repayments require permanent foreign exchanges since these transactions are not made in a national currency. The recurring lack of foreign exchange is called an external constraint. In the Argentine case, the required currency is the U.S. dollar which is permanently strengthened against its national currency, the peso.

The dollar replaces the peso as reserve of value and is configured as a means of speculation. This is because it works as a financial title (an expression of the denomination of monetary value) with a perceived guaranteed rise in value. This is the explanation why economic actors seek to position themselves in the US currency. In addition, those who generate dollars in the Argentine economy are empowered over others. We are referring to the agro-export sector, which has exceptional competitiveness due to its comparative advantages attributed to the climate and the fertility of one of the most prolific regions in the world, the Argentinean Pampa Húmeda. Exports (in the Argentine agricultural case, which are paid in U.S. dollars) are one of the only genuine entry points of the currency into the country. The other method to secure dollars is indebtedness.

Both to speculate in the domestic market by hoarding surplus or by sending capital abroad, the dollar is the unavoidable reference. Those who generate them through agro-export activity are strongly transnationalized. Its leadership is made up of few companies, and Argentine farmers are subordinated to its logic. This scheme reproduces and deepens the dependence of the Argentine economy.

The transnational agro-export companies work as a means of migration of the value produced territorially, dollarization of the surplus and its flight. Those who own the dollars will have the economic and political power. The agro-industrial company VICENTÍN, one of the few Argentinean traders, works in this area of the political economy.

Creditors using the U.S. dollar through debt issuance denominated in this currency exercise control and significantly influence the production and well-being of debtors and the societies in which these debtors operate. The rule of law is weaponized to extract resources, financial and economic, to satisfy these creditors ahead of any material adverse effects on the debtors and their societies. The creditors are prioritized.

4.2. Dependency

Following the dependency theorists in Latin America (among others - Prebisch, Cardoso, Faletto, Dos Santos, Sunkel, Hinkelammert, Silva Michelena), we identify countries of this region that are part of the capitalist order but located on the periphery of the system. The first element of this order is that Latin American peripheral economies structurally transfer value to central countries' economies. This happens through the payment of interest on external indebtedness, royalties, franchises, and so on (which have the effect of oppressing wage growth). For importation, profits are remitted to the parent companies in the central countries from subsidiaries located in Latin America. For instance, from 1912 to 1975, approximately 70 percent of the profits generated by external direct investment in Argentina were remitted abroad, with only 30 percent reinvested in the country. (E. Basualdo, personal communication, August 17, 2021).

The second element of this order is that in these countries, the cycle of reproduction of capital is not complete. Such a cycle requires accumulation capacity. An economy that has problems retaining the surplus it produces in its territory will have limitations to saving and investing, a cornerstone of the cycle of capital reproduction (Osorio, 2015).

Nevertheless, the conception of central economies today, with financial globalization, should be reinterpreted. It is not about developed countries versus underdeveloped or developing countries without nuances. The gaze must be directed at transnational corporations, those operating under financial services and mechanisms to dislocate the generated surplus and accumulating it. In some cases, transferring the surplus to tax havens while still under control of the transnational corporation.Workers from both the central and the peripheral nations are victims of these practices.

There is an aspect mentioned by Hilferding (1963), which also was alluded to by Kalecki (1956): the ruling elites of capital, if they can avoid it, will not develop the internal market of their own countries. Rather, they will have a propensity to orientate toward the foreign market. The development of the internal market would increase consumption in the territory, for which it is necessary to produce more. Something that implies an increase in the number of workers and the amounts of wages. This can empower workers. And that is something that influential global capitalists want to avoid.

This is further enhanced in Latin American countries, where the capital is sourced from agrarian pursuits and mineral mining. Historically, the region was integrated into the world economy as a supplier of raw materials for the foreign market. The local dominant sectors of these nations are those that arose from such an economic structure, imposing their worldview, traditions, thoughts, customs, and common sense. This culture permeates all aspects of the social life of these countries(Cardoso, 1999). The rule of law, both in its wording and in the criteria for its application, is included in this culture as a primary factor / mechanism in the persistence of the culture.

4.3. External constraints

Economies specialized in the production of raw materials face the issue of external constraints. This happens when these economies begin to grow. Existing industries, not yet technologically sophisticated, begin to demand more capital goods that are not manufactured in the country. They have to import them. In turn, economic growth causes the consumption patterns of the population to change and require products that are not manufactured locally. It should be added that the higher income sectors historically turned to tourism abroad. All these things increase the demand for foreign exchange, since foreign trade in goods and services is carried out in hard currency, most of the time in U.S. dollars. (Gaggero, 2014).

The uptick in demand for dollars due to increased imports is often not met with the supply of dollars that enter the country from its exports; we must take into account that imports are very elastic. In Argentina, it is estimated that each point of growth of its GDP will require an additional 3 billion dollars (Peirano, 2019). This cycle operates as a brake on economic growth (stop and go). The lack of income-generated dollars through foreign trade is compensated by the influx of dollars from external indebtedness. External indebtedness that generates interest expense, also payable in dollars, exacerbates the restriction. From 1983 to the present, interest payments in dollars on Argentina's foreign debt averaged 10 percent of the federal government's spending budget (Ortega, 2021).

We define external restriction as the cyclical lack of foreign currency necessary to finance imports and debt service suffered by a non-industrialized country that does not issue hard (reserve) currency and becomes obligated to debt service in other currencies (e.g., the U.S. dollar). This leads us to understand the extra value of a reserve currency in a country that does not issue it. The scarcity of the same in each event of external constraint will cause it to be revalued in relation to the local legal coin. Moreover, the hard currency will always be exchangeable for more things than the local currency. The exchange value of the dollar is higher. This will lead economic actors to seek to position themselves in dollars. The fluidity of the exchange rate for the reserve currency (often, U.S. dollars) suppresses economic opportunity in the country needing but not able to issue the reserve currency.

In countries that suffer under the burden of external constraints such as Argentina, the dollar will not only be a means of exchange—it will also be a strong tool for speculation due to its continuous rise in relative value. It would often work like a financial security that is always trading higher, imposing ever greater demands on those obligated to seek U.S. dollars for imports and debt service.

4.3.1. Agricultural exports and financial valuation

The leading activity in exports in Argentina (and therefore, the largest provider of dollars in the country, since sales abroad are made in that currency) is agriculture. The soybean complex alone (bean production and derivatives such as pellets, flour, and oil) represents 33.6 percent of total Argentine exports. If we add the complexes of the other three typical "Pampa Húmeda´s" crops (wheat, corn, and sunflower), together they comprise 51.2 percent of all the country's exports. INDEC 2021. The dollars that enter the country for this activity will therefore be subject to tensions.

The authors Arceo and Basualdo define the financial valuation model as

> …the placement of surplus by large firms in various financial assets (securities, bonds, deposits, etc.) in the domestic and international markets. This process, which bursts forth and is predominant in the Argentine economy since the end of the 1970s, expands due to the fact that interest rates, or the link between them, exceed the profitability of the various economic activities, since the accelerated growth of external indebtedness makes it possible to send local capital abroad by operating as a mass of recoverable surplus and/or by releasing profits for these purposes. (Basualdo, 2002: 7)

Debt service grows exponentially. Real production grows linearly. Ultimately, the value of extractive financial liabilities exceeds the value of productive material economic assets.

Constitutive of this model of turning abroad surplus produced in the territory is to monetize profits in dollars, thus avoiding legal restrictions and obtaining reserve currency. Argentinean pesos are accepted (more or less) only in Argentina. For this reason, to enable capital flight, dollars are required. The method to acquire dollars can be achieved through black market exchange. Alternatively, by purchase of securities or shares in pesos which are later sold abroad in dollars. Triangulating exports with foreign entities is utilized to hide transactions from the treasury (i.e., economically superfluous intermediaries are used to evade taxation).

Another tactic is padding invoice payments abroad, leaving the overpaid dollars in another country in a hidden account. Or, under-charging the income in dollars to hoard the surplus, thereby cheating the treasury. Still yet another method is to secure contracts payable in dollars for local transactions, which may be the strongest device, pressing the Argentinean government to establish an institutional framework that allows dollars to removed freely from the country.

A study in 2006 by the United States Federal Reserve revealed the bi-monetary nature of the Argentine economy. With 1,300 dollar bills per inhabitant, the country was first in the world ranking of dollar holdings per capita outside the United States. Barbería 2020. It is obvious that the majority of Argentines do not handle dollars. There is only a wealthy minority that places the country in the foreground in this art.

Thus, the ability to exploit the financial system through allowable financial services such as foreign currency saving, speculation, and trading is reserved for those with large capital surpluses. Only this small minority of individuals and entities can afford to protect themselves against the volatility of the local economy.

In brief, the means for taking dollars out of the country can be legal such as the remittance of profits from local branches of companies to their headquarters abroad.Or not legal such as manipulation of transfer prices, which is examined below.

4.3.1.1. Transfer prices

Intra-firm trade (e.g., between two branches of the same company located in different countries) represents around two-thirds of all world trade(OMC, 2009). Intra-firm trade responds to the strategy of transnational companies locating their activities in different countries while seeking lower labor costs, tax advantages, and stocks of raw materials (Hidalgo, 2012).

When we talk about transfer prices, we refer to the manipulation of the amounts (which are declared before the tax authorities) of the intra-firm commercial operations.To understand its importance, false invoicing (as pointed out in another part of this work) in Argentine international trade is equivalent to 4.4 percent of its Gross Domestic Product. Verónica Grondona (2014) estimates that transfer pricing manipulation due to under-invoicing and over-invoicing of Argentine exports and imports could range from 10 percent to 20 percent of the value declared to the treasury.

> Transfer prices are usually defined as the prices at which transactions are carried out between related entities, although this definition implies recognizing the existence of a price, of a contract between legally independent parties, something that is not fulfilled within a group economic. (Grondona, 2014: 6)

The author carries out an analysis of the tax evasion mechanisms of transnational companies for the purpose of evasion itself but which may have the effect of configuring capital flight. For the approach that we are interested in carrying out, oriented toward estimating how much economic surplus is produced in the territory that is migrated to other countries, disarticulating the process of accumulation is essential for estimating the national development transferred out.

Capitalist accumulation will be impossible in a state in which surplus achieved from principal exports flees permanently to foreign accounts without paying taxes. Productive and social investment is obliterated. The mechanisms include under-invoicing of exports, over-invoicing of imports, contracting and payment of simulated intra-firm services, self-loans between the branches themselves, among other manipulated and non-neutral activities. Together, these serve to distort the accuracy and completeness of the measurement of production of material goods and services within the State.

The Central Bank of the Argentine Republic (BCRA) is a public entity independent of the national State. Its mission is to protect the value of the local currency, maintain financial stability, as well as promote employment and economic development with social equity. Consequently, it regulates the amount of money that circulates; it is the fiscal agent of the government, and it executes the exchange policy of the State (Act Number 24, 144).

Since the availability of dollars is an essential issue for the Argentine economy, its financial stability, and the value of its legal tender currency, the BCRA imposes obligations through mandatory regulations; it issues (called "BCRA communications") the obligation to settle all amounts in dollars collected for sales of goods and services abroad. These dollars will be dumped in the official exchange market, with the exporter receiving the equivalent in pesos at the exchange rate recognized by the government. Circumventing these rules to preserve the dollars is an important vector for how to accumulate capital in Argentina

The manipulation of transfer prices does not only imply tax evasion. It is also appropriation of dollars that should have gone to the thirsty official Argentine exchange market, which needs that currency to finance strategic imports and public debt payments. If a soybean exporting company under-invoices its sale to its own branch abroad, it will pay less taxes to the treasury for the sale. Additionally, it will pay in fewer dollars than it actually received.

Here, the ruse of triangulations comes into play. The basic scheme is the following:

Suppose that a ton of soybeans costs 1 dollar, and assume that the price of the dollar in Argentina is 1 dollar = 2 Argentine pesos. A company in Argentina called "Víctor Argentina" exports 100 tons of soybeans to its own branch located in Uruguay, called "Víctor Uruguay." However, he invoices the sale as if it were 80 tons, not 100. He receives 80 dollars. When bringing those 80 dollars to Argentina, he settles them at the Central Bank, the official foreign exchange market, and receives 160 pesos for them. Then, the Argentine treasury charges a percentage of 30 percent of the exported value as export duties ("retentions"). "Victor Argentina," if he had received 100 dollars, later converted to 200 pesos, for the 100 tons of soybeans he exported, would have had to pay 60 pesos to the treasury. But since he declared 80 he paid only 48 pesos. He evaded 12 pesos to the treasury.

Then, the "Víctor Uruguay" branch sells the 100 tons of soybeans that it bought from its parent company in Argentina to the company "Holland AgriBusiness BV" from the Netherlands. "Holland AgriBusiness BV" will pay "Víctor Uruguay" 100 dollars. But Uruguay does not charge export duty ("retentions") because its legislation does not contemplate such a tax. Furthermore, in the soybean sales contract between "Víctor Uruguay" and "Holland Agribusiness BV," "Víctor Uruguay" requests a 20 percent in advance deposit to be made to an account that the company has in a New York Bank. In other words, "Holland Agribusiness BV" has to transfer 20 dollars to Wall Street.

As a result of the scheme, the owners of "Víctor Argentina" (which are the same as "Víctor Uruguay") will not only have evaded 12 pesos to the Argentine treasury. It will also have managed to get 20 dollars out of the country, snubbing the Central Bank's controls and deepening the shortage of dollars in the official exchange market.Regarding the materiality of the operation, the soybean was shipped in the port of Rosario (Argentina) and went directly to the port of Rotterdam (Netherlands). It never touched Uruguay. See Figure 4.1 below.

Thus, "Victor Argentina" will have 20 dollars outside the country and will use these in turn to speculate (because sooner or later its value against the peso will increase) and execute financial transactions.

The rule in exports of grains and industrial derivatives is triangulation with a trader located in a third country other than where the buyer is addressed. The exception is the direct sale to the country of final destination of commodity. About 97 percent of exports of this item made between 2020 and 2021 were triangulated sales with an intermediary in Uruguay (35 percent), Switzerland (23 percent), the United States (23 percent), and the Netherlands (16 percent) of total sales. (Muiño, 2022).

Some estimations point out that a few wealthiest Argentines have 400,000 million dollars abroad in their country, of which one only 90,000 million have been declared to tax agency AFIP (Oglietti, 2022). According to the INDEC, the balance of assets and liabilities (dollarized) of Argentine individuals abroad gives a positive balance in favor of the (Argentines) of 219 billion dollars. The relationship is inverted if we consider the government and the Central Bank, with a deficit balance of 105 billion dollars (INDEC, 2021). The private ones are creditors.

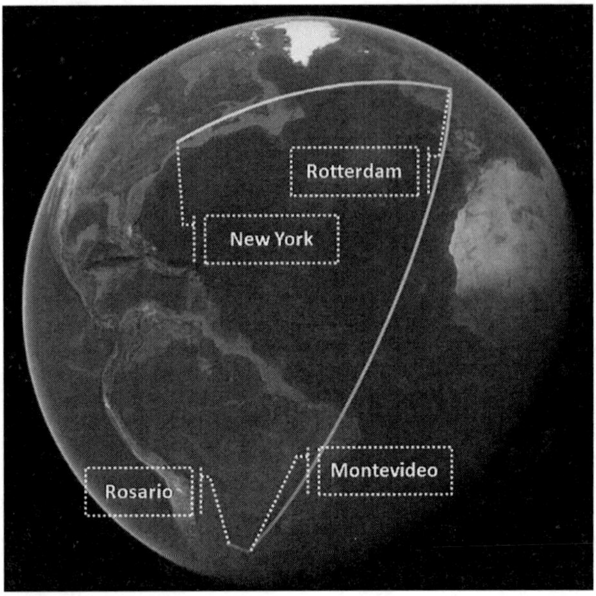

Figure 4.1: Triangulations.
Prepared by the author using Google Earth.

The public ones, debtors. We would have to ask what are the mechanisms of dollarization supported by the public effort of the majorities to sustain the speculation of the minorities?

In the Argentine case, the accumulation scheme of the capitalist leadership involves dollarizing its surpluses. The middle classes will attempt the same to preserve their limited savings capacity in the face of a local currency in continual devaluation. The lower classes, without even the capacity to generate surpluses, will suffer the consequences of an inflationary order, since the rising dollar is always a relative price of the items traded in the domestic market.

Transfer pricing comprises a means to manipulate financial liabilities to the state treasury and to hoard reserve capital, whether in domestic or foreign financial institutions, in the form of financial assets separate and apart from the production and exchange of material goods and services. The financial services layer atop the transfer of real goods and services extracts and maximize the grift of the more valuable currency (often, U.S. dollars) directly at the expense of the state treasury and indirectly at the expense of the general welfare. The processes of exporting and importing material goods and services are corruptly manipulated under a largely unchecked regime of non-neutral self-reporting of costs of production and prices of sales such that the profit, gain, and preferred currency flee under the direction of private capitalists, undeterred by legitimate interests of the State—its treasury and its society at large.

4.3.1.2. Agro-dollars

Commodities are an ideal market for speculation. As a standard, homogeneous, fungible commodity traded in large quantities, raw materials and their simple derivatives can function (and do) as a means of exchange and a reserve of value. Their availability in bulk enables them to be traded directly in the spot and futures markets. Commodities are a flexible vehicle for speculation (Hilferding, 1968).

The Argentine grain market is dollarized. Prices are not set in Argentina but abroad, primarily on the Chicago Stock Exchange (NYSE Chicago) in the State of Illinois, a Midwestern agricultural producer in the United States. The Chicago Stock Exchange specializes in agricultural commodities. For daily transactions made in Argentina, the quoted price in Chicago dollars is taken, converted into pesos at the current exchange rate, and the proportional amount for taxes (paid by exporters) and other logistic-related costs are deducted. The expected sum will be the price of the grain that will appear on the board of the local grain exchanges. The most important Argentine exchange is the Rosario Stock Exchange. Therefore, it will be the reference price that the exporting trader company (transnational in most cases) will pay to the Argentine field producer.

Inserted in the dependent dynamics, the export sector of grains and oilseeds will produce a surplus that, in large part, will be dollarized and go abroad. The rent will be de-localized from the territory[1]that originated it, migrating out of it, and not increasing the capital

1 For Marcelo Sili, the territory is "…the geographical space appropriated by a society under a system of intentions that organize and qualify that space. This system of intentions may well be multiple and diverse, which gives us a fragmented territoriality due to the fact that each actor has individual and different objectives from the rest of the actors, or there may be a collective and consensual intention that generates

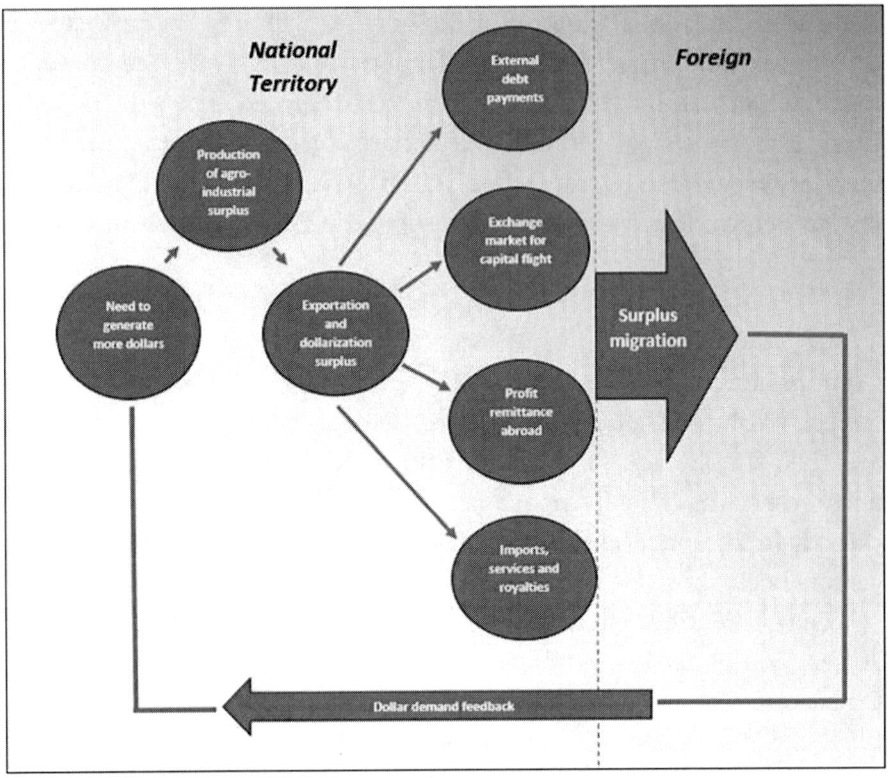

Figure 4.2: Dollarization and migration of the agro-industrial surplus.
Prepared by the author.

endowment of the country. Accumulation is not possible in this circularly vicious dynamic in light of the presuppositions of capitalism itself. See Figure 4.2 above.

The graph shows the circular dynamics of migration of the agricultural surplus. The need to generate dollars for the country leads to the encouragement, in any manner, to export grains payable in that currency. However, a significant proportion of the dollars received will not be allocated to strategic investment in the territory such as for the purchase of imported technological inputs. A segment of the dollars will never touch Argentine soil since they escape via the manipulation

a territory with unity of objectives and projects." SILI, M. (2005). La Argentina Rural, Buenos Aires. INTA Editions, Page 8.

of transfer prices. Another segment will be used to pay interest on the debt. Some will be utilized as a remittance of profits to the parent companies of the transnational. Additionally, a proportion of it will go to the consumption of imported goods by the wealthy classes. By not rooting the currency in the development needs of the territory, the need for foreign currency inflows is maintained or increased, restarting the cycle.

There are also political reasons. Whoever has a silo bag with grains in Argentina is sitting on a store of value in dollars. Hence, the historical dispute between the grain producing and trading sector on the one hand and the governments on the other. The great farmers and traders push to liberalize the foreign exchange market, allowing the currency to circulate without restrictions or access limits and at the price set by demand. This could increase the price of the currency rapidly, giving huge profits to the large agricultural producers and exporting companies that have their profits in dollars. On the government side, it would suffer the effect of an increase in internal prices (the dollar is a reference price—a price on which other prices depend, together with basic supply costs and salaries), adversely impacting wages and increasing the weight of the debt in foreign currency (the State collects taxes in pesos). These conditions in all likelihood lead to the general impoverishment of the population.

Free trade is not a neutral process. It is dominated, if not defined, by market participants with significant influence in the domestic political economy and savvy networks among market participants in foreign political economies. Analysis of the whole (e.g., overall GDP) presents aggregation risk; i.e., the likelihood of the data of the whole concealing the economic hardship on many of its parts. In sum, GDP presents the ecological fallacy as the group of persons collectively contributing to it do not benefit equally.

The granary market is one more area of political-financial speculation. See below.

4.3.1.3. The strong actors of the system

Argentine tradable goods with international competitiveness (to successfully penetrate the world market) include its agro-products. The static comparative advantages of soil and climate (products of natural factors) have been a determining factor for Argentina to be a great world exporter of biomass.

Since the military dictatorship of 1976, the Argentine State seems to have advocated "the commodity consensus" (Gaggeroet al., 2014) uninterruptedly. It does so with public policies that have become true persistent State policies since they were not modified by successive governments. This consensus consists of "not disturbing the main sector that obtains the dollars that the country needs."

Argentina has the largest (or second largest) global agribusiness export complex in the world. (Huergo, 2020) (Clarín, 2021). However, in a transnationalized economy scheme, the strategic management of these mega-agribusinesses is not domiciled in Argentina. The structure of international marketing, linking supply and demand, prices and logistics of the grain market, is not operated by Argentine producers. It is commanded by an oligopoly of transnational corporations that have dominated it for centuries: Archer Daniels Midland (Chicago, USA); Bunge (Saint Louis, USA); Cargill (Minneapolis, USA); Dreyfus (Rotterdam, Netherlands), and two newcomers (see below) stand out in this club.

Washington Post journalist Dan Morgan conducted an investigation of the history and power of grain traders worldwide. The work focuses on the five large cereal companies that monopolized the world grain trade in the 1980s: namely, Cargill, Continental, Louis Dreyfus, Bunge, and André. The investigation was motivated by an episode known as "the great cereal robbery."

In the midst of the Cold War, the Soviet Union managed to increase its grain purchases, taking them rapidly from 34 million tons in 1971 to 83 million tons in 1975. In 1972, the first explosive increase happened. Much of that grain was corn grown in Iowa and wheat from South Dakota and Kansas, bound for the USSR while not transparent to the United States Department of Agriculture (USDA). This change in the trade policy of the USSR of massive purchases of cereals from the US caused inflation in the price of food in the United States. That the strategic enemy of the United States has been able to make a purchase regardless of the United States Government provoked reflection about autonomy and power with transnational grain traders (Morgan, 1983).

Cereal sources are less diverse than other resources. Only a few countries have surplus production of this product (United States and Argentina, among them).However, arbitration and distribution of this surplus is concentrated in a handful of transnational companies.

> It is difficult to understand how the international grain companies could slip through history as discreetly as they did. Cereal is the only resource in the world even more important than oil for modern civilization. (Morgan, 1983:9).

The "great cereal robbery" makes Morgan conclude that the power of the cereal transnational corporation is the product of careful engineering in the management of power, organization, and focus in the way of acting and decision-making dating back to the 19th century.

> Of the companies that have the global oligopoly in grain trading, four traditional ones stand out: Archer Daniels Midland (ADM), Bunge, Cargill, and Louis Dreyfus, (called together "ABCD"). They control most of the international trade in cereals and grains and have great influence over the determination of international prices of food. With more than a century of historical persistence, they constitute an extremely peculiar group of companies. With a discreet attitude, they have changed very little in their long existence. They are among the largest companies in the world, but they are traditionally family businesses. In addition to grain trading, transportation, and storage activities, they play an important role in financing production through the delivery of technological packages and inputs (seeds, fertilizers, and agrochemicals). Its subsidiaries in many countries consume a large part of the raw materials they sell, so their prices are more like transfer prices: they store in their own facilities; they transport on their own railways and ships. Moreover, they are livestock and poultry producers, playing outsized rolesin the production of animal feed and participation in the biofuel markets. They are owners or tenants of land, and they are financial entities that actively participate in the derivatives markets. (Gómez Oliver et al., 2016:24)

Archer Daniels Midland, Bunge, Cargill, and Louis Dreyfus handle most of the world's grain trade. Their activities present a vertical integration with presence and control throughout the chain. They not only handle trading activities, but they are transport and storage companies acting as suppliers of agricultural inputs (seed, fertilizer, and agrochemicals). They have stockpiles and have their own means of land transport, including grain elevators, ports, and ships. In the same way, they process the raw material in their own facilities, obtaining oils, flours, and biofuels, as well as venturing into the manufacture of plastics, dyes, and starches. As Morgan (1983) argues: they are predominantly family businesses (though Archer Daniels Midland and Bunge are presently publicly traded).

In brief, consolidation and concentration of economic power in the granary markets, often in the form of family businesses, has enabled control over the pricing, production, and distribution of essential material goods to reside in a small group of individuals, families, and corporations that exert an outsized effect on the ability of millions of individuals in a multitude of countries to live and occasionally thrive. Sometimes, it is said that he who controls the present controls the past. In the granary markets—he who controls the availability and affordability of food materials (raw, intermediate, or final goods) controls the well-being of civilization.

4.3.1.3.1. Two new players in the international grain trade

The accelerated growth of China, a great exporter of technology and demander of raw materials and food for a population that is gradually increasing its consumption standards, has consequences in the agribusiness market. The company COFCO (China Oil and Foodstuffs Corporation) breaks into the league of companies that oligopolize the grain market.

COFCO is a Chinese state-owned, food processing holding[2]company. In 2014,COFCO acquired 51 percent of Nidera (a company with Dutch and Argentine capital) and 51 percent of Noble (a group based in Hong Kong), both in the agricultural and raw materials sectors. Later, it acquired 100 percent of both equity interests. COFCO is consolidated as one of the great players in Argentine agriculture, becoming the first exporter of the activity in 2019. (Arellano, 2021).

The COFCO holding company owns 20 companies, eight of which are listed on the stock exchange. It has 400 points of operation, from

2 A portfolio-holding company is a company that does not produce or market anything by itself. It is incorporated to own shares of other companies.

small grinding plants to huge ports located throughout China, staffed with 120,000 employees. This is an actor that is constituted in a different way: it is state-owned; it is a holding company, and it is listed on the stock exchange, characteristics that are different from the ABCD. Locally, on the coast of the Paraná River, it operates two of its own ports.

4.3.1.3.2. A special new market participant: GLENCORE PLC

GLENCORE PLCtakes its name from the acronym "Global Energy Commodity Resources." The acronym that follows means *Public Limited Company* (Public Limited Liability Company—it offers shares to the public). With headquarters in Baar, Switzerland, but domiciled in the tax haven of Saint Helier, Jersey, it ranks number 415 in market capitalization among publicly traded companies in the world according to the 2021 ranking of FORBES magazine. The company has a market value of 52.2 billion dollars—equivalent to the GDP of Uruguay (FORBES, 2021).

Dedicated to the areas of extraction, processing, and marketing of natural resources, GLENCORE, by 2010, had a 60 percent share of the world market in zinc; 50 percent in copper; 3 percent in oil; and 9 percent in cereals (Pidd, 2011). With the acquisition of Viterra Ltd,[3] a transnational of Canadian origin dedicated to the trade of agroproducts (headquartered in Rotterdam, Netherlands) in 2012,[4] GLENCORE sought to position itself as a leader in the global marketing of grains and its derivatives. It was the largest exporter of oils and flours in 2020, after controlling the most efficient grain extruder in the world (RENOVA S.A.) and having absorbed the market shares of VICENTÍNS.A.I.C.[5]

Both the origins and the growth of GLENCORE in the global order (i.e., the performance of the firm) are, to say the least, controversial. Its expansion seems to have been the result of financial ruse, legal

3 See https://www.viterra.com/ , official corporate website, accessed May 18, 2021.

4 EL CRONISTA. (2012). GLENCORE beat Cargill and won the Canadian Viterra, March 21 in El CronistaNegocios, website https://www.cronista.com/Negocios/GLENCORE-le-gano -to-Cargill-and-stayed-with-the-canadian-Viterra-20120321-0037.html , accessed May 18, 2021.

5 VALOR SOJA. (2021). Chau Oleaginosa Moreno: Now the main Argentine soy flour exporting company is called Viterra, in Bichos de Campo, May 3, website https://bichosdecampo.com/chau-oleaginosa -moreno-now-the-main-argentine-company-exporter-of-soybean-flour-is-called-viterra/ ,accessed May 18, 2021.

transgression, tax evasion, and operation with shell corporate forms, rather than the result of competitiveness achieved by the company's technological advancement. Its comparative advantage seems more accurately founded on manipulation of the legal and financial systems than on development of superior technological efficiencies.

The company first appears in 1974 under the name "Marc Rich & Co." Marcel David Reich (aka Marc Rich) was a Belgian businessman, who enjoyed Bolivian, Spanish, American, and Israeli citizenships simultaneously. His field of business was international natural resource brokerage and financial intermediation. Rich circumvented the 1970s Arab oil embargo by buying oil from Iran and Iraq, then selling it to US companies. With the profit obtained, he founded the company that took advantage of other embargoes, this time applied to countries under accusations of human rights violations. In this way, Rich's company was offered as a channel to do business with those countries. Along these lines, he carried out lucrative transactions with apartheid South Africa, the government of Nicolae Ceausescu in Romania, and that of Augusto Pinochet in Chile, among others (Rankin, 2013). His quest for profit and gain was not significantly limited by the lack of integrity of his (informal) business partners.

In 1983, Marc Rich was prosecuted in New York by prosecutor Rudolph Giuliani on charges of organized crime, illicit association, and tax evasion, among others. For such crimes, if convicted, an aggregate sentence of more than 300 years in prison could have been imposed. However, Marc Rich fled to Switzerland and was among one of the most wanted people by the FBI. He would be pardoned in 2001 by US President Bill Clinton on his last day in office. In parallel, the company's debt increased, since it operated aggressively in the world of risky financial transactions (Ammann, 2009).

The company became adept at making leverage buyouts of other companies, a mechanism in which the buyer does not put his assets at risk for the acquisition, but the creditors from whom he takes debt to pay for his purchase finance the transaction (Cox, 2011). Moreover, the buyer, without its own assets at risk, reports the purchase debt as owed by the company purchased. In a material sense, the company pays for its own sale: buy for one with the money of another. If the artifice ends well, acquisitions can be made with meager contributions from the purchasing principals and agents their own assets. For the year 1993, partly because of the debt load, the company, whose value had fallen, was acquired by its managers and directors (i.e., a management buyout) that came to own the majority of its shares. And it is at that moment that it adopts the name GLENCORE.

The trajectory of GLENCORE continued its questionable behavior, ethics, and lack of integrity—being accused of paying bribes in the Democratic Republic of the Congo (Allen Mills, 2008) and evading taxes in Zambia (Ford, 2001).

In 2011, it becomes a company that offered its shares to the public, choosing the London Stock Exchange to do so. By June of that year, the share price was 4.8 pounds, while as of June 2021 (10 years later), it was 3.2 pounds. The reasons for the declines and volatility of GLENCORE's shares are explained by the variation in international commodity prices, as well as by its indebtedness and recurring legal scandals.

In 2012, GLENCORE bought Viterra Ltd, a Canadian agribusiness company. In 2013, it merged with the Anglo-Swiss mining company Xstrata PLC. In 2015, it was close to bankruptcy due to its high indebtedness and falling commodity prices but managed to survive by issuing new shares (Mochinsky, 2015).

The company has been investigated by the Serious Fraud Office (United Kingdom's anti-fraud agency) and by the Department of Justice of the United States due to its suspicious financial maneuvers and allegations of payments of bribes. (Martinez-Galiana, 2019). In 2017, the company appears in the "Paradise Papers," the name of the investigation by an international consortium of journalists, based on multiple leaks of 13 million documents from two law firms and 19 tax havens, according to whichfraudulent maneuvers arose from various subjects and companies to evade taxes (ICIJ, 2017).

Likewise, GLENCORE was implicated in the 2020 FinCEN Files (another investigative chapter by the same international consortium of journalists already mentioned); this time based on a leak of FinCEN documents. FinCEN is the acronym for Financial Crimes Enforcement Network, an agency of the US Department of the Treasury that analyzes information on financial transactions suspected of money laundering, evasion, financing of terrorism, or other financial crimes(ICIJ, 2020). It is the financial intelligence unit (FIU) of the U.S. In the case of GLENCORE, Deutsche Bank issued two reports, the first of which identifies 773 transactions with dozens of companies implicating more than $566 million between November 2013 and April 2014. The second report discloses another 310 transactions of more than $259 million sent and received between May and June 2015. Many of these financial transactions involved the controlled entities of its Argentine partner, VICENTÍNS.A.I.C. (Mon, 2020).

On March 24, 2022, GLENCORE pleaded guilty to prosecutors of the Southern District of New York to bribing public officials to win contracts, and bribing judges to make lawsuits against him disappear. GLENCORE has operated a network to committing crime that included Nigeria, Cameroon, Ivory Coast, Equatorial Guinea, Brazil, Venezuela, and Congo. For this, he paid a fine of 1.1 billion dollars.[6]

Today, the company has profits of 11.6 billion per year (equivalent to the GDP of Equatorial Guinea), a presence in more than 35 countries, and 135,000 employees and agents. Its main shareholders are Qatar Holding LLC (9.1 percent), Ivan Glasenberg (9.1 percent), and BlackRock (6.7 percent). Apart from the accusations that weigh on GLENCORE for tax evasion and payment of bribes, the company has also been singled out for not recognizing the labor rights of its workers, pushing them to inhuman limits, as well as for the depredation of the environment that their industrial activities entail (Pantland, 2018).

In Argentina, it operates through Viterra SA, RENAISCO B.V., and the Buenos Aires branch of the Curtis legal consultancy.[7] Since it took over the operational capacity of RENOVA S.A. in 2020, it has become the country's leading exporter of soybean oil and meal. It has two private ports on the Paraná River.

6 See GLENCORE Entered Guilty Pleas to Foreign Bribery and Market Manipulation Schemes | OPA | Department of Justice, accessed September 2, 2022.

7 Seehttps://www.curtis.com/our-firm/news/curtis-advises-glencore-internatio nal-plc-on-us-legal-matters-in-acquisition-of-viterra-inc , and https://www.curtis. com/our-firm/offices/buenos-aires/overview , accessed June 14, 2021.

4.3.1.3.3. Supremacy of ABCD+Co+Gl

The segment Archer Daniels Midland, Bunge, Cargill, Dreyfus, COFCO, and GLENCORE (ABCD + Co + Gl) accounts for 49.05 percent of all Argentine exports of grains, legumes, protein meals, and vegetable oils (Di Yennno, 2021). Such dominance in the sector is politically enhanced by joining the powerful business chambers CIARA (Chamber of the Oil Industry of the Argentine Republic) and CEC (Cereal Export Center). These two trade associations under the leadership of ABCD+Co+Gl bring together all of the rest of the smaller companies in the grain and derivatives export activity. CIARA and CEC simply increase ABCD+Co+Gl's potency.

From their position in the export chain, ABCD+Co+Gl are an oligopsony as the only exit door for granary exports; they can lower the price of the raw material that they buy from farmers for export. This is verified by the indicated amounts of the theoretical FAS (Free Alongside Ship) published by the National Ministry of Agriculture, which would be the price that the exporter companies (ABCD+Co+Gl) should pay to the farmer. This price is opposed to the FOB (Free on Board), which is the price that the foreign buyer will pay to the ABCD+Co+Gl for exports. The theoretical FAS is calculated by subtracting from the FOB the expenses in taxes, port costs (fobbing), and commercial services. Let us look at an example to see how ABCD+Co+Gl imposes their power at the last link of export chain.

In 2019 (which we chose because it was prior to the pandemic), exports of unprocessed soybeans from Argentina alone were 3,472 million (INDEC, 2020). If the ABCD+Co+Gl traders represent 49 percent of exportation of all soybeans, 1,701 million was their share. This is equivalent to the price at that time for 5 million tons of exported soybeans. The quantity of 5 million tons was declared to the AFIP (Federal Administration of Public Revenues) under this declaration. However, in actuality, about 9 percent of exports are undeclared to the AFIP, approximating half-a-million tons according to the estimates showed above. Since ABCD+Co+Gl only intermediated: How much should they have paid to farmers from whom they bought those 5 million tons of beans?

Let us examine the first step ABCD+Co+Gl. According to the Ministry of Agriculture (FAS theoretical), taking the price in dollars per ton of soybeans in Chicago Stock Exchange, 36 percent would have to be discounted. That 36 percent is to cover export tax (which the exporting trader fully transmits to farmers), fobbing, and commercial services. In other words, for all the beans they bought during 2019 to export them later without adding value, ABCD+Co+Gl should have paid farmers $1,089 million. But how much were they actually paid? They were not paid those $1,089 million; they were paid only $1.021 million. The historical trend is that traders pay 4 percent below what is indicated by the official theoretical FAS under an analysis of the structure of real costs and benefits(Ortega, 2018). In other words, ABCD+Co+Gl appropriated an excessive surplus of $68 million. Figure 4.3 below depicts how the income from a ton of soybeans was distributed under this regime.

Let us go to the second step. From soybean exported in Argentina, it is estimated that 9 percent is not declared. This maneuver has two consequences. Firstly, the non-declared 9 percent ceases to be taxed (by escaping from the treasury's rules) the equivalent of 30 percent as export duties. Secondly, all dollars corresponding to that 9 percent will not be settled at the Central Bank (BCRA), receiving pesos in exchange, and

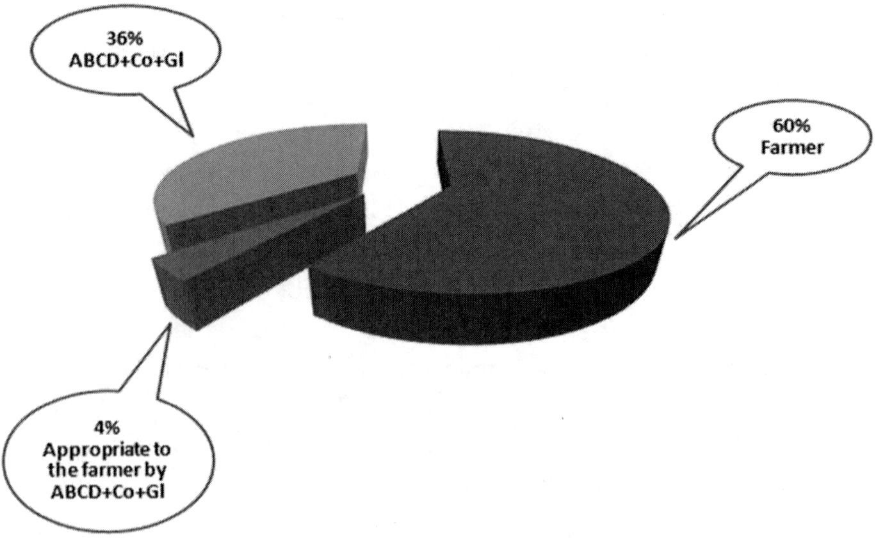

Figure 4.3: Appropriation of income from a ton of soybeans
Prepared by the author.

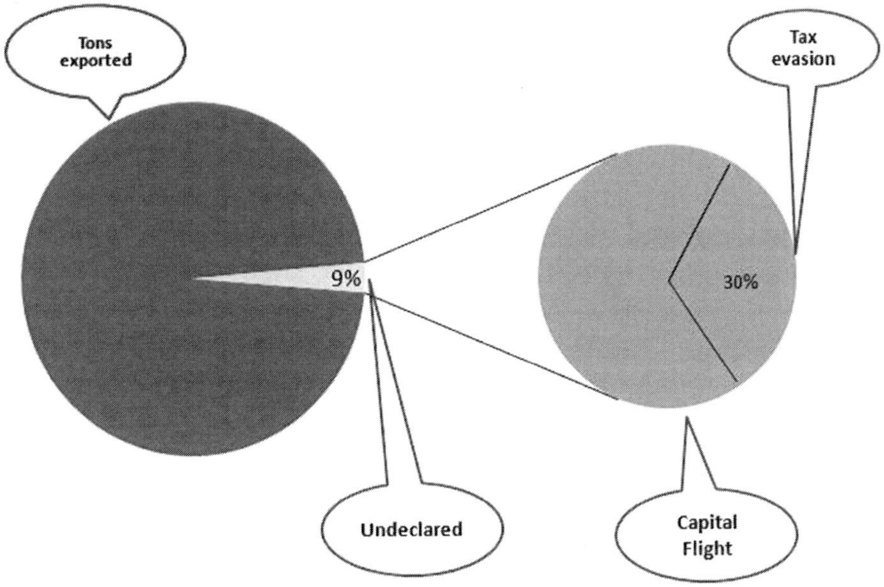

Figure 4.4: Tax evasion and capital flight regarding exported soybeans.
Prepared by the author.

thereby feed the official exchange market for foreign currency. Instead, those dollars will remain in some foreign account. This is capital flight. This exacerbated the external restrictions oppressing Argentina. See figure below.

The percentages may not move the reader until you consider the following: the grain export market is characterized by huge volumes traded. When we talk about a 9 percent that is not declared, or a 4 percent layer of value that the exporting trader takes from the farmer, we are talking about percentages based on millions of tons of products. Between grains and derivatives such as flour and oils, Argentina exported almost 60 million tons in 2019 (Terré, 2021). It is just a matter of multiplication to understand.

Due to the unchecked and underexamined market power of the cartel of buyers illustrated above, producers such as farmers are underpaid for their outputs and taxation authorities such as the Argentine treasury suffer from tax evasion. See Figure 4.4 above. This concentrated market power facilitates market manipulation at the expense of the general welfare of Argentina's political economy, as well as facilitate capital flight (i.e., U.S. dollars transferred to foreign accounts).

4.4. The Argentine agricultural producer

The export of grains and derivatives in Argentina is not presented as a foreign enclave system. This is because the large transnationals that dominate the business are not the owners of the land where the crops are grown. The Pampa Húmeda (Humid Pampa) is a sub-region of Argentina with an area of 600,000 km2 (231661.3 mi2). See Figure 4.5 below. Its topology is extensively prairie-like with an exceptionally flat relief. It has a raining regime favorable to agricultural and livestock activity. With a temperate climate, few regions in the world have the fertility of Pampa Húmeda, comparable only to the agricultural areas of Iowa, Nebraska, Illinois, and Minnesota in the Midwest of the United States. With 30 million hectares (74 million acres) cultivated, the Humid Pampa represents 80 percent of the country's planted area. It is the main area of production for grains and oilseeds in Argentina for export. See figure below.

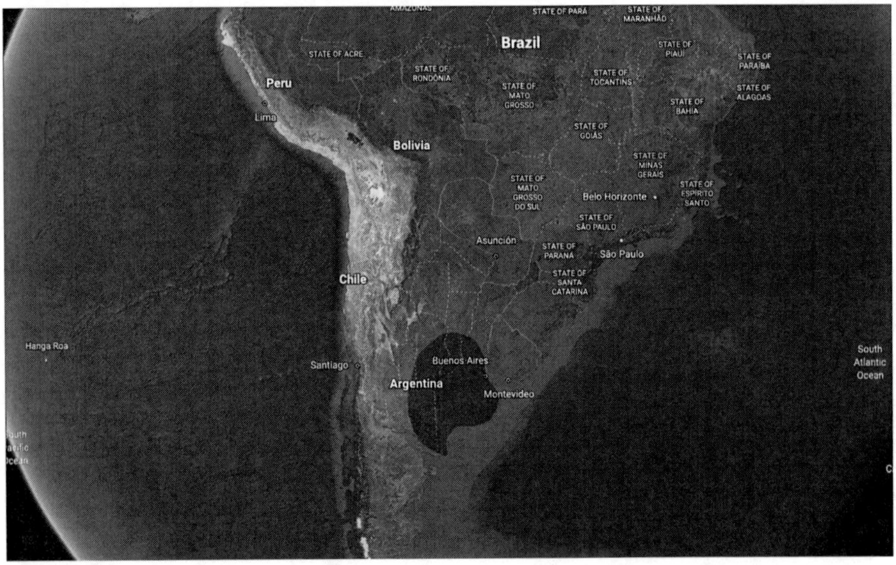

Figure 4.5: Pampa Húmeda location.
Prepared by the author using Google Earth

Producers of less than 100 hectares (247 acres) make up 38 percent of the farms in Pampa Húmeda but control only 3 percent of the land (Sili, 2011).

The agro-industrial productivity of Pampa Húmeda (because it is focused on exports) is one of the mechanisms for the entry of foreign currency into the country. Subsequently, it is subjected to appropriation, relocation, and flight of the capital surplus from the territory where it was produced. Producers that own more than 2,500 hectares (6,177.6 acres) control 39 percent of the land. This presents a consolidated model of the agricultural company in the country where 1.08 percent of agricultural exploitation by this model entity concentrates and controls 36.34 percent of the land (Verbitsky, 2008). The lack of proportionality between landowners and producers creates adverse conditions for Argentina.

How does foreign capital operate in agricultural activities in the territory? It does not do so directly by land ownership or as an enclave. It is not foreign capital that is directly in charge of agricultural production. When the transnational capital of the globalized food trade arrived in Argentina, these capitalists found that the agricultural activity already achieved high productivity as managed by its owners.

A property of 2,500 hectares (6,177.6 acres) or more is considered a large rural producer in Argentina. Comparatively, the United States Department of Agriculture (USDA) estimates that 575 hectares (1,421 acres) is a large farm, with 841.1 hectares (2,086 acres) a very large farm. We see then how the large estate is central in the mode of agricultural production in Argentina. Now, we will detail why.

Eduardo Basualdo and Miguel Khavisse (1994) analyzed the structure of land tenure in the Province of Buenos Aires, which is the most important nucleus of the Pampa Húmeda region, the fertile agricultural area where we find the crops of corn, soy, wheat, and sunflowers. The authors focused their observations on those that own more than 20,000 hectares (49,421 acres). The authors concluded that the owners of this type of large extensions continued to be the decisive actors in rural Argentina. Additionally, landowners increase their scale of production by leasing other properties. This central mechanism of extension agriculture is in use today by producers for export (Basualdo and Khavisse, 1994).

The large estate in Pampa Húmeda is economic not geographical. The land may be divided, even subdivided into different areas, but it is owned by the same family group. A family group that, to avoid the division of the land losing productive scale, keeps the estate together by placing it under control of a joint-stock company (or holding company), condominiums, de facto companies, or inheritances without partition among the successors. (Basualdo, personal communication, October 17, 2021). This power in the political economy, over agrarian production and exports / imports, in tax avoidance / evasion schemes, in capital flight of reserves, and so on is sustained through generations of families excluding the property and proceeds from the reach of the State and the public weal.

About 20,000 hectares (429,421 acres) are equivalent to almost the surface of the entire autonomous City of Buenos Aires-CABA, Argentinean Federal District, which has 20,300 hectares (203 km2, 78.3 mi2). There are 35 agricultural groups, most of them belonging to the traditional landed aristocracy of the 19thcentury, who collectively own a total of 1,564,091 hectares ("77 CABAs," 3,864,953 acres). On average, each of these groups owns 44,688 hectares. Each one ("2 CABAs," 110,426.4 acres) controlled by one of the following handful of families:

> Gómez Álzaga-Balcarce-Larreta; Duhau-Escalante- Avellaneda; Pereyra Iraola Anchorena; Beraza; Duggan; Santamarina; Santamanina-De Alzaga; Galli-Lacau-Rossi; Lafuente-Mendiondo; Lalor; Ballester-Tronconi; Paz Anchorena; Beamonte; Blaquier; Ochoa-Paz, Guerrero; Harriet; De Apellaniz; Anchorena Zuberbühler; Inchauspe; Sansot-Vernet Basualdo; Pueyrredón; Defferrar; Duhau Nelson; Bullrich; Pereda-Ocampo; Zubiaurre; Herreras Vegas; Arrechea; Lalor-Udaondo; FuchusFacht; Colombo-Magliaro; Ayerza-García-Zuberbühler; and Lanz.(Basualdo and Khavisse, 1994).

Such groups saw their dominance enhanced by the expansion of scale farming.Agriculturizationis the process of displacing livestock and more labor-intensive crops, or family production, in favor of cereal and oilseed crops.This process was accelerated with the opening to transgenic seeds[8] and direct seeding[9] for these crops. Such production increases the yields demanded by the international market. However, they did not have a rational accompanying system of public policies to protect small- and medium-sized producers or the environment. The sector was invigorated with hard technologies (e.g., tractors, agricultural machines, telecommunications, satellite information, agrochemicals) and soft technologies (e.g., novel business methods). In new management methods, the planting, fertilization, application of agrochemicals, and harvesting are no longer done by the owner of property. These works are outsourced to companies specialized in each of these activities, gaining economic efficiency. Thus, ownership and control are separated.

How does transnational capital impose its hegemony? It does so by association with local landowners. Local landowners are integrated vertically but with a subordinated role. The transnational capital represented by the companies Archer David Midland, Bunge, Cargill, Dreyfuss, COFCO, and GLENCORE, reserved for themselves the final stretch of the activity. That is, the production of industrial derivatives (e.g., flours, oils, pellets, biofuels) and their commercialization, linking with international demand for export. The last links to the global market dominate the chain. In a sense, transnational capital skims the cream for itself. See Figure 4.6 below.

In the figure above, we have represented the pyramidal structure of export agricultural activity in Argentina, where the large national producers are at the base and are integrated in a subordinate manner to a higher rung that are the transnational exporters, producers of genetics, and agricultural inputs. They are managed beyond the national territorial horizon, with logics and interests beyond the national interests of the base. At the top of the system is, as always, transnational finance

8 Transgenic crops are those that have been produced from an organism modified by genetic engineering and into which genes from another organism have been incorporated to produce the desired characteristics. For example, resistance to certain agrochemicals, which destroy all unwanted weeds, except for the genetically modified organism.

9 Direct Seeding consists of planting the crop without removing the soil and with a permanent cover of the soil with crop residues. It is a much faster and more efficient process than the opening of furrows through the plow.

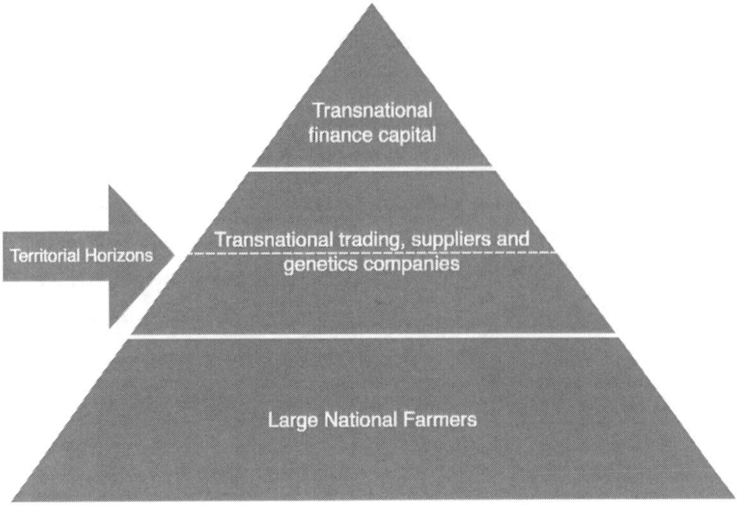

Figure 4.6: Vertical organization of the export activity.
Prepared by the author.

capital assigning value to production based not only on current supply and demand but also heavily on future speculation.

The lower rung, that of the large local agricultural producers, is functional and essential to this scheme of dependency. They embody subordination, operational and ideological. Their system of values and perceptions does not collide with the ideology of the big transnational traders that capture a large part of the value produced. On the contrary, they align with them. And a similar mindset happens with medium-sized producers. Closing contractual ties with large exporting companies, or integrating cooperatives and local federations, they are imbued with the same vision that favors the leadership of the traders and the anti-state and anti-regulatory discourse. In this sense, the local producers favor the international financial interests at the expense of material domestic concerns.

The figure above illustrates how powerful foreign market participants endowed with large amounts of capital in the global political economy control and significantly influence from a distance the lives and well-being of producers and others in the domestic economy of Argentina. Domestic material well-being is subordinated to foreign capital interests. This occurs less under the weight of military command and control than under the influence of ideology: the subordinated accept and adopt the ideas of the dominating financial managerial class, whether emanating from Wall Street, Europe, or London. Thereis no need to govern from the outside with tanks and turrets where the ideas on the inside conform with the capitalists' decision-making and profit contagion.

4.5. The Paraná River

The competitiveness of Argentine agro-exports is based on two natural geographic factors. One, Pampa Húmeda's fertility. The other, the magnificent Paraná river that runs through an important extension of the Pampa Húmeda, which is part of the Cuenca del Plata[10] that empties into the Atlantic Ocean. It is an easy and cheap outlet for grains production and logistics. On the banks of the Paraná River, the largest export agro-industrial complex in the world extends its influence throughout much of Argentina. It is called "Polo Rosafe." See Figure 4.7 below.

This port agro-industrial complex extends over 70 km (43.4 miles) of the Paraná River coast to the North and South of the city of Rosario, with more than 30 ports and 21 grain storage and processing plants (Arellano, 2021). Act 22,108 of the military dictatorship in 1979 allowed companies, national or foreign, to have private port terminals for the export of grains. However, under legislation enacted during the succeeding regime of democracy, decree 2284 in the year 1991 superseded the National Grain Board, which had been the entity that regulated the activity of grain exports. The Paraná River was thus free to be managed by transnational companies.

Having installed the silos and the grain processing plant on the river coast and having the capacity to ship the raw material or the industrial derivative for export from this plant reduced freight inefficiencies and

10 The Plata Basin, with an area of 3.1 million km2, is the fifth largest in the world after the Amazon, Congo, Nile, and Mississippi. Named after the Rio de la Plata, a waterway that flows into the Atlantic and gives its name to Argentina, which comes from the Latin "Argentum" (Silver).

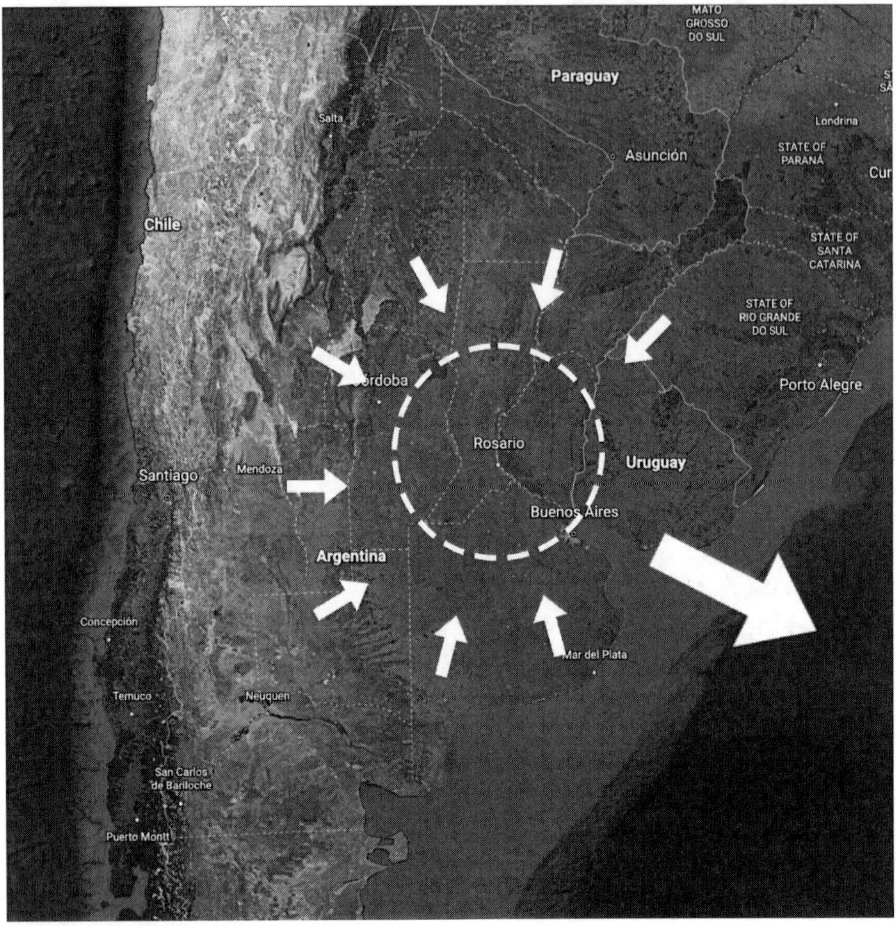

Figure 4.7: Polo Rosafé
Prepared by the author using Google Maps.

provided extraordinary competitiveness. Sixteen port terminals are operated by transnationals. Cargill has 3; Archer Daniels Midland with 2; Bunge with 3; Dreyfus with 2; COFCO with 2; and GLENCORE with 2. The turnover of agricultural products for export that runs through this river is approximately 28,000 million dollars per year according to several calculations (Arellano, 2021).

As a waterway for exporting agricultural products, the Paraná-Plata Basin is comparable to the Mississippi River in the United States. While the Argentine river is dredged and buoyed by a transnational company, the American River is in the care of the United States Army. Different strategies create different levels of well-being.

Poignantly, the consolidation of market participants into imperious market power with capacity to manipulate, excuse, and justify its production and allocation of capital was accompanied by liberalization through means of democracy. In practice, this became neoliberalism and domination by capital, whose interests held sway. The absence of enforceable and enforced regulation controlling and limiting the interests of those with greater power in the political economy (e.g., wealthy capitalists, investors, and traders) in a material sense allows the initially best-positioned politically and financially supported few to affect in a materially adverse way the general welfare. This is leverage over the political economy, whether democratized in theory or not.

4.6. Conclusions

The largest agro-industrial port complex in the world, adjacent to one of the most efficient grain-producing regions in the world, is the main source of dollars generated through exports in an economy that suffers from external restrictions such as Argentina. Such a complex isoperated by transnational companies, which are oriented to profit with extraordinary returns (using finances) without commitment to the needs of national development. Profit contagion rules.

But in this complex, there are also two agro-exporting companies that are Argentineans. One is General Oil Company Deheza. The other, VICENTÍN. These companies will be discussed in more detail forward.

References

ALLEN-MILLS, T. (2008). "Congo sapped of riches as Denis menaces Boulevard Saint-Germain"The Australian, June 17 2008, https://web.archive.org/web/20091014162011/http://www.theaustralian.news.com.au/story/0,,23873480-643,00.html, Accessed June 14, 2021.

AMMANN, D. (2009). The King of oil, New York, St. Martin's Press.

ARELLANO, L. (2021). Argentina sangra por las barrancas del Paraná, Buenos Aires, Ágora.

BASUALDO, E. and KHAVISE, M. (1994) ."La Propiedad Rural en la Provincia de Buenos Aires" en Desarrollo Económico, 34–134.

BASUALDO, E. M., and KHAVISSE, M. "La gran propiedad rural en la provincia de Buenos Aires." Desarrollo económico (Buenos Aires) 34, no. 134 (1994): 197–216.

BASUALDO, E., et al. (2002). "Las transferencias de recursos a la cúpula económica durante la presidencia Duhalde" en Revista Realidad Económica Número 186 - 16 febrero al 31 de marzo de 2002, Buenos Aires.

CARDOSO, F., et al. (1999). Dependencia y Desarrollo en América Latina, Buenos Aires, Siglo XXI.

CLARIN. (2021). "Rosario dejó de ser el líder agroexportador del mundo: quién ocupa su lugar", en Clarin, https://www.clarin.com/economia/rosario-dejo-lider-agroexportador-mundo-ocupa-lugar_0_I_RFhUj0C.html, accesse October 2022.

COX, B., et al. (2011). "GLENCORE I.P.O Mimics Blacksonte an Draws Skeptics", The New York Times, May 3, 2011, https://www.nytimes.com/2011/05/04/business/04views.html, Accessed June 14, 2021.

DI YENNO, F.,et al. (2021). "Ranking de exportación de empresas agroindustriales según ventas en la campaña 2020/21", *Informativo Semanal*, August27, BCR.

EL CRONISTA. (2012). "GLENCORE beat Cargill and won the Canadian Viterra", March 21 in El Cronista Negocios, website https://www.cronista.com/Negocios/GLENCORE-le-gano-to-Cargill-and-stayed-with-the-canadian-Viterra20120321-0037, Accessed May 18, 2021.

FORBES. (2021). "Global 2000, 1 World's Largest Public Companies" Forbes, May 13, 2021, https://www.forbes.com/lists/global2000/#1941e9b15ac0, Accessed June 14, 2021.

FORD, L. (2011). "Mining firm under fire over tax payments in Zambia", The Guardian, April 15, 2011, https://www.theguardian.com/global-development/2011/apr/15/mining-firm-tax-payments-zambia, Accessed June 14, 2021.

GAGGERO, A., et al. (2014). Restricción Eterna, Buenos Aires, Crisis.

GOMEZ OLIVER, L. and GRANADOS SANCHEZ, R. (2016). "Las cuatro grandes empresas comercializadoras y los precios internacionales de los alimentos". Economía Informa. UNAM. México D.F, 400, 24–38.

GRONDONA, V. (2014). "Fuga de Capitales IV. Argentina, 2014. La Manipulación de los Precios de Transferencia".WoorkingpaperN°58. Buenos Aires, CEFID-AR.

HIDALGO, R. (2012). "Organización Mundial del Comercio: viejos dilemas y nuevos retos", Revista Cubana de Economía Internacional, CIEI, N°1, February, 2012, http://www.rcei.uh.cu, Accessed April 19, 2022.

HILFERDING, R. (1963). El Capital Financiero, Madrid, Tecnos.

HUERGO, H. (2020). Cómo se conformó en el Gran Rosario el complejo agroindustrial más grande y concentrado del mundo, Clarín June 28, https://www.clarin.com/rural/conformo-gran-rosario-complejo-agroindustrial-grande-concentrado-mundo_0_F6lILfErl.html, Accessed October 21, 2022.

ICIJ-INTERNATIONAL CONSORTIUM OF INVESTIGATIVE. (2017). "Paradise Papers", https://www.icij.org/investigations/paradise-papers/, Accessed June 14, 2021.

ICIJ-INTERNATIONAL CONSORTIUM OF INVESTIGATIVE. (2020). "FinCen Files", https://www.icij.org/investigations/fincen-files/, Accessed June 14, 2021.

INDEC-Instituto Nacional de Estadísticas y Censos. (2020). "Comercio Exterior", Vol. 5, N°4 https://www.indec.gob.ar/uploads/informesdeprensa/complejos_03_21311B84F340.pdf, Accessed June 26, 2021.

INDEC-Instituto Nacional de Estadísticas y Censos. (2021). "Comercio Exterior", Vol.5, N°14, https://www.indec.gob.ar/uploads/informesdeprensa/ica_12_20B2C4146816.pdf, Accessed January 6, 2022.

INDEC -Instituto Nacional de Estadísticas y Censos. (2021). "Balanza de Pagos, posición de inversión internacional y deuda externa", Informe Técnico, Buenos Aires, INDEC.

KALECKI, M. (1956). Teoría de la dinámica económica: ensayo sobre los movimientos cíclicos ya largo plazo de la economía capitalista, México DF, FCE.

MARTINEZ-GALIANA, X. (2019). "Una nueva investigación por sospechas de soborno hunde GLENCORE en la bolsa", El Economista, December 5, 2019, https://www.eleconomista.es/mercados-cotizaciones/noticias/10239990/12/19/Una-nueva-investigacion-por-sospechas-de-soborno-hunde-a-GLENCORE-en-bolsa.html, Accessed May 14, 2021.

MON, A., et al. (2020). "FinCEN Files: operaciones millonarias entre GLENCORE y VICENTÍN quedaron en la mira de Estados Unidos", La Nación, September 17, 2020, https://www.lanacion.com.ar/politica/fincen-files-operaciones-millonarias-GLENCORE-vicentin-quedaron-nid2453165/, Accessed May 17, 2021.

MORGAN, D. (1983). Los Traficantes de Granos, Buenos Aires, Editorial Abril.

MOSHINSKY, B. (2015). "The four- decade story of GLENCORE´s rise and fall"Insider, October 7, 2015, https://www.businessinsider.com/glencores-history-and-what-happened-to-the-company-2015-10,Accessed May 28, 2021.

MUIÑO, G. (2022). "Mitos y verdades", El Cohete a la Luna, April 3, 2022, https://www.elcohetealaluna.com/mitos-y-verdades/, Accessed April8, 2022.

OGLIETTI, G., et al. (2022).Argentina, tan rica afuera como pobre adentro, celag.org, April 7, 2022, https://www.celag.org/argentina-tan-rica-afuera-como-pobre-adentro/, Accessed April 11, 2022.

OMC-ORGANIZACIÓN MUNDIAL DEL COMERCIO. (2009)."Estadísticas del comercio internacional", https://www.wto.org/spanish/res_s/statis_s/its2009_s/its09_toc_s.htmA, Accessed April 8, 2017.s

ORTEGA, J. (2018). "Apropiación del excedente agroalimentario generado en el territorio: El caso Cargill en Argentina", Tesis de Doctorado, Madrid, Universidad Complutense de Madrid.

ORTEGA, J. (2021). "La dolarización del comercio granario y su administración en el concurso preventivo: cuando la productividad y el empleo pierden para que gane la especulación", Derechos en Acción, Autumn 2021pp 115–147, La Plata, UNLP.

OSORIO, J. (2015). "Teoría de la Dependencia Hoy" [Conferencia], Facultad de Ciencias Sociales, Universidad de Chile, Santiago de Chile, September 2, 2015.

PANTLAND, W. (2018). "GLENCORE, enorme y despiadada empresa de explotación de materias primas".Informe especial, April 25, 2018, Industria ALL Global Unión, http://www.industriall-union.org/es/informe-especial-GLENCORE-enorme-y-despiadada-empresa-de-explotacion-de-materias-primas, Accessed June 14, 2021.

RANKIN, J. (2013). "Marc Rich: controversial commodities trader and former fugitive dies aged 78", The Guardian, June 26, 2013, London.

PEIRANO, M. (14 de agosto 2019). Desarrollo industrial en argentina [Conference] Universidad Nacional de San Martín, San Martín, Argentina.

PIDD, H., et al.(2011). "The rise of GLENCORE, the biggest company you've never heard of", The Guardian, May 19, 2011. London.

SILI, M. (2005). La Argentina Rural, Buenos Aires. INTA.

TERRÉ, E. (2021). "Argentina embarcó granos por 56,5 millones de toneladas en el 2020, un 6% menos que el año anterior", BCR, https://www.bcr.com.ar/es/mercados/investigacion-y-desarrollo/informativo-semanal/noticias-informativo-semanal/argentina-17, Accessed January 23, 2022.

VALOR SOJA. (2021). "Chau Oleaginosa Moreno: Now the main Argentine soy flour exporting company is called Viterra", in Bichos de Campo, May 3, website https://bichosdecampo.com/chau-oleaginosa -moreno-now-the-main-argentine-company-exporter-of-soybean-flour-is-called-viterra/, accessed May 5/18, /2021.

VERBITSKY, H. (2008). "Radiografía de la pampa", Pagina 12, June 15, 2008, https://www.pagina12.com.ar/diario/elpais/1-106061-2008-06-15.html, Accessed April 5, 2021.

Chapter 5

Development as a protected legal asset

The greed of the powerful leads them to circumvent the rules that they themselves created for their benefit.

Keywords: control through punitive power, criminalization of poverty, white-collar crimes, bad development crimes.

5.1. Synthesis

In this chapter, we ask ourselves whether the law has anything to say about the harmful dynamics leveled against the possibility of development of the people (general welfare) that we have been describing. Is development a protected legal asset and right with norms that sanction those who impede it? Is the achievement of development a human right? Does law only legitimize *de facto* power, or does it also challenge and protect the vulnerable? Is a new theoretical conceptual framework necessary in the face of systemic and structural behaviors that parasitize and direct the efforts of the majorities that result (not accidentally) in a concentration of wealth in a minority? Are there laws that classify as crimes the corporate acts of the appropriator of wealth and income from the less powerful, who comprise the overwhelming majority? Is the general welfare a meaningful concept and theory under the rule of law, especially where the rule of law is legislated, enforced, and adjudicated under oligarchic and plutocratic influences?

These are the questions that we will address below without having the presupposition and hubris to find an answer for everyone. Our intention is primarily to stimulate vital debate involving the comparatively silent and subordinated supermajority.

5.2. Development as an asset protected by rule of law

A legal asset is an entity, material, or abstract, which is protected bylaw. Something considered valuable, whose enjoyment must be guaranteed to the subject of law, protecting him against unjust disturbances by third parties. According to Franz von Liszt, legal assets were those goods which the law recognized and safeguarded.

> All legal assets are vital interests of the individual or of the community. The legal order does not create interest, it creates life; but the protection of the law elevates the vital interest to legal asset.(Von Liszt, 1999:6)

Zaffaroni (2000), from a limiting conception of the punitive power of the State to protect individual freedom, points out that the protected legal right is the relation of availability of a person with an object. That is, the legal right insulates the relationship of the person to the object of the right, in this case—freedom to develop against actual / potential impairment from others' oppressive actions.

The actions that we have been considering in this work affect the development of the territories. The territory is not just an extension of soil;it is the community that lives and interacts in that geographical area and builds its collective project in the place. It is the natural environment and the relationship that those who inhabit that space establish with it. It is the culture and institutions that are formed there. It is their legitimate aspiration to develop.

For the United Nations, human rights are inherent to all persons without distinction of any kind such as race, sex, nationality, religious belief, or other status. These include the right to life and liberty; not to be subjected to slavery or torture; freedom of opinion and expression;

education and work, among others.[1] Human rights are a legal dimension that do not address in particular delinquent facts: its scope is to deal with the relationship of public power vis-à-vis potential violations of essential rights shared by or extended in the community.

The right to development is a human right. The United Nations General Assembly in its resolution 41/128 on December 4, 1986 established as a recognized and protected human right the right to development. Specifically,

> 1. The right to development is an inalienable human right by virtue of which every human person and all peoples are entitled to participate in, contribute to, and enjoy economic, social, cultural, and political development, in which all human rights and fundamental freedoms can be fully realized.
> 2. The human right to development also implies the full realization of the right of peoples to self-determination, which includes, subject to the relevant provisions ofInternational Covenants on Human Rights, the exercise of their inalienable right to full sovereignty over all of their natural wealth and resources.

We believe that actions that impede the development of peoples require an international, multilateral approach. The monitoring of transnational corporations is necessary. While the transnational corporation is not the subject of international law, individually and collectively they may have more power over the realization of the right of human development than most countries of the community of nations.

The transnational's power may overwhelm a given State's power. Our concern in this paper is evaluating whether the national current law has criminal laws that would sanction these "developmentcide" behaviors—conduct that in fact seriously impairs the human right of development. Comparatively, criminal offenses under national laws were ordinarily conceived with a view to protecting legal assets such as private property, public treasury, or the economic order, with the goal of preserving and enforcing the rules of the market economy. They were not designed to punish "developmentcide." The ecosystem

1 See United Nations General Assembly, Universal Declaration of Human Rights, December 10, 1948.

of State rules of law do not contemplate generalized harm to the many as a specific breach of the established legal order.

The preexisting category of crimes make the development of a community unworkable in many material respects. A special framework to deal with corporate conduct that in fact impairs human development but which is not recognized as criminal by the law needs enactment and enforcement. The liberal conception in the classical sense of criminal law and its function of containing the punitive power of the State (Zaffaroni, 2000) to protect individual property and freedoms does not support the creation of specific criminal laws focus in describing and proscribing corporate behaviors that threaten and impair the development of the general welfare.

Development is a broad concept and vulnerable to different interpretations. It is difficult to conceptualize and provide a specific description about conduct that would constitute the proximate cause of the effect of a community's failure to develop. Due process considerations are implicated (e.g., does the rule of law clearly inform as to what's prohibited conduct?) The criminalization of such actions would enter into the realm of assumptions and speculations, potentially becoming an arbitrary regime without due process of law (e.g., the parties subject to the law do not really know what the law allows / prohibits!) Any political position could imaginably be interpreted to constitute an attack on community development, contingent on the subjectivity of the interpreter.

Nonetheless, community development as a legal asset should be conceived and recognized in a worldview that provides a way to understand the consequences of some existing socially harmful corporate actions. It would be a new way of understanding old problems (Böhm, 2019). This enlightening knowledge could properly be harnessed in the articulation of practical imperatives that not only directly prohibit (corporate) acts unduly oppressive to the community's residents and guests but also indirectly encourage the rehabilitation of the community from the preexisting ravages of profit contagion.

The practices of some transnational corporations that operate outside the sovereignties of States (or more precisely, parasitizing the sovereignties of States to their advantage to accumulate capital and advantage in the political economy at the expense of the citizens of the territories) imply the violation of the community's right to development and support its own general welfare composed of its residents and guests. Indeed, community norms and expectations subservient to transnational corporations imply a world order without adequate opportunity for far too many.

We note also that the transnational corporation may indeed coup the State through the open or covert negotiation of deals and sidedeals with the leaders of the State (i.e., working inside the sovereignty). Thus, the rule of law must be evaluated both through assessment of the facts behind its creation and through the details of its enforcement. Lip service to community development is inadequate.

Does the law say anything about the abuse of creating symbolic assets and selling them in the present, backed only by expectations of something that may exist in an uncertain future? Does it have something established in relation to abstract constructions of corporate subjects with more prerogatives than the human persons that initiated, authorized, and established them? The issue is less can these individuals hide behind these constructions (because in fact they do) but more should these individuals obtain impunity by such constructions? Rule of law without moral and ethical force is equivalent to tyranny.

How is it that financial instruments (e.g., stocks, bonds, derivatives) create legal and enforceable market structures that take surplus earned in one country to migrate it to other countries far from the enjoyment of those who worked to produce it? Presently, the laws of the market leverage the power of financial instruments to create communities and states that suffer from debt overhang imposed by their own corrupt / unknowing leaders in their own venues and jurisdictions in cahoots with transnational corporations' financial interests. The community's current and futureinterests in self-development have been lawfully transferred (i.e., sold out) to financial speculators and traders from foreign venues and jurisdictions without due consideration of the general welfare. In fact, input as to community well-being from the (disaffected) community is not even sought under conditions of profit contagion.

5.3. Law as a discourse

Generally, the rule of law legitimates real power. This is because the rule of law is a cultural creation of its time, constituting one of the discourses of the power. However, at other times, the rule of law can be used to challenge unjust practices and the subjugation of the weakest.

Discourse is a symbolic construction that seeks to represent reality. The discourse is not neutral. In uttering itself, it is signifying what it seeks to relate from a certain position of power, and it does so following the interests of its issuer. What is more, the discourse not only seeks to represent reality but rather is intended to create and reproduce it (Nietzsche, 2006). However, just as the map may not reflect the territory, the discourse may not mirror reality.

> In every society the production of the discourse is at the same time controlled, selected and redistributed by a certain number of procedures that have for function to conjure the powers and dangers, to dominate the random event and to avoid its heavy and fearsome materiality.(Foucault, 2013:14)

Moreover, the rule of law is a discursive form. It represents the entire surrounding social reality from its technique, modes, and perspectives—these are synthesized in a particular manner, favoring particular interests. It does not consist solely of legal texts, and it is not neutral. Those who speak it (e.g., lawyers, academics, and above all judges) are part of the discourse. It is enough to see their modes, language, and even clothing to understand that there are hierarchies, authorizations, and vetoes to articulate the legal discourse (Ruiz, 1986). The rule of law demonstrates and reinforces the hierarchy operative in the political economy.

More often than not, the rule of law has a legitimizing function of power. Legal dictates and their interpretations do nothing but normalize (that is, giving norms, "make normal") what power wants. Let us recall that trafficking in human beings (slavery) was once legal, and until very recently, the legislation reserved a marginal place for women. Hence, constructions such as partnerships through actions and the institutionalization of virtual finance are neatly legislated to preserve the status quo of those who use these tools. However, the rule of law has a paradoxical characteristic.

Power is not an instrument; it is not a thing you possess. Power is a relationship, where there is a subject who acts with power and another who resists him. This resistance is not an external factor to power but constitutes it. Power is not a thing that someone has. Power is an exercise (Foucault, 1991). In this sense, the legal norm can be understood as a truce agreement in the social battle of opposing forces. Depending on the outcome of this battle, the rule of law is not only the status quo of the powerful; it may also represent and provoke change and progress. Conquest via rule of law is not inevitable: through legal resistance, it is possible to protect the weakest, regulating and mediating the social progress of those who were disadvantaged (Cárcova, 2012). Examples of this include, among other instruments of the rule of law, legislation that protects laborers; social security imperatives; and equality between men and women.

It is in the exploration of this democratic and progressive side of the law that we will see which tools have the capacity to deal with the concrete case. We will expose where the dynamics of abuse of financial instruments of capital are memorialized and effectuated to allow escape from accountability for impairments to the rights of development of so many following the patterns described in previous chapters.

The rule of law is a tool of language, creating commands and standards according to and often supportive of the interests of those with adequate influence to impose or change these concepts. Legislatures and regulatory regimes are moved less by the developmental needs of the general welfare than the incentives, implied or express, offered through maintenance and reinforcement of the status quo. Positive change for the many may occur, but its details, limitations, and pace of realization are determined by society's leadership, front-and-center like politicians and/or in the back- or boardroom beyond transparency. Thus, the rule of law upholds, as well as transforms, power.

5.4. Who is persecuted by the penal system?

Max Weber defined the State as the entity that monopolizes the legitimate use of violence (Weber, 2002). One of the uses it makes of it is through criminalizing the conduct it considers harmful and threatening. The recognizable instrument through which the State criminalizes conduct and represses it is represented by its primary criminalization agencies (e.g., Congress through the dictation of penal laws that carry a punishment initiates and authorizes the possibility of criminal punishment) and those of secondary criminalization (e.g.,police and the judiciary that set these laws in motion and carry out the enforcement regime) (Zaffaroni, 2000).

What will be the conduct that the law will establish as socially undesirable by making it a crime punishable by repression and punishment; and in what cases, and with what diligence will this law be complied with or not? Everything is the result of a political decision. In other words, politics determines who and how many citizens will be punished and put in prison. The norm is created, preserved, and enhanced through the rule of law operative in the political economy.

Throughout history, the punitive system has always aimed to persecute those sectors that are "annoying" to the scheme of power of its time. Weak minorities are often the subjects eligible for persecution prosecutable for the unpleasantness they cause to the system. Or even because their persecution serves as a scapegoatfor the sufferings of society. Thus, the imposition of penalties channels the violent impulses of the members of the community, diverting it to a sector that power has no interest in protecting, intentionally sacrificing it.

Interpreting the thesis of Deleuze and Guattari (1998) of desire as a productive impulse, and of how this impulse is manipulated by capitalism, we could say that for the configuration of the punitive apparatus, the cruel drive is channeled according to what suits the power that reigns. The desires of violent nature nestled in the psyche of the members of a society, its morbidity for enjoyment of the suffering of others, its sadistic impulses—these are "statized," culturized, institutionalized, and ordered to be functional and useful to capitalism. Neoliberalism will know how to herd these violent impulses present in the community and direct them against designated enemies potentially presenting a vulnerability of the regime. Enemies are leveraged under the criminal justice system to reinforce and expand the powers with the capacity to instrumentalize the rule of law (e.g., oligarchic interests).

Heretics and infidels in the Spain of the Inquisition, unionists in 19th century Europe; Jews and Gypsies in Nazi Germany; dissidents in the Stalinist USSR in the 20th century; the poor and excluded in Latin America today—these populations have been subjugated and punished in their own different societies. The essential factor in the capacity and practice of sending someone to prison is not so much a measure of his/her dangerousness to the community at large, but the weakness of the persecuted person in the face of power. They cannot successfully resist.

We understand neoliberalism as the ideology of capitalism in its financial phase. It advocates the absolute sovereignty of capital, regardless of the workforce and the environment—notwithstanding the essentialness of labor and the milieu. It conceives of the supremacy of capital in all aspects of the organization of society, no matter the consequences on nature and life. It has the despot's will and, like all great discourses, seeks to impose its hegemony as the only universal, cultural, moral, desirable, and possible course. In other words, it is the totalitarianism of capital that prosecutes its means and methods as if there were no alternatives.

Illogically, capital sees itself as indispensable and the labor force as dispensable. This inversion of potentiality is both unreal and self-serving. Capital creates its mythology independent of the facts on the ground.

The State (neoliberal in this case) through its ideological apparatuses (Althusser, 2003) creates an enemy that that same State will then pursue through its repressive apparatus. In this case, it is the penal system. It does not invent these prosecutable and punishable subjectivities to defend society; it does so to protect the regime. (Zaffaroni, 2000).

The persistent and draconian punishment of those involved in the trafficking and consumption of illegal drugs in or to the U.S. may be seen as illustrative victims of the regime's quest to control not only the minds and bodies of individuals (e.g., the prohibition of mind / mood altering substances such as marijuana) but also the capital obtained by those successful in the distribution and logistics. Control over the currency of the drug transaction is as much a feature of the regime's efforts (e.g., punishments imposed against money laundering drug proceeds) as control over the person's liberty. Specific crimes are utilized to augment the capitalists' power and influence.

5.5. Bad development crimes

Financial capitalism expands through the activities of obtaining extraordinary profits and gains of finance; of management of rhizomatic corporate structures for fraud; of capital flight and tax evasion; and from other unlawful but related conduct. Since the law (like criminology) is a discourse of power, the existing under enforced and deficiently designed punitive approach to financial and corporate fraud lacks a systemic treatment that locates it as crime that does significant harm to the community (which may be surpassed only by crimes against humanity such as genocide). Corporate, tax, and financial crimes that occur in a sustained and systemic manner are a profitable way to do business. They are not the enemy the State (coopted by its powerful elite) wants. The journalistic coverage (e.g., expressions of the mass media companies that are not neutral observers since they are financial and transnationalized actors) serves to placate the vindicative impulses of the community in one sense and exacerbate them in the other. Prosecutions of some (e.g., Bernie Madoff) represent as much token enforcement as specious justification of the fairness and equality of the criminal justice system in effect.

The citizenry live in a state of mind that makes it capable of lynching a pickpocket, while at the same time being condescended to by the top-down driven giga-millionaire state bailouts (financed with the public resources that could have been dedicated to health, housing, education, and security) to banking and capital-managing scammers and speculators. The elite create the narrative of their own deservingness.

Sociologist Edwin Sutherland (1949) created the concept "white collar crimes" to refer to those that were committed by respectable people, of a high social status, and inserted in privileged positions in the community. The American focuses on the peculiar practices of the area where these prestigious individuals work, which are generating a "practical sense" of "how things should be done." (Bourdieu, 2008). In the field of the administration of big business, the breakdown of the law is perceived as necessary; it is "naturalized," and whoever does it is not perceived as a delinquent. Financial and corporate crimes are neutralized as if they are acts done by all for all—ordinary and common. Of course, comparatively very few occupy the seats of power (e.g., directors and officers) driving corporate policy, practices, and procedures.

Moreover, due to questions of cultural hegemony (Gramsci, 1981), the victims themselves (the great majorities) do not see any of this as a threat, and even feel empathy and admiration for them. Thus, criminal practices are consolidated and institutionalized in an unwritten manner, with impunity for apparent perpetrators in many cases. The propagandization of the base of workers, including victims at many levels, is effective. Their place in the hierarchy of the political economy is deserved pursuant to such ideas. They have been instructed whom to agitate against (e.g., the scapegoats of the moment) and with whom to fall in with (e.g., purveyors of the predominant ideology).

To call actions that cause harm to the community and exceed the dangerousness of ordinary crimes, Herbert Jäger (1989)created the concept of "macrocriminal." It points more to the quantitative dimension of the harm caused by the criminal act, or the hierarchy within the State held by the actors. Its approach has to do with the inadequacy of separate national legal systems to address crimes against humanity, and in our case—transnational corporate and financial conduct that seriously impairs the general welfare across numerous States.

Macro-criminality is comprised of harmful actions that should not be considered in isolation but as part of an organized collective program to impose unjust conditions in the widest sense. The co-optation of the State and its sovereignty is essential for this execution. It is from the State where macro-criminality is carried out. Hence, it is clearly a human rights issue.

We believe that it is necessary to specify the concept more, to include in a theoretical framework that helps the application of existing regulations, those crimes of massive harmfulness that prevent the development of the general welfare in many States seen from the perspective of emerging countries. That road is being built, in our opinion, with the conception of the crime of bad development. From Maria Laura Böhm:

> The crime of bad development is the set of interrelationships and activities in the context of international, transnational, regional, and national economic policies and undertakings that entail or have materialized the risk of hindering the satisfaction of basic needs at the collective level and thus participate directly or indirectly in the exercise of cultural, structural, or physical violence that prevents the sustainable and comprehensive development of a population in terms of economic, cultural. and legal peace. (Böhm, 2019: 105)

The author builds for the debate characteristics that the criminological category of impairment of right of development would and should have. Nevertheless, it does not constitute a new legal criminal type or category. It is a theoretical framework to reconcile certain existing legal criminal categories if and when they attack and impair the collective capacity to obtain goods and services materially necessary, with the effect of adversely affecting the general welfare, including generational consequences.The characteristics of the crime of poor development are as follows:

- First, that it is the cause and result of violence in its cultural and physical expressions, which it reproduces.
- Second, it is an aggravated form of white-collar crime, both because of the damage caused and also the opacity of the instruments, including the corporate form and financial instruments that comprise the legalized tools to commit the social and individual harms.
- Third, it is an aggravated form of the criminality of the powerful since its authors (i.e., those who initiate and authorize the development and extension of the legalized tools of subjugation) are located at the top of corporate and State capitalism.
- Fourth, it implies aform of macro-criminality by omission since it is not the State that executes it by action, but rather by its inaction, tolerance, and even protection allows its dispersion and depth.

- Fifth, it is legitimized by the international mass media.
- Sixth, it causes environmental damage to favor the flight of resources from the territory.
- Seventh, it makes the population socially, occupationally, and educationally precarious.
- Eighth, it hinders the satisfaction of basic needs in the short- and long-terms of the victimized society.
- Ninth, it is global, given the transnational nature of its perpetrators, yet its victims are local.
- Tenth, it is perpetrated synchronously and diachronically.
- Eleventh, it harms society in national and international dimensions, corroding the very notion of democracy, and
- Twelfth, being a conceptual category, the crime of bad development cannot be criminally categorized in one legal way since it involves a number of several separate and distinct legalized infractions. The idea to typify by new laws is not enough to complete the protection since the behaviors are multiple and overlapping—too complex to be described in a oversimplified typification of a single line. (Böhm, 2019).

We believe that the theoretical framework of the crime of bad development helps us to approach the particular case that we will study later. In Böhm's approach, the crime of bad development attacks assets such as a healthy environment, the health of the population, its culture, protection against exploitation, and the education of the communities' minorities (i.e., those marginalized subgroups in the political economy) under the legalized regime in the territory.

For our part, we will add that the management of corporate fraud and financial abuse as a constant means and legalized instrument for the accumulation and absorption of the value produced by a national community (preventing the territorial reinvestment of the surplus for a growing welfare) is a crime of bad development for the reasons that follow:

- It is an aggravated form of white-collar crime. It is initiated, authorized, and extended in application by the members of the leadership of a capitalist society (i.e., one such as a neoliberal regime that, in brief, excessively privatizes society's benefits and socializes society's detriments).

- It is facilitated by the State for protection and concealment (i.e., those who effectuate the social harms and bad development are hidden and insulated with impunity). The mass media legitimizes it. It makes work precarious.It stops national development by becoming a legalized machine for the private hoarding and direction of economic surplus.
- Finally, because there are laws that, although they may sanction some of the behaviors that accompany the operation of this machine (e.g., pollution of waterways), they are not sufficiently or even adequately applied by the secondary criminalization agencies of the State (i.e., collectively, its criminal justice system, including public prosecutors, criminal investigators, and the judiciary).

5.6. Conclusions

Power shapes the rule of law. However, this is not a linear process. Resistance to power also functions in the visioning, operating, and revisioning of the rule of law, hence its paradoxical function. However, the struggle is permanent. It is not enough for an isolated or sporadic social conquest to crystallize into a norm. The norm is shaped dynamically, requiring a persistent rational system of specific social preferences that constrain and prohibit some conduct while permitting and fostering the development of other conduct. The State, a space of permanent tension, is formally in charge of doing so.

In Argentina in the year 2020, there were 106,559 people imprisoned; of these 36,032 for robbery and simple theft. Meanwhile, for crimes such as fraudulent bankruptcy or insider trading, the number was zero.[2] In a material respect, the regime's preferences and ranking of priorities are expressly and impliedly discoverable through examination of who goes

2 Data according to the Argentinean National Statistical System on the Execution of Sentences (SNEEP, 2020).

to prison for what and who does not notwithstanding his/her actions and omissions. Criminality is an interpretation of the underlying predicate actions and omissions; it is a layer of language, applied or not, contingent on the designers and implementers of the rule of law. It is not enough to categorize a predicate act as unlawful; it must also be rigorously and seriously enforced.

While the theoretical and conceptual crime of bad development would need specificity to provide due process in the State of its potential enforcement, an important distinction about due process needs contemplation and further debate: 1) procedural due process, which would examine the legislatively defined crime, including whether these material components and the synthesized crime itself comport with the constitutional regime effective in the given jurisdiction; 2) substantive due process, including whether the material components and the synthesized crime have been drafted not only constitutionally on its face per 1) but whether it serves to address the social harm—no more and no less.

While the difficulty of this due process conformity seems immense, the failure to engage in this formation of criminal law seems worse. In brief, a good society and political economy, including its criminal justice system, would be characterized not so much by great winners (a few) and desperate losers (comparatively many) but how it treats the lucky and the unlucky; the honest and the dishonest; the greedy and the temperate. However, under conditions of profit contagion that permeate society, the political economy, and the criminal justice system, the rule of law should be a mechanism that dampens the worst instincts and conduct and encourages the best in men, women, and children.

Next, we will see the application (possible, although in many cases unsuccessful, due to the passivity of the secondary criminalization agencies) of criminal categories existing in the legislation that would and should be reframed under the theoretical construct and criminality of bad development. We will delve into corporate fraud and tax law violation that could have applied hypothetically to the VICENTÍN case.

References

ALTHUSSER, L. (2003). Ideología y aparatos ideológicos del Estado. Freud y Lacan. Buenos Aires, Nueva Visión.

BÖHM, M. (2019). "El delito del mal-desarrollo", Letra: Derecho Penal, N°8, pp 78–116.

BOURDIEU, P. (2008). El sentido práctico, Buenos Aires, Siglo XXI.

CÁRCOVA, C., et al. (2012). "Análisis funcional del Derecho", Las Teorías Jurídicas Post Positivistas, Buenos Aires, Abeledo-Perrot.

DELEUZE, G. y GUATTARI, F. (1998). El Anti Edipo, Barcelona, Paidós.

FOUCAULT, M. (1991). Microfísica del poder, Madrid, Ediciones de La Piqueta.

FOUCAULT, M. (2013). El orden del discurso, México, Tusquets.

GRAMSCI, A. (1981). Cuadernos de la Cárcel, México D F, Ediciones.

JÄGER, H. (1989). Makrokriminalität: Studien zur Kriminalität kollektiver, Gewalt, Frankfurt, Suhrkamp.

NIETZSCHE, F. (2006). Sobre la verdad y mentira en sentido extra moral. Madrid, Tecnos.

RUIZ, A. (1986). "La Ilusión de lo Jurídico", Crítica Jurídica, N°4, May, 1986, México, UAP.

SNEEP. (2020). "Informe Nacional 2020", https://www.argentina.gob.ar/justicia/politicacriminal/estadisticas-e-informes/sneep-2020, Accessed June 19, 2023.

SUTHERLAND, E. (1949). El delito de cuello blanco, Buenos Aires, Editorial B de F.

VON LISZT, F. (1999). Tratado de Derecho Penal, Madrid, Reus.

WEBER, M. (2002). Economía y Sociedad, Madrid, FCE.

ZAFFARONI, R., et al. (2000). Derecho Penal Parte General, Buenos Aires, Ediar.

Chapter 6

Neoliberalism and the State

A predatory company is one that returns misery to the population in indirect exchange for the wealth it has received from the State.

Keywords: neoliberalism is statist, privatization of profits, socialization of losses

6.1. Synthesis

In the leadership of agro-export companies operating in Argentina, there is a minority that are nationally capitalized. One of them, VICENTÍN S.A.I.C., shocked the industry of agricultural production when it surprisingly announced its default at the end of 2019. Today, this firm is in a bankruptcy reorganization plagued by irregularities and with an uncertain fate. Its directors are criminally charged with fraud.

In this chapter, we will summarily ascertain the path of the growth and demise of this company. Their business logic was subordinated by a financial strategy that was not dissimilar from transnationals that operated in the same field, with three exceptions. Firstly, the latter were not transnationalized so quickly and untidily. Secondly, they did not make mistakes of macro- and microeconomic speculation like their Argentine peer. And lastly, and most importantly, they possessed more global power.

Table 6.1: Ranking exporting companies of grains and derivatives.

Agro-export companies	Exports in million tons per year			
	2018	2019	2020	2021
ADM	6,63	11,19	8,72	8,1
BUNGE	6,83	9,57	8,7	8,06
CARGILL	9,62	11,94	12,71	9,38
DREYFUS	5,91	6,83	6,91	6,28
COFCO	10,2	14,8	11,72	9,31
GLENCORE (Moreno-Viterra)	5,77	7,85	10,39	7,92
VICENTÍN	***6,77***	***8,48***	***0,23***	***0***
AGD	6,68	8,98	7,42	6,14
REST	14	19.1	22,98	19,13
TOTAL	72,41	98,74	89,78	74,32

Prepared by the author with Bolsa de Rosario's information

6.2. The leadership of granary traders in Argentina and a default

The activity of selling grains and derivatives abroad in Argentina, the main export item in the country and therefore a generator of dollars in a national economy where they are scarce, is led by Archer, Midland Daniels, Bunge, Cargill, Dreyfus, COFCO, and GLENCORE—first through Oleaginosa Moreno then through VITERRA (its controlling firms). The club is completed with the companies that we show in Table 6.1 above.:

From this ranking of companies, we identify those with Argentinean capital. They are Aceitera General Deheza (AGD), Molinos Agro, Argentine Federated Farmers (AFA), the Association of Argentine Cooperatives (ACA), and VICENTÍN S.A.I.C.[1] Regarding the latter, the table shows its drop in sales for the 2019 and 2020 campaigns, and their disappearance in 2021. What happened with VICENTÍN?

On December 5, 2019, the Argentine agricultural and agro-industrial sector was altered. One of the largest exporting agribusiness companies communicated to the media that it was delaying payments

1 S.A.I.C. is the acronym for "Sociedad Anónima Industrial y Comercial" (Industrial and Commercial Joint-Stock Company).

due to financial stress. VICENTÍN S.A.I.C. had fallen into default. The news was a surprise to the approximately 2,600 creditors of the company, among which were banks, input suppliers, and farmers who sold the raw material to the firm for export. VICENTÍN processes industrial flours, oils, biofuels, and other material derivatives or exports these as raw materials.

How could a default of that magnitude come about unexpectedly? The company's annual financial statements, as required by the General Law of Companies 19,550 (LGS), had been prepared in a timely manner, reflecting its financial strength. Such instruments had been exhibited before the shareholders' meeting, who approved it, and before the administrative and tax control authority, which did not raise any objections. The balance sheets were also endorsed by KPMG, a company that together with Deloitte, PwC, and EY, make up the "big four" of global public auditors, which comprise the most prestigious firms in the world in auditing (and related financial services including consultation services). As if that were not enough, VICENTÍN also submitted its partial accounting statements, with monthly updates, to the creditor banks that had requested these to grant it new loans. None of these reports showed that the company was imminently headed into a financial crisis.

Perplexity increased when it transpired that the Banco de la Nación Argentina, a state credit entity, was the largest creditor of the company now in default, to which it had lent the equivalent of $300 million in total. Of these, $86.6 million had been disbursed during the month prior to the default.

It is also known that 2 days before the public announcement of the cessation of payments, VICENTÍN had sold 16.67 percent of the shares it owned in RENOVA S.A., the largest grain extruder in the world, to RENAISCO, a company in the Netherlands owned of GLENCORE. The value of the shares sold was equivalent to 23 percent of the all estimated value of VICENTÍN by the court where on February 10, 2020, 2 months after communicating its cessation of payments, it was presented in a judicial call to creditors (Chapter 11, in American law) under the framework of Argentinean Law 24,522 on Contest and Bankruptcy (LCQ –Ley de Concursos y Quiebras – in Spanish). In such a required presentation, the debtor must detail all of its assets. Among the presented statement of financial condition, it was not possible to find the 122.7 million dollars received from RENAISCO.

The creditors found out that 122.7 million dollars escaped them; that the company, which in July 2019 documented before its lending banks that its assets were $616 million, now declared they had shrunk to only $41 million (less than 7 percent of what it had indicated a few months earlier in July of 2019).

What had happened? Why a firm which everyone perceived as a family business, now lead seem the front-runner of shady transnational financial management? At times, it is believed that things have changed, when in fact they were the same as they had always been. Let's see who VICENTÍN S.A.I.C. was and is.

6.3. A growth sheltered by the State

The inception of the VICENTÍN agro-industrial group is grounded (according to the company's website)[2] in the second decade of the 20th century. It starts as a small store (storage of seeds and grains) with general branches, located in the City of Avellaneda in the North of the Province of Santa Fe, Argentina. At that time, the company is dedicated to ginning cotton[3] and to the manufacture of seed oil from the aforementioned crop. The corporate structure was formed in 1929, when VICENTÍN S.A.I.C. (Sociedad Anónima Industrial y Comercial) was founded.

In the 1940s, when in Argentina and the rest of Latin America, the United States implemented policies to promote import substitution industrialization (ISI), VICENTÍN in 1943 installed a plant for vegetable oils of flax, peanut, and cotton. (Gaggero et al., 2020).

But the strongest industrial growth came in 1966, at the beginning of the military dictatorship of Juan Carlos Onganía. The *de facto*

2 VICENTÍN S.A.I.C., website https://www.vicentin.com.ar/historia?lang=es, accessed on August 1, 2021.

3 Separate the seed and impurities from the cotton fiber, the last one that will be used in the textile industry.

Figure 6.1: Geographical location of the headquarters of VICENTÍN S.A.I.C.
Prepared by the author using Google Maps.

government granted the company free land in the departments of General Obligado and Vera, collectively, a cotton production area (Chirino, 2020). It incorporated seed grinding and a solvent extraction process.

In 1976, after a brief democratic interregnum, the country suffered a new civil-military dictatorship, this time calling itself the "National Reorganization Process." Its objective was to annihilate all dissent and to impose the neoliberal model, as had already happened in Chile. One of the targets attacked by the repression was unionist organizations. VICENTÍN was no exception. In the company, 14 union delegates were detained or disappeared. The objective was to discipline (as in other areas of the country) labor demands, favoring a new pattern of distribution whereby the participation of workers' income in relation to GDP went from 50 percent (1975) to 30 percent in 1983 (Graña et al.,2011).

In 1979, always under the "National Reorganization Process," the dictatorship made a modification to the current regulations, authorizing exporting firms to have private ports. In this way, VICENTÍN became the port in the town of San Lorenzo under the complex Rosafe on the

Paraná. At the end of the civil-military dictatorship in 1982, the *de facto* government nationalized (takes charge of) $2 million of VICENTÍN´s indebtedness.

In 1989, with the wave of neoliberal policies spreading throughout the world, the "Paraguay-Paraná Waterway" was institutionalized through international agreements. It is a river transport corridor of more than 3,400 km (2,112 miles), which flows through the Paraná and Paraguay rivers, through which exports of grains and derivatives leave the Plata basin. The waterway allows continuous navigation among the ports of Argentina, Brazil, Paraguay, and Uruguay, and, in fact, constituted a setback for State sovereignty. This is because the basin was left open to the installation of ports, dredging and beacons managed by private companies, most of the time transnational. The results, the commercial flows that pass through there, remained outside of State control. See Figure 6.1 above.

However, in 1991, with decree 2284/91, several of the regulatory instruments of the economy that the State had were eliminated. This included the abolition of the National Grain Board, an entity that intervened in the purchase and sale of grains to agricultural producers to support the price, while performing certain supervisory functions of grain shipments at ports. With this, the regulation of the granary trade was transferred, in practice, from the State to the oligopoly of the large agribusiness companies.

In 1994, the government authorized transgenic soybeans. This drove the expansion of cultivation, covering 55 percent of the almost 37 million hectares that were planted[4] (approximately, 14 million acres). The soy complex comprises more than a quarter of Argentine exports(INDEC, 2020). By 1997, a third VICENTÍN soybean crushing plants began operating in the "Rosafe" port complex. See Figure 6.2 below.

In 2001, Argentina suffered the worst financial crisis in its history with the fall of the convertibility regime (fixed exchange rate of 1 peso for 1 dollar, supported by the inflow of foreign currency through

4 See National Institute of Agricultural Technology (INTA), website https://inta.gob.ar/sites/default/files/inta_informe_estadistico_del_mercado_de_soja.pdf , accessed January 29, 2022.

privatization and indebtedness) that involved a transfer of public resources to a small group among the private sector (Escudé, 2006). In a context of a giga-devaluation of the peso, the Argentine currency lost 74 percent of its value against the dollar. On the eve of devaluation, a privileged group of companies and individuals, with information management, managed to acquire dollars at the favorable exchange rate of 1 peso for 1 dollar. Then, the US currency climbed to the value of 3.6 pesos. VICENTÍN was one of those who participated in this maneuver, which left a profit of 260 percent. It turned 135 million pesos into 135 million dollars, earning 351 million pesos (Cafiero, 2002).

In 2002, VICENTÍN, like other persons with debts in dollars and at the same time Argentinean bonds issued in this currency, benefited by decree 214/2002, called "asymmetric pesification." Under this system, all dollar-denominated debts were converted at a rate of 1 peso for every 1 dollar. Interestingly, holdings in bonds or securities denominated in dollars were converted at a rate of 1.40 per dollar, yielding a 40 percent conversion gain.

In 2005, VICENTÍN Paraguay SA began its activities as a subsidiary that functioned as a marketing agent, either acquiring soybeans from Paraguayan farmers, or triangulating exports to evade the treasury. Also, VICENTÍN adds its fourth grinding plant in Rosafé. In 2007, it added the biofuels sector to its businesses, taking advantage of Argentine legislation to establish a promotional regime for its production,[5] producing a mixture with fossil fuels. In the same year, it formed a joint venture with GLENCOREand Molinos Río de la Plata, resulting in RENOVA. VICENTÍN now had four manufacturing plants: Avellaneda, Ricardone, San Lorenzo, and Timbúes.

5 Biofuels means bioethanol, biodiesel, and biogas, produced from raw materials of agricultural, agroindustrial, or organic waste origin. Definition according to Law 26,093 called "Regulation and Promotion Regime for the Sustainable Production and Use of Biofuels of the year 2006."

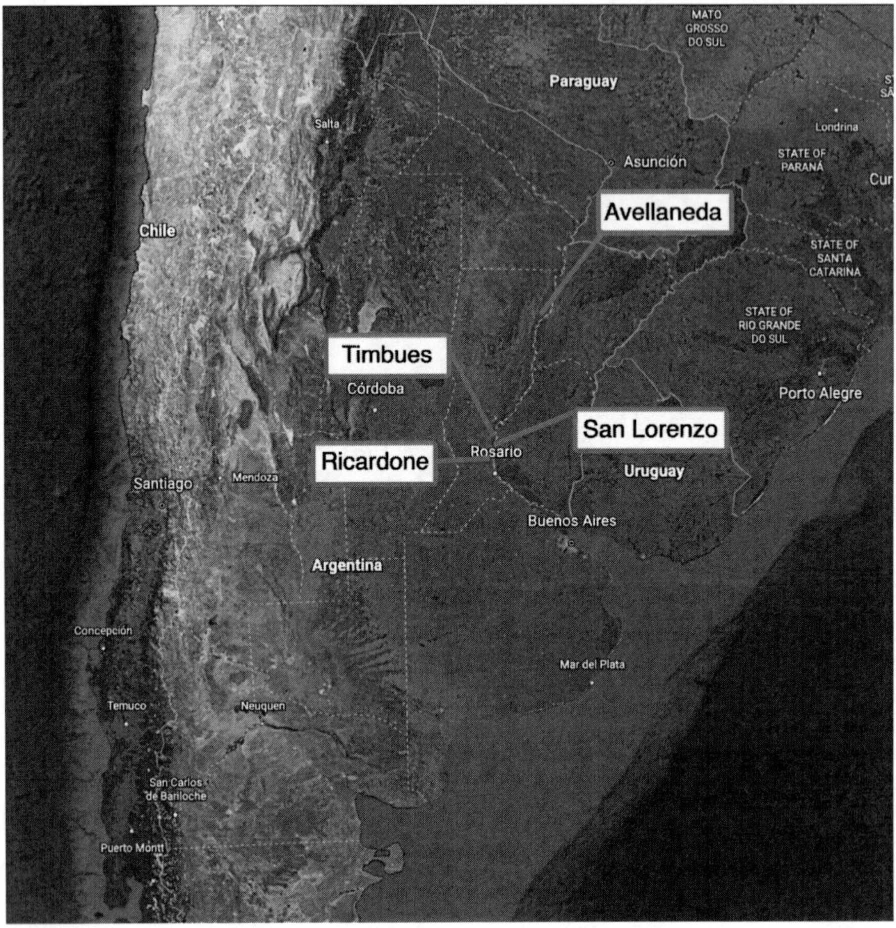

Figure 6.2: Manufacturing VICENTÍN's plants in Santa Fe.
Prepared by the author using Google Maps.

6.4. The fall

Finally, on December 5, 2019, VICENTÍN defaulted on its debt. Its indebtedness with the Banco de la Nación Argentina had doubled since 2015, going from $150 million to $300 million. Most of the credits occurred in the last year. In 2019 alone, 72 loans were granted, 28 of them in the month prior to the cessation of payments even though VICENTÍN was already in default. In the November before the default, it received $86.6 million (Valli, 2020).

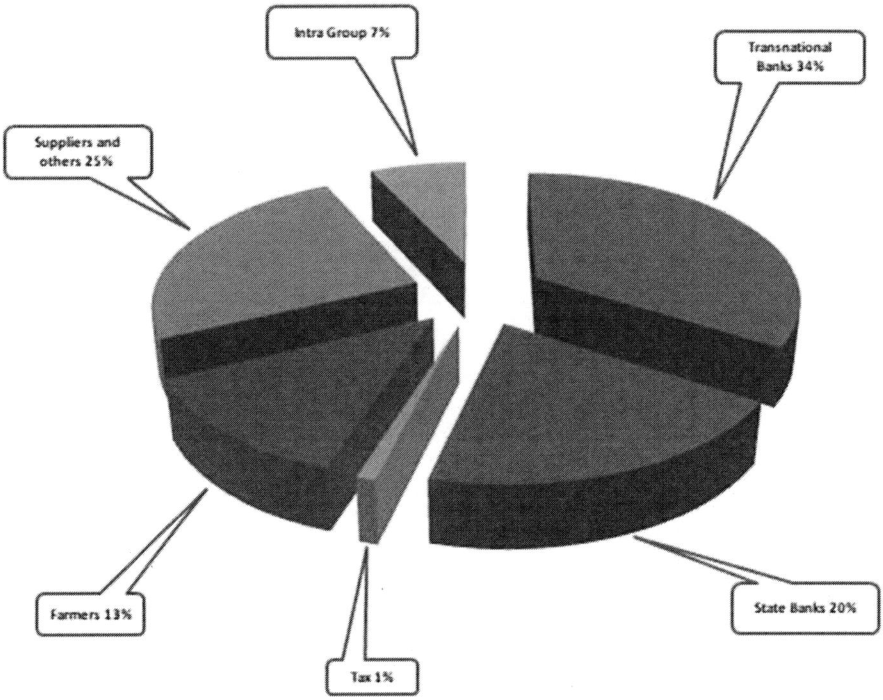

Figure 6.3: VICENTÍN's debt by creditors.
Prepared by the author

The debt in default is one-and-a-half billion dollars, distributed among more than 1,700 creditors. Among them, 34 percent are transnational banks, 20 percent public banks of the Argentine State (the "Banco de la Nación Argentina" is the largest creditor among all VICENTÍN lenders), 1 percent is the national, provincial, and municipal tax agencies, 13 percent farmers, and 25 percent service providers and others. In addition, VICENTÍN's non-core companies claim to collect from its parent VICENTÍN their own reported credits. Despite the confusion of the recording and reporting of entity assets among controlled companies (subsidiaries and related parties) and its controller, VICENTÍN S.A.I.C., the controlled group claims 7 percent of all of VICENTÍN's debt. See Figure 6.3 above.

VICENTÍN S.A.I.C. is a limited company that does not make an offering of its shares in a public stock market. It has 106 shareholders, most of them descendants and in-laws of its founder (in 1929) Don

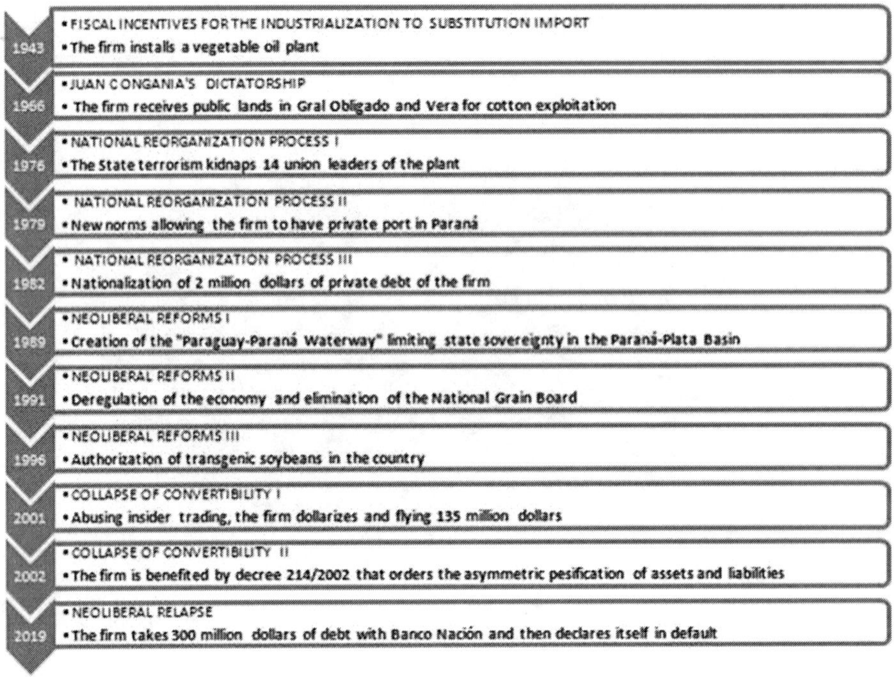

Figure 6.4: VICENTÍN and its growth thanks to the help of the State.
Prepared by the author.

Pedro VICENTÍN. The shareholder with the largest holdings owns only 3.3 percent of the capital. Its course and relationship with the Argentine State can be summarized in the following figure.

The considerations made reveal that the anti-state discourse of the sector of capitalized actors in agribusiness is fallacious. The State was always a tool of accumulation for them, even to extremes that implied the violation of human rights. VICENTÍN was no exception. Importantly, so-called free market capitalism and neoliberalism depends on the State to impose and enforce a regulatory and legal regime that protects its expansion, profits, and gains. The State is the strong arm of private profit contagion, a species of property law and liberalism that allows individuals through legalization of fictions such as corporations to secure or imperil at will economic resources, with the result that profits and gains may be privatized and losses socialized (e.g., through special State-sanctioned bailouts supported by appropriated public funds). See Figure 6.4 above.

The company is currently facing the possibility of bankruptcy. The most likely scenario is that its most valuable assets, especially RENOVA, will be appropriated by transnational companies at auction or fire-sale prices. Public effort, private profit, and centralization and consolidation of capital—nothing new to see here.

6.5. VICENTÍN, financialization, and rhizomatic corporate structure

For Gaggero and Zanotti (2020), the company had different phases of development and growth. The first was the production and export of oils; the second the diversification and internationalization of activities around the parent company of the group, VICENTÍN S.A.I.C.; third, the corporate splitting and transnationalization of the corporate structure.

In the second stage of diversification, VICENTÍN expands. From the industrialization of cotton, grains, oilseeds, and the export of these, it goes on to include activities such as meat refrigeration, biofuels, wine, and port services. These new activities were carried out by other companies controlled by the parent company VICENTÍN S.A.I.C. The same names are repeated in the directories of the controlled companies as in the directory of the controlling company. Thus, VICENTÍN becomes a group that expands into a "rhizomatic" structure of no less than 23 companies. (Arelovich, S., personal communication, August 14, 2020).

We can see in Table 6.2 below that VICENTÍN has participation in 20 corporations in different share proportions. Anyway, it does not matter if VICENTÍN has 100 percent of shares (i.e., VICENTÍN Paraguay) or 0.4 percent (i.e., Friar). VICENTÍN rules always. Also, we can see that several corporations are owned too by VICENTÍN Family Group (VFG), a separate holding company created by VICENTÍN in Uruguay. VICENTÍN had purposely transferred credits from non-core companies step by step to its shell company VFG, which is located in a corporate-friendly jurisdiction, taking advantage of intra-firm commerce rules to avoid and evade taxes.

VICENTÍN S.A.I.C. was turning from its productive activity toward the management of financial businesses (i.e., financial managerialism

Table 6.2: VICENTIN's corporation structure.

Vicentín SAIC	Vicentín Paraguay (Py)	
	Rio del Norte	
	Diferol	***VFG***
	Vicentín Europa	
	Tastil	
	Vicentín Brasil (Bra)	
	Biogas Avellaneda	
	Terminal Puerto Rosario	***VFG***
	Playa Puerto	***VFG***
	Enav	***VFG***
	Juviar	***VFG***
	RENOVA	
	Renopack	
	Emulgrain	
	Friar	***VFG***
	Sottano	***VFG***
	Buyanor	***VFG***
	Oleaginosa San Lorenzo	***VFG***
	Sir Cotton	***VFG***
	Algodonera Avellaneda	***VFG***

Prepared by the author with data from Gaggero et al.(2020)

as a strategy and realization of private profit contagion). It is configured as the capital manager of its own controlled companies (non-core) that it assisted financially, including the absorption of their losses.

VICENTÍN begins to involve its controlled companies in credit requests to national and foreign financial entities. In this sense, the scheme used by VICENTÍN S.A.I.C. was this: VICENTÍN S.A.I.C. or a non-core company asks for credit, and another non-core company or VICENTÍN S.A.I.C. acts as joint guarantor simultaneously. These cross-guarantees gave lenders confidence, resulting in the payment of financial support. The capital thus obtained could be destined for the requesting company or be transferred to any other entity of the group. The reason given for requesting the loan also had a subtle often covert dynamic. It has been substantiated that the credit was requested to "pre-finance" exports from VICENTÍN S.A.I.C. and, after obtaining it, it was used to reinforce the position of a non-core entity to pay previous debts or for anything else(Iribarne, 2021). Thus, the amounts financed were diverted to ends not disclosed in the credit application.

Likewise, the employees of a group company could work in one company but appear on the payroll providing services for another. The IT systems and the accounting department were one, shared by all the companies in the group. In fact, most of these companies had their legal address in the same building as VICENTÍN S.A.I.C.

The characteristics identified above should not be underestimated in importance. The self-reporting structure presents high risk of manipulation and transfer of financial and other assets and liabilities. Without a stable set of books and records verified independently, the recording of transactions and reporting of account balances of the group are not likely trustworthy.

6.6. The day of the Battle of San José

On April 25, the Battle of San José is commemorated. It was fought in the struggle for South American independence in 1811 against Spain, led by patriots of what would later be the Argentine Republic and the Eastern Republic of Uruguay. On that day, some 203 years later, three meetings of three different corporations were held. All domiciled, together with a branch of VICENTÍN S.A.I.C., in Uruguay (specifically, in the World Trade Center Complex, Luis Bonavita 1294 Street in liberated Montevideo). Ironically, it is clear that in these assemblies, no discussion of the independence of the country took place.

The Official Newspaper of Uruguay is the legal bulletin through which commercial companies must publish certain acts. In the edition of July 24, 2014, the three assemblies mentioned are published. In one of them, Insurel SA changed its name to "Industria Agroalimentaria LATAM SA;" in the other, Monterey International SA to "VICENTÍN Family Group SA."In the last one, Jusmel Corporation SA to "V.F.G Inversiones y Operaciones Especiales SA." In all three cases, 30 million Uruguayan pesos were established as new capital for each. VICENTÍN had created a triad of holding companies where the share ownership of its controlled companies was going to begin to migrate. Currently, we are in the third stage of corporate unfolding and transnationalization of the group. (Gaggero et al., 2020).

In Uruguay, it is easy to become a limited company. Through a search of the web, one can discover legal and accounting service companies that sell incorporating services to form the desired legal structure, registering it, and formally appearing to commence operations, even if only as a shell company (in effect, an empty legal suit that any buyer can wear). By April 25,2015, VICENTÍN acquired three of these "suits" to start the offshoring processes of the companies in its group.

Of all the works that tried to clarify what the corporate tangle of the VICENTÍN group companies was like, the work by Gaggero and Zanotti (2020) is by far the clearest, even far above the forensic audit ordered by the judge in the preventive bankruptcy process. It is reflected

Table 6.3: VICENTÍNFamily Group's corporation structure.

Vicentín Family Group (Uru)	**Industria Agroalimentaria Latam SA (Uru)**	Vicentín Chile (Chi)	
		Sir Cotton (Arg)	Playa Puerto (Arg) Vicentín Desarrollos(Arg) Logística Rio Arriba (Uru) ***Servicios Fluviales (Arg)*** ***Terminal Puerto Rosario (Arg)***
		Buyanor (Arg)	Celint (Arg)
		Oleaginosa San Lorenzo (Arg)	
	VFG Inversiones y Actividades Especiales SA (Uru)	South America Food (Uru)	Alimentos Refrigerados (Arg)
		Algodonera Avellaneda (Arg)	Sudeste Textil (Arg) Diferol (Arg) ***Servicios Fluviales (Uru)*** ***Friar (Arg)***
		Friar (Arg)	Friar (Uru)
		Patagonia Bio Energía (Esp)	Patagonia Bio Energía (Arg)
		Sottano (Arg)	
		Enav (Arg)	Juviar (Arg)
		Capible (Uru)	

Prepared by the author with data from Gaggeroet al.(2020).

as the offshore holding company[6] called "VICENTÍN Family Group SA," which in turn owns the shares of two subsidiary holding companies: "Industrias Agroalimentarias Latam SA" and "VFG Inversiones y Actividades Especiales."These two subsidiary holding companies are the owners of equity share packages of more than 20 companies.

As VICENTÍN S.A.I.C. is an agro-export company, it is logical that it chooses Uruguay to transfer its corporate structure. Not only because of the proximity of that country to Argentina; or because it shares the River Plate basin as a riparian State; or for the facilities it provides to form corporations: it also chooses Uruguay because export duties are not paid there, which is the heaviest tax that those who sell soybeans and their derivatives abroad face in Argentina.

6.7. Conclusions

VICENTÍN S.A.I.C. made a rhizomatic structure of corporate vehicles through which it became transnationalized. This structure was the platform that the company used to finance its activity. In board of directors' Minutes, we see constant movements of money toward non-core companies, joint credit requests, guarantees of third-party debts, and transfers of capital reflected without a productivity foundation explaining it. No justification of how these movements were related or sustained is in the Statute of VICENTÍN S.A.I.C. The Statute is "the maximum internal law" of the firm. It is its constitutional norm. It establishes the corporate purpose of the company (what the company should be dedicated to and what it was set up for), the powers of those who make it up, and gives its directors a framework for action, establishing their responsibility before the partners. Partners are the owners of the firm on whose behalf that board of directors exercises the administration. See Table 6.3 above. In brief, the Statute functions as the articles of incorporation and bylaws of the company.

6 Holding companies are companies that do not have productive activity; they only own shares of other companies, which may be operating and/or additional layers of holding companies.

VICENTÍN S.A.I.C. is a company whose objective, according to its Statute, was agricultural and agro-industrial commercial activity. Finance was a secondary objective, ancillary to all of this. It seems that one day finances became central.

According to the file where the preventive contest (functionally equivalent to Chapter 11 in United States) is processed,[7] the company's debt is $1,573 million. The nominal or book value of its assets is $1.253 billion. However, the market value of VICENTÍN's assets, what in economic reality could be obtained by selling them, does not exceed $700 million. (Arelovich, S., personal communication, August 14, 2020). There are 2600 creditors whose debts are outstanding.

The inflation of book value well in excess of market value suggests gross manipulation of books and records without a credible nexus with reality. To reach such an exaggerated level of book value, absent a catastrophic fall in asset prices, transactions must have been recorded with inflated values; i.e., the transfers in of assets and capital were overstated and accompanied by transfers out of assets and capital that had the effect of liquidating the corporation while maintaining a superficial appearance of economic and capital gain. The corporation was covertly bled dry while reporting false and materially misleading gains. Value was transferred on terms highly unfavorable to the corporation.

Something must have been done wrong. The development and use of an enterprise of commercial entities in which to obtain and transfer capital, as well as to earn and divert revenues arising from and assets related to material production and sales of products and services provided by the enterprise, comprise the art of financial managerialism. Opacity rules, and nothing is as it seems for long due to the inadequately checked ability to transfer in and transfer out financial assets and financial liabilities according to the command and control of owners, directors, and officers of the enterprise. They initiate and authorize financial transactions on less than arm's length.

7 Cases "VICENTÍN S.A.I.C. S/ Concurso Preventivo", CUIJ No. 21-25023953-7, Court of First Instance for Civil and Commercial Matters, Second Nomination, Judicial District No. 4, Reconquista, Province of Santa Fe.

References

CAFIERO, M. and LLORENS, J. (2002). La Argentina Robada, Buenos Aires, Ediciones Macchi.

CHIRINO, J. (2020). "La ´Propiedad Privada` de VICENTÍN", El Diario del Centro del País, June 28, 2020, https://www.eldiariocba.com.ar/cultura/2020/6/28/la-propiedad-privada-de-vicentin-23570.html, Accessed August 1, 2021.

ESCUDÉ, C. (2006). Festival de Licuaciones. Buenos Aires, Lumiere.

GAGGERO, A., et al. (2020). "El Proceso de vaciamiento de VICENTÍN S.A.I.C., Un análisis reciente de las transformaciones de su estructura corporativa, la dinámica financiera y el intercambio comercial", Informe final, Buenos Aires, BNA.

GRAÑA, J., et al. (2011). "Producción de la riqueza social y su distribución: productividad y salarios en Argentina. Medio siglo en perspectiva latinoamericana e internacional", Cuestiones de sociología, N°7, La Plata, UNLP.

INDEC-Instituto Nacional de Estadísticas y Censos. (2020). "Comercio Exterior", Vol. 5, N°4https://www.indec.gob.ar/uploads/informesdeprensa/complejos_03_21311B84F340.pdf, Accessed June 26, 2021.

IRIBARNE, A., et al. (2021). "Informe final cuerpo de auditores forenses", VICENTÍN S.A.I.C. S/ Concurso Preventivo, Juzgado Civil y Comercial Segunda Nominación, Reconquista.

VALLI, P. (2020). "Para la nueva gestión, hubo fraude en el crédito del Banco Nación a VICENTÍN", Perfil, January 25, 2020, https://www.perfil.com/noticias/politica/para-la-nueva-gestion-hubo-fraude-en-el-credito-del-banco-nacion-a-vicentin.phtml,Accessed August 1, 2021.

Chapter 7

Assets fleeing on corporate vehicles

What in psychiatry is the abnormality of dissociative identity disorder, in law is the normality of legal personality: The corporation as sociopath.

Keywords: disregard of the legal entity, emptying of company, bankruptcy fraud, fraud in transnational acquisition.

7.1. Synthesis

The management of business to obtain quick and extraordinary profits can lead to conduct that constitutes crimes. If this happened on a regular and sustained basis, under the passivity of the State and with damage to the population of an entire territory, we would be under the criminological category of crimes of bad development (Böhm, 2019).

As we said, bad development is a concept that cannot be outlined in a single stroke as a specific crime in the classic sense, that is, as the definition of a typical unlawful behavior. However, and perhaps in a non-systematic and scattered manner, there are established categories of criminality in our current legislation that can repress and remediate crimes of bad development.

For academic purposes, we conjecture that there is a plurality of behaviors displayed by a group of companies in the VICENTÍN case that could be considered crimes of bad development. Inside this conceptual framework, they would fall into various categories provided for in the Argentine and American legislations and codes of criminal conduct.

From the panorama studied, we chose the most important event related to the Argentinean economy: the sale by VICENTÍN of a part of the RENOVA company, the evaporation of the payment received for these transactions, the profusion of corporate vehicles to carry out the schemes, the contraptions of transnational corporate control deployed in it, and the damage resulting from all of this initiated by the partners of VICENTÍNand to the detriment of its creditors and to the community at large.

When considering this group of actions, our hypothesis (traced for scientific purposes only) is that they fall under the criminal type provided for by Argentine legislation as Emptying of Company (analogous to the American unlawful activity of corporate waste).

7.2. Who rules in VICENTÍN?

The governing, administrative, and supervisory organizations established by the General Companies Law 19,550 (Ley General de Sociedades -LGS-) in relation to Private Corporations in the Argentine Republic are the Assembly of Partners, the Board of Directors, and the Supervisory Commission. Corporations may, if they wish, make a public offering of their shares. For this, they require the authorization of the National Securities Commission according to the Capital Market Law 26,831. This is not the case of VICENTIN S.A.I.C., which is not listed on the stock exchange. It is a company where the shareholders are third generation descendants and in-laws of its founder, Don Pedro VICENTÍN (i.e., a privately held corporation).

On the date of its entry into default, VICENTÍN S.A.I.C. was a company consisting of 106 shareholders, a board of directors of 15 members (who were also shareholders at the same time), and a supervisory board of six members. Most also held a seat on boards of directors and supervisory boards of the non-core companies in the group.

The VICENTIN S.A.I.C. command was held by the directory board and within the directors by a subgroup of specific people. In practice, they did not base their authority on shareholder percentages (no one owned more than 3.6 percent of the capital in the firm) but on a series of family relationships, politics, business management of other companies of the group or related entities, and the norms of operating procedures.

Mentioned in other parts of this work, the effective control by shareholders over board decision-making is not widely a characteristic of corporations. In VICENTÍN S.A.I.C., the informality of treatment among people who had family relations was added, and it was customary for shareholder partners to receive dividends without demanding much of them, including compromising their efforts or asking too many questions. This was combined with a status-based privilege system through which shareholders and family members could access paid jobs within the company or non-core companies that were distributed according to political criteria (i.e., performance-based).

7.3. Insolvency as a result of the corporate enterprise Ponzi scheme

This unprofessional management facilitated the course of the insolvency of VICENTÍN S.A.I.C. without an insider sounding the alarm. If we had to outline in a stroke how insolvency was achieved, we would say that it was a corporate Ponzi scheme.

VICENTÍN S.A.I.C. applied for loans from banks under the pretext of financing needs for exports of grains and derivatives and for other productive motives that would enhance profit. To lenders, it feigned solvency by exhibiting manipulated balance sheets. One of the mechanisms used to misrepresent solvency was to alter net worth, showing liabilities as if they were assets. The vehicle most used by VICENTIN for turning a liability into an asset was grain purchase-sale contracts with a "fixed price."

Grain price is volatile. Argentina takes the international prices established (most of the time) in Chicago, and the value of the grain is dollarized. Therefore, in a country where dollars are scarce, the grain serves as a reserve of value and a means of speculation. Agro-export companies, however, need to have available stocks of this raw material to meet a specific schedule of shipments for the export of flour or vegetable oil or to meet emerging inventory demands. Hence, one of the contractual modalities used is the sale of grains from the farmer to the exporters in the "price to be fixed" modality. This means that the farmer sends the grain to the exporting company but does not get paid immediately for it. The farmer has to "fix the price" of the grain he sold, and only then will he be paid.

How is the price set? The farmer, within the period agreed in the sales contract (which cannot exceed 180 days), chooses a specific day (the one he thinks is best for him) from the price of the grain (which he has already sold to the agro-exporter) in the Cereal Stock Market. After chosen, it is communicated to the agro-export company and only then does the latter pay the farmer the price of the day of his choice. Why is this important in the dynamics of VICENTÍN S.A.I.C. business operations? Because the grain with a "price to be fixed" that the agro-export company has, for which it has not yet paid, cannot be accounted as an asset owned by the company. He has not yet paid for it, which he will only do at a time in the future chosen by the farmer. For this reason, the grain with a "price to be fixed" that the company has, is either not recorded on the balance sheet, or it is recorded, but with an estimate of the liability.

VICENTÍN S.A.I.C. accounted for the grain that it had at a "price to be fixed" (for which it had not yet paid) as if it were an asset belonging to the firm. With that, it improved its asset value and gave the appearance of solvency.

The contracts were characterized by contingent values. These values were apparently manipulated by the company such that the value of the company's net assets (total assets less total liabilities) was artificially inflated by its management through the reporting of contractual values that not only were not realized (i.e., obtained in fact) by the company, but the values were not currently realizable (i.e., obtainable in the future) under conservative assumptions and estimates by the company.

In 2017, VICENTIN S.A.I.C. declared that it owed (liability) farmers 11 million dollars for grains purchased at a "price to be fixed." In 2018, it owed 122 million dollars. In 2019, the date of default, the company could no longer sustain the scheme under the commitment of 474 million dollars for grain contracts that it must pay to farmers under the "price to be fixed" contractual schemes. In 2019, there was no extraordinary record harvest that would explain a 388 percent increase in the amount of grain received at a "price to be fixed" by VICENTÍN compared to the previous year. In conclusion, VICENTIN S.A.I.C. was falsifying its balance sheets, inflating assets by accounting for the grain "price to be fixed" as something it owned and for which it had already paid (Iribarne, 2021). In material respects, the production value of the grain contracts was neither entirely paid for nor entirely recoverable from farmers.

The other method that VICENTIN used to inflate assets on the balance sheets was, on the eve of the date of presentation of its financial statements, to have its non-core companies transfer money to the accounts in the name of VICENTÍN. Thus,swelling current assets thereby convincing the lender of his financial solvency. After lender review, the money went back to the non-core companies (Iribarne, 2021). The temporary transfer of funds to the parent company was essentially unrecorded and unreported loans to the parent company, resulting in the overstatement of net assets on a non-consolidated basis by the parent company.

VICENTÍN's credit loan requests were secured with guarantees given by the non-core companies of its own group.

Thus, the firm continued receiving credits that it did not earmark for productive investment. Hence, these loans did not produce profits that would have allowed it to repay capital and interest. When the scheme could not continue any longer, the company went into default and requested the preventive (cf. American Chapter 11 bankruptcy proceedings) contest.

7.4. Bankruptcy and crimes under Argentine law

The plurality of behaviors that led VICENTIN S.A.I.C. to its insolvency would fit into several of the crimes typified in the Argentine Penal Code. In principle, simple fraud (article 172 of the Penal Code), fraudulent administration (art. 173 inc. 7 CP),[1] emptying of the company (art. 174 inc. 6 CP), false balance sheet presentation(art. 300 inc. 2 CP), authorization of improper acts (art. 301 CP), and in the case where bankruptcy is judicially declared-fraudulent bankruptcy (art. 176 CP). Additionally, potential categories of criminal conduct include those that have to do with infractions of the Penal Tax Regime, Law 24,769 for aggravated tax evasion, and infractions of the Penal Exchange Regime, Decree 480/95 for violations of the regulations that impose declaration of foreign trade operations and liquidation of foreign currency.

It is interesting to note that the acts of VICENTIN could have a criminal nature, due to the transnationalization of the company beyond the Argentine jurisdiction. Note that one of the potentially swindled credit institutions was the International Finance Corporation (IFC), headquartered in Washington D.C., for 270 million dollars lent to VICENTÍN S.A.I.C. that it cannot recover. IFC is VICENTIN S.A.I.C.'s second largest lender.

The vast majority of debt transactions within the financial sector are made in United States currency. The guarantees that VICENTÍN S.A.I.C. gave to IFC were for payments for its exports, payments that should be made directly to Natixis bank in New York, IFC's financial agent. In the respective contracts, in case of controversy, the jurisdiction of the courts of the Southern District of New York was established. It was in these courts where the consortium of creditor banks[2] of VICENTÍN (led by IFC) requested a "Discovery" to trace the assets of the Argentine

1 "CP." is the abbreviation of "Código Penal", equivalent to Title 21 of United State Code. "Art." is the abbreviation of "Artículo," equivalent to section in English. "Inc" is the abbreviation of "Inciso," equivalent to subsection in English.

2 The group of transnational creditor banks is made up of the International Finance Corporation (IFC, the financial arm of the World Bank Group), the Netherlands Development Finance Company (FMO, the Development Bank controlled by the State of the Netherlands), Internationale Nederlanden Groep (ING, the Netherlands),

company. Several deposits and transactions, including those of the controversial sale of RENOVA S.A., were made through JPMorgan Chase, also of New York. All of these circumstances could together form the basis forcriminal investigation and prosecution under U.S. jurisdiction.

For now, we are going to analyze the most important of all in terms of a patrimonial appropriation (patrimonial more in the sense of privately controlled and inheritable wealth and income than in the sense developed by Piketty that more specifically articulates distributions of wealth and income among socioeconomic strata of the population) of the entire plexus of maneuvers under suspicion of fraud by VICENTÍN. It is a transnational company, an asset in the country which made no real investment in capital. It existed and capitalized simply by abusing corporate and financial vehicles. Now, it is accused of a fraud against creditors and is deeply affecting the future of Argentina's agro-industrial export production. We are referring to the sale of a financial interest of 16.67 percent of RENOVA S.A. by VICENTIN S.A.I.C. 2 days before it announced its own default.

7.4.1. An umbrella for the debtor: The preventive contest

Presently, the company is under preventive contest, law 24,522. The preventive contest (also called call for creditors) is a universal judicial process, where the debtor in crisis, under the tutelage of a judge, calls on the creditors to verify their credits against the company. Once all the credits have been registered and recognized, the debtor proposes a renegotiation of the debt to his creditors. Such renegotiation may consist of a reduction in the amount, a delay on the payment date, capitalization of the debt with company assets assigned to creditors, reorganization of the company with the participation of creditors, among many other variants.[3]

the Dutch entity Rabobank, and the French Natixis, and the Credit Agricole network of cooperative banks.

3 Preventive contest is similar to "reorganization" bankruptcy from Chapter 11 US Code.

Throughout this period, the company continues to operate, led by its original directors, but with limitations in the disposition of its assets and always under judicial surveillance. This judicial oversight is implemented mainly through a bankruptcy receiver. The trustees who carry it out are expert professionals in economic sciences and audits. If the agreement proposal (renegotiation of the debt) is approved by a majority of creditors representing two-thirds of the unsecured capital owed (that is, creditors who do not have privileges such as mortgage, pledge, or assignment of collections to their benefit such as secured creditors), the judge approves the agreement and declares the contest to be finished, having established controllers for monitoring of compliance with the agreement.If, on the contrary, a majority of the creditors are not obtained, or the judge does not approve the agreement, or if the rescue process fails (e.g., a third party takes over the company with creditors' approbation), or the agreement is otherwise not fulfilled, the company would be declared in bankruptcy and creditors are paid by dividing their assets pro rata (cf. liquidation of assets under the American bankruptcy regime).

There is a peculiarity in Argentina. In Argentina, the preventive bankruptcy dilutes markedly the value of the debts of the bankrupt company by the mere passage of time. By virtue of article 19 of the LCQ, the claims against the debtor are frozen at their value in pesos (except if it was agreed in dollars) on the date the process begins. A bankruptcy process requires at least 2 years. In a country with a constant devaluation of its currency, this is equivalent to liquidation of the claimed debt. In the case of VICENTÍN, the creditors whose debts were recorded in pesos, in a market where the grain follows the value of the Chicago stated price, which is in dollars, had their claims substantially impaired. In a year of the process, the grain creditors who registered their debts in pesos had already lost half of their value without mediating any haircut (Ortega, 2021).

The preventive contest is a civil and commercial process, which is managed by a judge of the designated jurisdiction. If there are accusations that the debtor behaved fraudulently to harm creditors, the investigation to determine whether a crime occurred would take place in a criminal court—our next area of focus.

7.4.2. What is the criminal behavior that best describes VICENTIN's conduct?

The directors of the VICENTIN's board are under investigation in criminal jurisdictionsof different courts. In the Federal Court of Reconquista, for aggravated tax evasion, Law 24769, Criminal Tax Regime. In the Federal Prosecutor's Office No. 11 of Buenos Aires, for fraud against a Public Administration, art. 174 inc.5 CP. This is because one of the frauds would have been committed against the Banco de la Nación Argentina, a financial institution of the Argentine State. Additionally, the Prosecutor for Organized Crime and Complex Crimes of Rosario Office, Ministry of the Accusation of the Province of Santa Fe, is conducting a criminal investigation for simple fraud (art. 72 CP) and false balance sheets (art. 300 inc. 2 CP).

While the investigations progress (slowly, as usually happens in complex crimes, when the investigated are subjects with power), the relevance of other criminal types is emerging.

Simple scam is comparatively easy to prove. The typical action is to defraud the victim by deceiving or abusing trust through false balance sheets that exhibited by the accused to the lender to induce the lender to extend credit. For example, acts with the malicious intent of misleading the lender to grant the company a loan that it will not be able to repay because, in fact, it was insolvent may form the predicate and evidence to support fraud. It has the disadvantage, however, that the criminal investigation does not enter the field of corporate plots, both of VICENTÍN and its non-core, and of the transnational companies that acted in collusion in order to obtain improper patrimonial advantages. With the simple scam, VICENTÍN is a victimizer and, everyone around, victims, a seemingly black and white issue. Yet, the actual scenario has more nuances, including the criminal participation of others.

It is in consideration of this that we focus on studying the criminal action that apparently fits more specifically with the conduct of the directors of VICENTIN. Specifically, how they carried out the disposal of the largest grain extruder in the world RENOVA S.A. This action is the emptying of the company in violation of art. 174 inc. 6 CP.

We are sensitive to the totality of facts and circumstances attendant to the use of the parent company to obtain and distribute economic resources, including financial assets, among its related parties and favored business partners worldwide. These acts were supported under patrimonial regimes(domestic and foreign)that functioned like crony capitalism. Its rule of law served less the goals of justice than the profit contagion of a group of private individuals.

7.5. RENOVA and its transfer to GLENCORE: Emptying of the company

In the question of how the 16.67 percent of the shares that VICENTÍN had in RENOVA was disposed of, we recognize material elements present in corporate fraud. The motive to centralize, accumulate, and distribute capital without investing in the earning businesses to the expense and detriment of others under impunity created by a mantle of fictional companies drove the enterprise's scheme of siphoning and diverting economic and financial resources to a select and privilege few. The receipt and transfers of capital were characterized by conduct not supportive of the lawful commercial future of the enterprise but committed to enrich unjustly a select group of controlling persons—enterprise be damned!

VICENTIN's board behavior falls into the framework and category of crime provided for in art.174 inc.6 (emptying company), since they intentionally impaired the normal development of the firm, deliberately reducing its value. They did this by transferring the assets of VICENTÍN S.A.I.C. to other companies in their economic group, or to other associated companies (e.g., favored business partners). All of this to the detriment of the shareholders in the firm, the scores of creditors, and the political economy in general.

We will outline how through the abuse of legal personality (article 144 of the Civil and Commercial Code of the Nation -CCyCN- and article 54 of the LGS), the assets of the company RENOVA S.A. were transferred for the benefit of other companies in the group as well as associated companies. With this, the bulk of creditors and the shareholders of

VICENTÍN were deliberately harmed. Likewise, it caused undue hardship and uncertainty in the political economy in general.

RENOVA is a joint-stock company. The share capital was divided giving 50 percent to VICENTIN and 50 percent to VITERRA.

One day, surprisingly, VICENTÍN sold 16.67 percent of its shares in RENOVA to a semi-unknown company, RENAISCO B.V. (a company controlled by GLENCORE).[4] It did so 48 hours before publicly announcing that it had fallen into default with 22 working days remaining to appear in preventive contest.

Our hypothesis is that VICENTÍN's intention was to remove those assets from its ownership. Assets that would have constituted the mass of economic and financial value disputed by creditors in a possible bankruptcy and send them to their non-core companies.On top of this, we believe the main driving force was to ensurethat it provided GLENCORE, through one of its controlled companies, and at a fire-sale price unsupported by sound business logic, control of the entire RENOVA Timbúes plant.

The 16.67 percent of RENOVA S.A. (transferred for 122.7 million dollars) would be nominally equivalent to 9.7 percent of all the assets of the firm VICENTÍN. This is calculated according to the valuation made by the contest and bankruptcy receiver (legal overseers of the company during the bankruptcy) of the assets of the firm. However, the contest and bankruptcy receiver has been strongly questioned by the creditor control committee[5]for reproducing and uncritically repeating the arguments of the debtor company and for ignoring the criminal cases in progress against the board of VICENTÍN that are being heard in parallel. They overstated the assets of VICENTÍN. More detailed calculations value the exit of RENOVA as a loss of 17 percent of the debtor's assets immediately before it is presented in the creditors contest proceedings.

4 RENAISCO B.V. is one of VITERRA's subsidiaries, which is subsidiary of GLENCORE. VITERRA is owner of 100 percent of RENAISCO's shares. Also, VITERRA appears owning 67, 6 RENOVA S.A's. See pages N°88 and N°42 "VITERRA 2020 annual report"https://www.viterra.com/dam/jcr:5e692425-6bda-4cbe-98bc-8d394e627 50a/Annual-report-2020-.pdf, accessed September 5, 2022.

5 The Control Committee is a body made up of representatives of the creditors and workers of the firm in crisis, who assure the correctness of the process. (Arts. 14 inc. 13 and 42 of the Contest and Bankruptcy Law 24522 -LCQ-).

An overstated net asset value operates to neutralize objections until the interested parties, including creditors, become aware of the material exaggeration.

Where did the money received from the sale go? The money that VICENTIN received from RENAISCO was not used to pay creditors. VICENTIN depleted all that money in the 6 working days following the sale. Where did the money go? For payments to the companies of its group, payments to its subsidiary RENOVA, and payments to the other owner of RENOVA (VITERRA). VITERRA is a company also controlled by GLENCORE. The money from the sale made a loop and returned to its starting point. Financial interests in the debtor were consolidated under the legal protection of a favored business partner, outside the bankruptcy / preventive proceedings.

7.5.1. Transfer timeline

VICENTIN S.A.I.C. and VITERRA SA were the owners of RENOVA by halves. See Figure 7.1 below. The sequence of the maneuver of how VICENTÍN got rid of 16.67 percent of RENOVA, was as follows:

- On November 4, 2019, two directors of VICENTIN board, who simultaneously were also proxies of the non-core VICENTÍN Paraguay, on behalf of the latter, sold 16.67 percent of the shares of RENOVA to VICENTIN S.A.I.C., but to its Uruguay Branch. A branch does not have legal personality of its own, but is only an office of a firm, authorized to operate in another political jurisdiction. In other words, they were selling RENOVA to themselves. Furthermore, the money that VICENTÍN would have paid VICENTÍN Paraguay for the purchase could never be traced.
- On December 2, 48 hours before VICENTIN communicated its default to the community, the President and Vice President of VICENTIN directed the sale of 16.67 percent of the shares of RENOVA (which they had acquired from their non-core VICENTÍN Paraguay 28 days before) to RENAISCO B.V. That same December 2, they also sent RENAISCO and VITERRA (in their capacity as co-shareholders of RENOVA and as subsidiaries

of GLENCORE) an agreement proposal that, in case of silence of the recipients, would have been accepted. The proposed agreement guaranteed GLENCORE's total control over RENOVA, avoiding any market competition. The means to ensure that control was a commitment to reform RENOVA's Statute (cf. articles of incorporation and bylaws). Such reform of the Statute contained:

  - o A provision granting Class A shares to RENAISCO and VITERRA and Class B (Class B shares have fewer or limited voting rights) to those retained by VICENTÍN. With this maneuver, because GLENCORE owned RENAISCO and VITERRA, they guaranteed GLENCORE's control over RENOVA.
  - o Maintain the prohibition of a sale of RENOVA S.A. shares to any firm that does not belong to the VICENTIN or GLENCORE group. If an agreement is reached to remove this prohibition, give VICENTIN and GLENCORE the preferential first right of purchase.
- On January 3, 2020, just 6 working days before VICENTIN S.A.I.C. files for preventive contest process, VICENTIN's board of directors decides to cede the use of the portion of the RENOVA plant that it preserved. That is, 33.33 percent of the plant's capacity, which corresponds to 33.33 percent of the shares that VICENTIN still has in RENOVA, after having sold 16.67 percent. And to whom do they give that use? Toits subsidiary VITERRA. With this, GLENCORE already controls, in fact, 100 percent of the RENOVA plant.
- On May 21, 2020, 77 working days after submission to the contest, the RENOVA S.A. shareholders' meeting (VICENTÍN+ RENAISCO+ VITERRA) was held. The Statute of RENOVA was reformed, with the institutional changes proposed by VICENTIN S.A.I.C. on December 2, 2019 when it sold RENOVA's 16.67 percent. Control by GLENCORE is guaranteed.

7.5.2. The subjects and the object

RENAISCO B.V. is a company whose activity and domicile is complex to trace in Argentina. According to the Bloomberg agency, it is domiciled

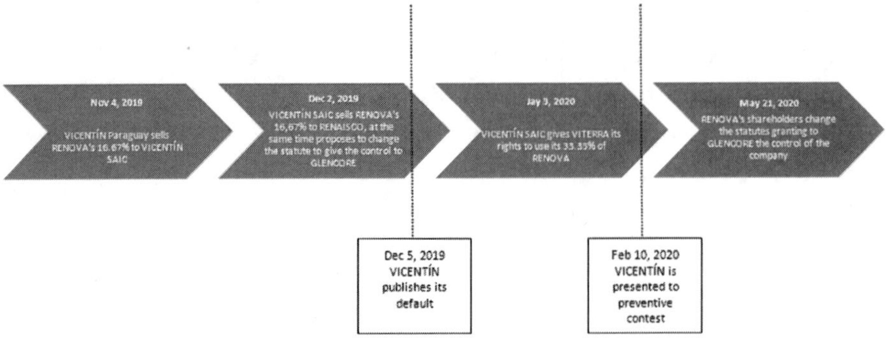

Figure 7.1: Transfer timeline.
Prepared by the author.

in Rotterdam, Netherlands.[6] The Netherlands is listed among the top 10 jurisdictions that most facilitate corporate tax abuse globally according to the *Tax Justice Network*.[7] RENAISCO is legally structured in a " BeslotenVennootschap" (B.V.) -private company in Dutch-, a very malleable and flexible corporate form, which limits the liability of the partners to the integrated share capital. To form them, a share capital of one Euro (€1) is enough, and they can be established by foreign individuals or companies. A BV can be formed in a few days, with few or no restrictions and founded and operated by a nonresident of the Netherlands[8].

Viterra Ltd[9]is a transnational of Canadian origin dedicated to the trade of agro-products, based in Rotterdam, Netherlands. GLENCORE PLCis the owner of VITERRA, having acquired it in 2012 (El Cronista, 2012) and of RENAISCO B.V.

6 See https://www.bloomberg.com/profile/company/1360950D:NA, accessed May 16, 2021.
7 Tax Justice Network. (2021). Tax Haven Rankings Show Countries Setting Global Tax Rules Do What They Can To Help Businesses Ignore Them, March 9, website https://www.taxjustice.net/press /classification-of-tax-havens-shows-that-the-countries-that-set-the-global-tax-rules-do-the-possible-to-help-companies-ignore-them /, accessed online May 16, 2021.
8 See https://es.intercompanysolutions.com/establecer-una-compa%C3%B1%C3%ADa-holandesa-de-bv/, accessed online on May 16, 2021.
9 See https://www.viterra.com/, official corporate website, and accessed May 18, 2021.

RENOVA S.A. is the most efficient grain extruder in the world. The soybean crushing business basically consists of transforming the grain into oil and flour. Biodiesel can also be produced with soybean oil. The RENOVA Timbúes crushing plant is located on the banks of the Paraná, with its own shipping port on the river. On the other hand, RENOVA has another plant focused on biodiesel production. This plant is in San Lorenzo, on the banks of the Paraná too, and is one of the most productive in Argentina. Which means that whoever owns RENOVA S.A. would be able to extrude at costs lower by up to 50 percent than those of its competitors. It is not that RENOVA S.A. has an inaccessible technology, but rather since it was recently designed and has ports in Paraná, it has a hyper-efficient layout and the latest technology on the market (Grassi, A, personal communication, March 31, 2021).

RENOVA has more than one manufacturing plant. The most coveted is Timbúes, the diamond, as it is the world leader in crushing with the most modern and efficient facility. Other plants owned by RENOVA are located in San Lorenzo, Quequén, and Bahía Blanca.

The RENOVA Timbúes manufacturing plant was built to work in the "fasón" mode. This modality consists of the producer delivering the grain to RENOVA, RENOVA processes it industrially, converting it into oil or flour. RENOVA does not export that oil or flour, but it gives the producer the flour and the oil. It is the producer that must export them. RENOVA will charge an amount only for its manufacturing processing services. In other words, working fasón implies selling only the grain processing service, disregarding the export of flour and oil.

RENOVA Timbúes was thought to be the fasón factory of only two exclusive clients: VICENTÍN and GLENCORE.

For the GLENCORE PLCgroup, the acquisition through RENAISCO B.V. of 16.67 percent of RENOVA S.A. represented a great advantage. With this ruse, they controlled RENOVA. We reiterate that the property of RENOVA S.A. is divided into 50 percent of VITERRA, 16.67 percent of RENAISCO B.V. (both financial interests controlled by GLENCORE PLC), with the remaining 33.33 percent still in the hands of VICENTIN S.A.I.C. VICENTÍN S.A.I.C. ceded the exploitation of that remaining 33.33 percent to VITERRA SA. In conclusion, GLENCORE today controls the operation of 100 percent of RENOVA S.A.

The maneuver has borne fruit for the Swiss–British transnational. Despite being the upstart in the grain traders'market, it has rapidly transformed into the primary exporter of soybean oils and meals in Argentina. This could only be possible due to the *de facto* absorption of RENOVA S.A. and the market share of VICENTIN S.A.I.C. (Longoni, 2020).In brief, the consolidation of these largely domestic agricultural companies under the foreign control of the Swiss–British transnationalsignificantly altered the productive landscape of Argentina, directly ceding economic and financial interests and indirectly ceding influence in the political economy to actors independent of the well-being and development of Argentina broadly.

7.5.3. How the VICENTIN directory orchestrates the sale?

Minutes of the Board of Directors of sharing companies is mandatory documentation that must be maintained. This is the record of the discussions of the members of the Board of Directors, the company's administrative and policy-making body. The debates between the directors and the resolutions to which they arrive as administrators of the firm are recorded there. When there are disagreements, these are recordedas are members' voting records. Meeting minutes are reviewed and approved by all of the directors that participated in the meeting (art. 73 LGS). So,let's see how VICENTIN's Board behaved; how it made decisions during the sale of RENOVA and the crisis.

In the Minutes of the Board of Directors No. 2461 of November 29, 2019,6 days before the announcement of the default, the Board of Directors mentioned the issue of the sale of RENOVA S.A. for the first time. It is stated succinctly and without detail, alluding to the intention to sell 16.67 percent of RENOVA S.A. It is not specified why it is being sold, or for what amount, or the destination of the funds obtained. There are no reports or documents attached for such an important change and operation. It is not stated (as it had not been done in the previous minutes) that the company is in a financial crisis. According to the minutes, the board meeting lasted only one hour.

Later, in the Minutes of the Board of Directors No. 2463 of December 3, 2019, 2 days before the public announcement of the cessation of payments, the board of directors of VICENTIN S.A.I.C. confirms the sale and transfer of the shares of RENOVA. There is no reference to the proposed reform of RENOVA's bylaws, which was part of the sale agreement, and that this reform would further reduce the share rights of VICENTIN's shares in RENOVA. The reason for the sale is not indicated, or the price and terms of the sale disclosed. The destination of the proceeds is unknown. The meeting lasted barely an hour.

In two meetings of 1 hour each, the sale of one of VICENTÍN's most valuable assets, and the company's transition to a subordinate role with respect to its partners (i.e., VITERRA and RENAISCO) is not rationally explained. The logical explanation is the urgency to dispose of the asset to and ensure GLENCORE has control of the plant before communicating the default and submitting to a bankruptcy.

And, regarding the financial crisis of the firm? The directory never mentions it. An outdated comment on January 3, 2020, a month after publicly announcing its default, the first reference to the current financial crisis of firm is noted in the minutes of board. In other words, the press and members of the community apparently knew about the default well before the board itself.

As a cause of its financial crisis, the Board blamed exchange rate uncertainty (it had never been mentioned in the previous Minutes), the high interest rates (it had not been mentioned before either), the 3 percent differential that it must pay for rights of export when soybeans are exported as beans and not as industrialized products (they had not mentioned it before either), the results of the 2019 presidential elections (they had not mentioned it before either), and the commercial conflict between the US and China (about which promising prospects had been noted in previous Minutes). Given this crisis, recognized for the first time, VICENTÍN nonetheless hastened to cede the usage quota of 33.33 percent of RENOVA S.A.'s installed capacity for the benefit of VITERRA SA.

7.5.4. *Was the transfer of 16.67 percent of the shares of RENOVA S.A. made with an intention to harm the mass of creditors?*

We conclude yes. This is evidenced by the fact that it is implemented through an operation full of inconsistencies, obscure aspects, contradictions, gaps, and indications that support an argument of fraud against creditors. The doctrine, jurisprudence, and even civil legislation (see art. 969 of the old Civil Code; arts. 336 and 340 of the Civil and Commercial Code of the Nation (creditor fraud); arts. 115 and 119 of the Contest and Bankruptcy Law) present legal structures and series of requirements and presumptions impossible for the operation in question to circumvent within the law. The contest and bankruptcy receiver, despite its passivity and complacency with VICENTIN, mentions this operation in its report as likely to be revoked for creditor fraud.[10]

In subsequent statements, the Board stated that the sale was made precisely because of the challenges the company was experiencing, with the aim of having funds to pay off its debts with creditors (TELAM, 2020). This need to sell to pay does not appear anywhere in the records analyzed. Only the existence of the financial problems of VICENTIN S.A.I.C. ismentioned later in the Minutes of the Board of Directors No. 2467 of January 3, 2020. Then, in the Minutes of the Board of Directors No. 2468 of February 7, 2020,the decision to present itself to legal process and contest among creditors appears; this is done just 3 days later on February 10, 2020. In other words, they prepared the presentation for one of the largest calls for creditors in the country's history in just 72 hours, suggestive of business assumptions and estimations operative in the Board but not disclosed in the minutes.

The conduct of the Board was manifestly intransparent with respect to material pending issues. The failure to disclose and discuss these issues suggest the existence of a scheme of concealment and breach of duty to the corporation.

10 General Report of the Receiver, according to article 39 section 8 of the LCQ. Cars VICENTÍN S.A.I.C. s/ Preventive Contest.

7.5.5. The pact and collusion between the owners of RENOVA

The transfer of 16.67 percent of the shares of RENOVA is carried out by means of an irrevocable offer of sale and shareholders' agreement[11]initiated by VICENTIN to RENAISCO with notification to VITERRA, as the latter was a shareholder of RENOVA.

Despite its obscurity, if we take the time to read the contractual instrument of the irrevocable offer, we will recognize one more mile stone in the transference of a portion of VICENTIN S.A.I.C. to another company's name among its associated companies, thus putting it beyond the reach of creditors. All of this accomplished before the imminent presentation in a preventive contest of VICENTIN.

The formalization of the contract for the sale of a part of RENOVA takes place (once again) in the form of an "irrevocable offer." Clearly, the risk of abuse of process is high when the same natural person is simultaneously on both sides of the transaction. The same personis to sign twice but in different capacities. The abuse inherent in the form and substance of the "irrevocable offer" characterized by circumstances in which the offeror and the offeree are the same natural person is real and considerable, arising from self-dealing and lack of an arm's length agreement.

What is more, VITERRA annual report and financial statements expressly acknowledge that VITERRA by itself directly acquired 16.67 percent of RENOVA without even mentioning RENAISCO.[12]

The definition of contract according to article 957 of the CCyCN is *the legal act through which two or more parties express their consent to create, regulate, modify, transfer, or terminate legal property relations.* If such a definition depended on the transactional management of the members of the VICENTIN board of directors, it should be reformulated and read

11 Attached in the case Preparatory Criminal Investigation (IPP) CUIJ no. 21-08421855-0, "Representantes de VICENTÍN s/ Estafa" and accumulated proceedings before Dr. Miguel Moreno, Prosecutor of the Special Unit for Economic and Complex Crimes of the Public Ministry of the Accusation of the Second Judicial District of Rosario.

12 VITERRA 2020 ANNUAL REPORT, https://www.viterra.com/dam/jcr:5e692425-6bda-4cbe-98bc-8d394e62750a/Annual-report-2020-.pdf, accessed October 24, 2022.

as a "contract is a legal act in which a person unilaterally modifies the rights of third parties as he pleases."The RENOVA transfer does not escape this; it exemplifies it.

The form adjusted to the law to reflect the real legal structure of RENOVA S.A., and VITERRA, as well as RENAISCO B.V. and VICENTIN S.A.I.C.'s participation in it, should be interpreted as a *Joint Venture* structure.

Materially, RENOVA S.A. operates in a *Joint Venture.* In fact, the RENOVA S.A. website defines itself as a *Joint Venture.*[13] VITERRA also does so when it says on its website "RENOVA is a joint venture between GLENCORE Agriculture and Vicentin."[14] But before the law, it did not assume that legal form. Let's see why.

Joint Venture is a contractual modality accepted by Argentina, from Anglo-Saxon law, through jurisprudence (Binstein, 1989).

The Joint Venture is an associative contract, by means of which two or more persons, whether natural or legal, agree to operate a common business for a certain time, agreeing to participate in the profits resulting from it, as well as being liable for losses in solidarity and unlimited form (Argumedo, 2020: 1).

There's the explanation. To avoid this joint and unlimited liability, the members of the RENOVA *Joint Venture* (VICENTÍN, VITERRA, and RENAISCO) disguised it as a public limited company.

In the *Joint Venture contract,* there is no legal personality other than the member companies. The institute is authorized in Argentina (today) in article 1,454 CCyCN as a "business collaboration contract," which says: *There is a collaboration grouping contract when the parties establish a common organization for the purpose of facilitating or developing certain phases of the activity of its members or to perfect or increase the result of such activities.*

The group thus formed does not have a lucrative purpose for itself, since its profits will go directly to its participating companies. Therefore, it adjusts to RENOVA'smethod of operation whereby its directors are not paid by RENOVA. It is diametrically separatedsince VITERRA,

13 See https://renova.com.ar/compania.php, consulted on May 23, 2021.

14 See https://www.viterra.com/Media/News/GLENCORE-Agriculture-becomes-majority-owner-of-RENOVA, accessed November 28, 2021.

RENAISCO, and VICENTÍN do not have joint and unlimited liability with respect to third parties as mandated by art. 1,459 CCyCN. The deception of dressing up as a corporation was for this purpose.

In this way, we better understand the inextricable web of the clauses of an irrevocable offer of sale and shareholders' agreement. Such a web does not coincide with the operation of a separate and individual legal entity, a Limited Company that RENOVA claims to be but is not.

In VICENTIN S.A.I.C.'s board of directors' minutes No. 2461 dated November 29, 2019, two directors of VICENTÍN were authorized to offer its sale to RENAISCO B.V. As of that date, one of the authorized parties was President of VICENTIN S.A.I.C. and, concurrently, Director of RENOVA S.A. The other authorized person was a director of VICENTIN S.A.I.C. and, concurrently, President of RENOVA S.A. Both names were duplicated as both bidder and seller.

A common practice among incorporated entities is to reproduce through the efforts of key officers and directors (often, individual controlling persons) into a collection of parties related by these key persons under an umbrella enterprise can commit acts under a variety of subsumed entities without imperiling the existence of the enterprise. Risk is divided, allocated, and isolated in the disposable / transferable entity. These entities may be non-consolidated subsidiaries, affiliates, or otherwise related parties. This type of organizational structure and presentation functions to preserve key persons' control but mitigate both personal and enterprise risks.

7.5.6. Changes in the Statute

On December 2, the President of VICENTÍN S.A.I.C. signed the irrevocable share transfer offer and the proposed shareholders' agreement to amend RENOVA's Statute and, by means of that reform, gave more shareholder rights to the shares of VITERRA and RENAISCOinrelation to those of VICENTIN. The offer is addressed to the president of VITERRA in Argentina, who at the same time is Vice President of RENOVA. It is also addressed to another Director of VITERRA who, at the same time, is also Director of RENOVA. The directors of VITERRA register their emails on the contractdocument which directly note the

"GLENCORE" domain. The same applies to the other recipients of the irrevocable offer, the directors of RENAISCO. In their emails, you can also see the domain "GLENCORE." All roads do not lead to Rome but to Jersey, the offshore tax haven home of GLENCORE.

This constant overlapping of the same people in different companies seems to be paying off. The irrevocable offer made on December 2 was immediately accepted, both in Buenos Aires on behalf of VITERRA and in Rotterdam on behalf of RENAISCO. That same day, the first payment is transferred to VICENTIN S.A.I.C. for the shares sold in the amount of 30 million dollars. A transfer that is not made from Buenos Aires or from Rotterdam. Rather, it is made from New York through JPMorgan Chase and to VICENTIN S.A.I.C. accounts in MARIVA and NACIÓN banks. The set of December 2 communications was apparently seamless: entities in Avellaneda, Buenos Aires, Rotterdam, and New York each acting in concert in real time.

The following day, December 3, VICENTIN receives a second payment from RENAISCO for 37 million dollars through JPMorgan Chase to VICENTIN's accounts at Banco MARIVA.

In reviewing the language of the Share holders' Agreement Offer (preliminary draft proposed to reform the RENOVA Bylaws),we have the following. Given the rhizomatic structure of companies controlled both by VICENTIN S.A.I.C. and by GLENCORE, the offer outlines a type of entity that we will not find in the Civil and Commercial Code of the Nation or in the General Law of Companies: namely, "company affiliated." This is what VICENTIN names the companies controlled by GLENCORE and VICENTÍN such that they can become shareholders of RENOVA. This new company described in the offer as an "affiliate" becomes a shareholder of RENOVA.

The "affiliates" that have already managed to enter are called "parties." These are the companies that, belonging to the trunk of VICENTIN or GLENCORE, managed to enter RENOVA by disposition of those shares, resulting in an institutionalization of RENOVA as a " cosa nostra" only of and for VICENTIN and GLENCORE. Free market competition may exist as a theory but less so in practice.

What this irrevocable shareholder agreement offer called "parties" corresponds to parties in a *Joint Venture* with the logic of such an association. Only here, to avoid the joint and several liability of the members, the business group that is RENOVA dressed upas a corporation does not correspond to it. Such use of legal personality falls within the provisions of 144 of the CCyCN and 54 of the LGS, which would make RENOVA's legal personality unenforceable both by GLENCORE and VICENTÍN.

In article 2 of the proposal to reform RENOVA's Statute, it is well marked who will be the future hegemon of RENOVA: GLENCORE, of course. Acting through VITERRA and RENAISCO, both will together represent 66.67 percent of RENOVA's Class "A" shares. Thus, a block is constituted that can exercise political will at any time against a VICENTÍN that is relegated to 33.33 percent of the shares Class "B." To complete assurance of the preponderance of GLENCORE, it is established that Class "A" shareholders will have the right to elect three directors from the five that make up the RENOVA board of directors. Among these three, the president has the golden vote. Meanwhile, the Class "B" shares of VICENTÍN, already out of favor in this game, do not give the right to elect a president or vice president, only two lowly directors.

In article 7, the entrance of anyone who is not affiliated with GLENCORE or VICENTIN is prohibited. Something inappropriate to the spirit of a corporation (*intuito rei*) but typical of a Joint Venture that is *intuito personae.*

The free transfer of shares in the Statute proposal that we have been analyzing is only possible among affiliates. If it is intended to offer it to a non-affiliate, the parties must be previously notified so that they can exercise their right to preferential purchase with price advantages. The closed system that guarantees the hegemony of GLENCORE is completed with the commitment that the reform of RENOVA's Statute will be made at the first meeting following the date of the sale of 16.67 percent to RENAISCO. Thus, all of these detailed changes are internalized statutorily.

The fact is that we are not dealing with a joint-stock company, only with the appearance of one. This is corroborated by the distribution of powers for the use of RENOVA's installed capacity. RENOVA should be a separate legal entity from its partners GLENCORE and VICENTIN.

GLENCORE and VICENTÍN could not apportion RENOVA and reserve pieces of it for their exclusive use. A person is precisely an entity that is indivisible. However, here we witness the stripping of RENOVA into pieces and withoutdue deference to the proportion of shareholding of those who comprise it. We explain below.

For the RENOVA plant in Timbúes, geared toward oilseeds production, VITERRA reserves for itself the use of 68.82 percent of the plant, when its shareholding is less than this percentage.

For the plant that RENOVA has in San Lorenzo, oriented to the production of biodiesel and lecithin, VICENTÍN captures the use of 33.33 percent of its installed capacity, while MOLINOS AGRO (which is not an affiliated company) takes another 33.33 percent by virtue of previous contracts signed with VICENTIN S.A.I.C., not with RENOVA.

For the RENOVA plants in Quequen and Bahía Blanca, oriented to the processing of grains and oilseeds, VICENTIN S.A.I.C. keeps 50 percent of the use of the installed capacity compared to another 50 percent of VITERRA.

For RENAISCO, nothing. An indication that RENAISCO is a merely an empty corporate shell / holding company.

The participation of RENAISCO in this scheme seems to be explained by the intention of GLENCORE and VICENTÍN to evade what is regulated by article 6 subsection C of Law 25,156 on the Defense of Competition. If GLENCORE used VITERRA SA to acquire the 16.67 percent that VICENTÍN sold, the operation would be framed as an economic concentration and control of the company. This is because VITERRA would have more than 50 percent of the share capital. Thus, it would have had to notify the Court for the Defense of Competition (TDC in Spanish acronym) so that the latter could authorize the operation. The TDC could have rejected the potential sale on the grounds of economic concentration. What's more,even if it had been approved, the TDC had 45 working days before expressing approval. A term that exceeded the 22 working days that VICENTIN S.A.I.C. had remaining to present itself in preventive bankruptcy. Any intervention by the TDC would have interfered with the transfer of RENOVA to the benefit of VITERRA. The RENOVA shares would then have remained within the equity of VICENTÍN, remaining within the reach of its creditors. That is why the "RENAISCO artifice" was used to avoid it.

It is obvious that we are not dealing with a legal entity that has capacity, assets, and a will of its own. RENOVA is about a legal fiction devoid of individuality, autonomous existence,its own will, and which is subject to the exploitation of another: namely, VICENTIN and GLENCORE.

The statements above illustrate the unreality of the RENOVA. It has not been operated and used as an independent and real person, but it has served as a corporate shell under which and through which to allocate financial and property interests to the detriment of specific creditors and the general welfare, if not also some minority shareholders.

7.5.7. Mr. L.A.

On May 21, 2020, with VICENTIN S.A.I.C.'s preventive contest already open, an ordinary and extraordinary general meeting of RENOVA S.A. was held in compliance with what was agreed in parallel with the sale of 16.67 percent to RENAISCO and that we noted above. The shareholders of RENOVA (VICENTIN+VITERRA+RENAISCO)were part of the meeting. The representations by each one of the shareholders were identified by the representatives of each one, namely:

VICENTIN S.A.I.C.:	Mr. A.M.
VITERRA SA:	Mr. L.A.
RENAISCO B.V.:	Mr. L.A.

Mr. L.A. is then the agent and representative of VITERRA and RENAISCO (controlled by GLENCORE) at the same time, therefore having a double and potentially conflicted identity. But it so happens that Mr. L.A. was also a trustee of the RENOVA board of directors; that morning, Mr. L.A. had a triple identity.

Mr.L.A. is a member of the CURTIS firm. CURTIS is a transnational legal services company headquartered in New York, United States.[15]

15 See https://www.curtis.com/our-firm/offices, accessed February2, 2022.

One of the firm's main clients is GLENCORE, to whom CURTIS, among other services, provided advice on the acquisition of VITERRA.[16] Legally, the identity of Mr. L.A. was not three-fold but four-fold.

The abuse of legal personality is clearly taking shape, which makes it unenforceable in accordance with the provisions of art. 144CCyCN and 54 of the LGS. The same individuals trading with themselves on both sides of the counter (and above and below it, too) are wearing multiple corporation guises. At a minimum, we have a series of conflicts of interest, actual and potential, that should have invalidated the assembly. Article 241 of the LGS prohibits directors from voting on their own management approval. In item 4 of the agenda, Mr. L.A. (RENOVA trustee) approves his own management, voting (in the simultaneous capacity of representative of VITERRA and RENAISCO) the approval of his management as trustee of RENOVA. Mr. L.A. should have excused himself from voting on this point as established in 241 of the LGS. He did not.

Likewise, in point 6, the conversion of the 438,233,700 shares that RENAISCO had recently acquired was decided. The RENAISCO shares were transformed into RENOVA Class "B" ordinary, nominative and non-endorsable shares (shares with fewer political rights, and more limitations on transferability), then converted to Class "A" ordinary shares. Class A shares give more political rights and are easily transferable. Mr. L.A. did not excuse himself from voting on this issue either, since this maneuver seems more in tune with the interests of GLENCORE than with the social interest of RENOVA. GLENCORE was placing his own shares in RENOVA on steroids without contributing a dime.

The art. 248 of the LGS establishes that the shareholder or his representative who in an operation has an interest contrary to that of the company has the obligation to abstain from voting at the meeting. For Halperín (1998), interest contrary to society is not only antagonism or interests in conflict with said society, it is enough to try to procure a particular utility or advantage over the advantage of society to compose the material element of impairment.But here, no one restrained.

16 See https://www.curtis.com/our-firm/news/curtis-advises-glencore-international-plc-on-us-legal-matters-in-acquisition-of-viterra-inc, accessed February 2,2022.

In the Minutes of the ordinary–extraordinary meeting that we have been following, in point five, it was decided not to set remuneration for the directors of RENOVA. This demonstrates the fictitious character of the function. Their directors are, in fact, paid by the companies to which they actually belong. From the eight Directors of RENOVA, four were simultaneously directors of VITERRA, and fourwere also directors of VICENTÍN. They decide to modify the Statute, closing the RENOVA office andrevising its registered address from Calle 14, No. 495 inthe City of Avellanedato an address in the city of Rosario. Calle 14, N° 495 was and is VICENTÍN's domicile. VICENTÍN was in troubles. Time to move.

(They were right. Shortly after the move, Calle 14, No. 495 was the venue of two judicial raids.)

Likely, GLENCORE plans to retain 100 percent ownership of RENOVA.[17] If such total transfer has not yet occurred, it is because there were problems with the Court for the Defense of Competition, and there was a prior contract preventing it. In the words of VICENTIN itself, which it expressed in its 2019 financial statements, it was unable to dispose of all its shares in RENOVA because:

> Unfortunately, there was a share retention agreement that prevented the sale of 33.33 percent of the share package, for which only the partial sale of the free 16.67 percent could be carried out, a flow that was not sufficient to meet the expectations of the producers, who in the last days before the change of government increased their sales for fear of changes in the level of payment of export duties.[18]

17 See "GLENCORE offers USD 325 million to get VICENTÍN out of RENOVA" https://elabcrural.com/glencore-ofrece-usd-325-millones-para-sacar-a-vicentin-de-renova/, "For U$S 325 million, GLENCORE wants the other part of RENOVA in the hands of Vicentin" https://www.infocampo.com.ar/por-325-millones-de-dolares-glencore-quiere-quedarse-con-la-planta-de -renova/, "The formal proposal of Vicentin and the negotiations for the sale of RENOVA," https://news.agrofy.com.ar/noticia/185220/propuesta-formal-vicentin-y-negociaciones-venta-renova,

"GLENCORE offered US$325 million to keep the rest of Vicentin's shares in RENOVA" https://www.cronista.com/apertura-Negocios/empresas/ GLENCORE-ofrecio-us-325-millones-para-quedarse -with-the-rest-of-the-shares-of-Vicentin-in-RENOVA-20200407-0003.html, accessed May 2021.

18 VICENTIN S.A.I.C. (2020). Annual Financial Statements Closed on October 31, 2019, Avellaneda.

As evidenced above, it is all a simulated act to perpetrate the transfer of 16.67 percent of VICENTIN to GLENCORE subsidiaries. On the one hand, the latter strengthens its control over RENOVA by taking ownership of a total of 66.67 percent of the share package (VITERRA plus RENAISCO). On the other hand, VICENTIN S.A.I.C's creditors are removed from the reach of RENOVA S.A. The physical persons are always the same. It is the hat they wearfor each transaction that changes.

7.5.8. The path of money

In the VICENTIN S.A.I.C. proceedings regarding the preventive contest, the Receiver's General Report, on the occasion of complying with the mandate established by subsection 8 of article 39 of the LCQ (acts that may be revoked),disclosed the sale of 16.67 percent of the shares of RENOVA S.A. to RENAISCO B.V.

Through access to the "Discovery"[19]ordered through the U.S. District Courtfor the Southern District of New York, litigation involving the transnational lending banks that had accused VICENTÍN of fraud, more evidence was obtained supporting the argument that the transfer of 16.67 percent of RENOVA S.A. was made to defraud creditors.

Let's see what was done with the money received by VICENTIN from the sale (i.e., the audit trail). Of the 122,700,000 dollars that VICENTIN acknowledged having received for the sale, 26,300,000 dollars were retained by RENAISCO B.V. to pay RABOBANK, which was also a creditor admitted in the insolvency proceeding, for a debt due arising from events prior to the filing of the preventive contest.

Without going into the questions of how this overturns the *paripassu*and the *pars condition creditorum,* one of the factors that most evidenced the valuation that the debt with RABOBANK was actually 25,900,000 dollars is the apparent disappearance of 400,000 dollars "lost along the

19 "Discovery" is the name given to the US federal civil procedure that aims, in a phase prior to the lawsuit (it is as a preparatory measure), to secure and obtain documentation, evidence and track the location of assets of the probable defendant. It is regulated by 28 US Code § 1782.

way." RENAISCO did not return this discrepancy and overpayment; nor does VICENTIN seem to care much about claiming it either.

Of what remained from the payment of these 122.7 million dollars to VICENTIN, part of the remainder went to the companies of its group. A change of hands to avoid satisfying some creditors (and preferring others). In effect, this is company emptying (i.e., corporate waste).

Thus, VICENTÍN Europe received 16,400,000 dollars, and FRIAR SA 5,690,799 OLEAGINOSA SAN LORENZ0 S.A. received 257,666 dollars. Moreover, VICENTÍN DESARROLLOS SAgot US$20,550; RENOPACK SAgot US$2,371, and SERVIPACK S.R.L., got 570,660 dollars. Regarding the latter, VICENTIN S.A.I.C. claims that it is not part of its group. However, the current Vice President of VICENTIN S.A.I.C. is the partner and administrator of SERVIPACK S.R.L.[20] Meanwhile, SERVIPACK operates from a property that is owned by VICENTIN S.A.I.C.[21]

So far, we have calculated that 18.6 percent of the proceeds from the sale VICENTÍN S.A.I.C. were remitted to its own companies. But there is more.

VITERRA shares ownership of RENOVA with VICENTIN; therefore, VITERRA also received proceeds from what VICENTIN obtained. In fact, what VITERRA received was 9,561,176 dollars for an allegedly existing debt of VICENTÍN. In turn, VITERRA claimed more money, since it appeared as a verified creditor for 14 million dollars in the preventive contest of VICENTIN. See Figure 7.2 below.

With regard to RENOVA, which considered itself a proper company, we should reflect and consider the evidence adduced throughout this manuscript: RENOVA does not function as an independent company in practice. Instead, it functioned as a cost center for both VITERRA and VICENTIN S.A.I.C. From this cost center, an amount of 122.7 million dollars was transferred out from tranches and funds in the name of VICENTÍN that properly should have been within the reach of the creditors of the preventive contest. After initially removing these

20 See Official Bulletin of the Province of Santa Fe website https://www.santafe.gob.ar/boletinoficial/ver.php?seccion=2019/2019-02-20contratos.html

21 See https://www.cronista.com/apertura-business/empresas/Vicentin-quienes-son-los-integrantes-del-nuevo-directorio-que-por-primera-vez-no-pertenecen-a-la-familia-20201016-0001.html

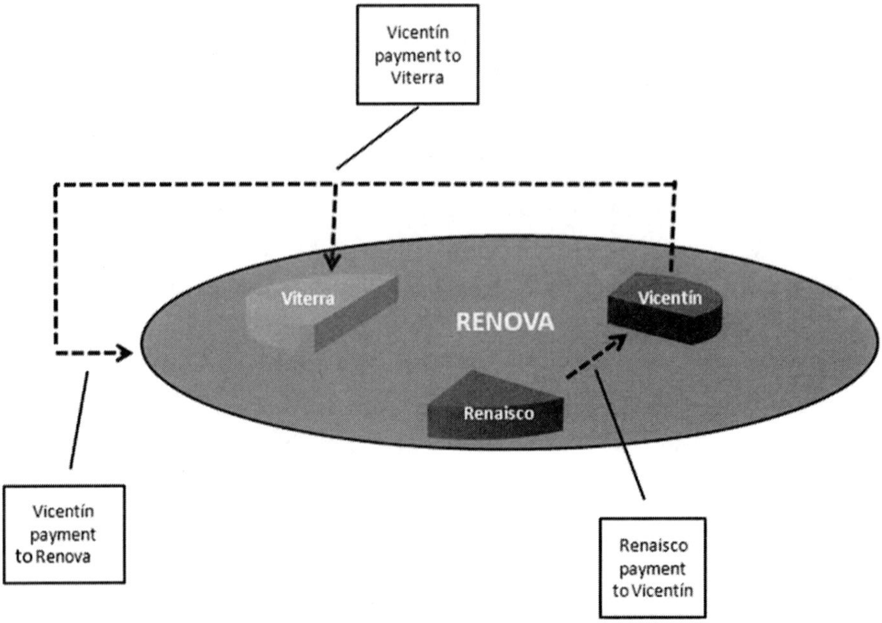

Figure 7.2: VICENTÍN sells RENOVA capitalizing RENOVA.
Prepared by the author.

proceeds of 122.7 million, a significant part of which was returned into RENOVA S.A. through a backdoor—one that no longer had the name of VICENTÍN. This was a way to avoid creditors. See Figure 7.3 below.

We have already explained above how 9.5 million dollars (from what VICENTIN received for the sale of RENOVA) went to VITERRA. It remains now to explain that another 25.1 million dollars went directly to RENOVA for payment of a debt that VICENTÍN reportedly had with the company. VICENTÍN "owed itsown creature." In addition, RENOVA (like VITERRA) appears as a verified creditor in the preventive contest proceeding.

The abuse of legal personality that these operations demonstrate leaves us with no other option than to resort to graphics in order to understand the complex engineering of the fraud that has been carried out.

Following the trail of the money received from the sale of the 16.67 percent of RENOVA, shows us who the ultimate beneficiaries were.

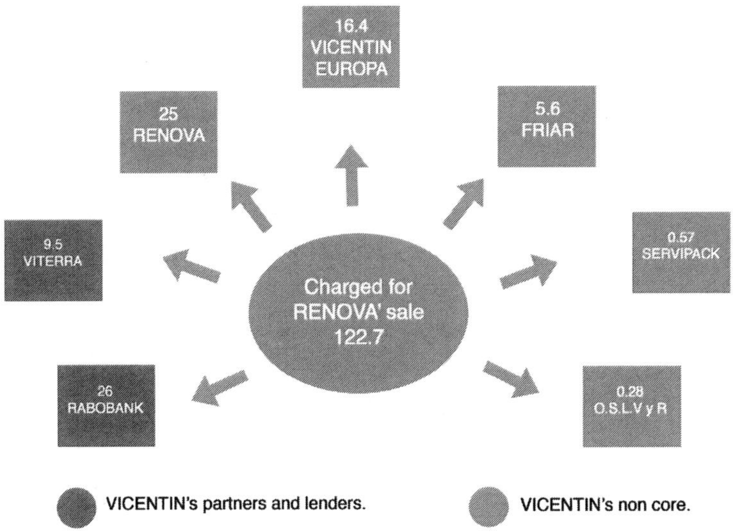

Figure 7.3: Where did the money from the sale go? (In million dollars)
Prepared by the author.

About 68 percent of the money from the sale of RENOVA S.A. went to companies controlled by VICENTÍN S.A.I.C. and to creditors of VICENTÍN S.A.I.C. prior to the presentation in the preventive contest. These proceeds were returned to RENOVA S.A. itself and protected under a legal mechanism that could not be attacked by creditors. Conveniently, all of this activity was transacted during a sale made 48 hours before the announcement of the bankrupt's order of cessation of payments (cf. Automatic stay under American-style bankruptcy law).

Transfers of funds and assets among the related and affiliated parties described above suggest the risk of preferential transfers (i.e., some transferees receiving unlawful favor at the expense of others) and fraudulent conveyances (i.e., transfers of value of funds / assets for inadequate consideration received to defraud lawful creditors of the bankrupt). The financial transactions in which the bankrupt and relatedparties were on both sides of the transaction pose a high risk of unlawful intentional disposition of assets to harm some creditors and favor others. In brief, the reported business purposes of such transactions may be questioned.

The set of transactions entailing the conduct described above and penalized by 174 subsection 6 is demonstrated below.

7.5.9. The imputed criminal category to which the conduct applies: Emptying of Company (article 174 subsection 6 CP)

The directors of VICENTIN S.A.I.C., who had to act with loyalty and with the diligence of good businessman (art 59 LGS), hid the financial crisis of the firm they managed. At the same time, they hastened to reduce the company's assets by disposing of part of its most valuable asset and transferring the product of that operation to other firms. The 122.7 million dollars obtained from the operation were not used to improve the offer of the Extrajudicial Preventive Agreement (art. 69 LCQ) that the board of directors in Minutes No. 2468 of February 7, 2020resolved to alleviate the crisis. Nor were they used to, even partially, satisfy the firm's most aggressive creditors. They did not even remain as company assets to face the preventive contest from a more solid position.

As reported by the same company, these 122.7 million dollars were spent at a dizzying pace before filing for preventive bankruptcy. Here, we reproduce a publication of the company. See Figure 7.4 below.

In other words, payments to "suppliers" are overwhelmingly made between the date that 16.67 percent of RENOVA S.A. is sold (December 2) and December 5, the date on which it publicly communicated its default due to "financial stress."[22] In other words, 96.71 percent of the funds received in hand by VICENTIN S.A.I.C. for the sale of RENOVA were spent quickly (at the rate of 1 million dollars per hour) during those 96 hours before the creditors found out that their debtor was in default.

Then, according to the forensic audit carried out in the VICENTN S.A.I.C. proceedings preventive contest, it was possible to find out

22 See "Communication from VICENTÍNS.A.I.C. where it informs that it has started a payment restructuring process based on a situation of financial stress that affects them." In Reconquest Today, website https://www.reconquistahoy.com/38306-comunicado-de-vicentin-S.A.I.C.-donde-informa-que-ha-iniciado-un-proceso-de-reestructuracion-de-pagos-a-partir-de-una-situation-of-financial-stress-that-affects-them, accessed June 23, 2021.

A la opinión pública:

Ante versiones periodísticas que insisten en afirmar que Vicentin S.A.I.C. vendió en diciembre de 2019 acciones de Renova sin ingresar los fondos al país, se aclara: Vicentin S.A.I.C. vendió el 02/12/2019 el 16,67 % de acciones de Renova S.A. en la suma total de U$S 122.700.000. De ese total, el comprador descontó un total de U$S 26.300.000 millones, para cancelar el capital, intereses, comisiones por pago adelantado y honorarios legales, de un préstamo con garantía de esas acciones en favor de Rabobank. El importe remanente que ascendía a U$S 96.400.000 fue utilizado para pagar a productores y proveedores de Vicentin S.A.I.C. a través del Sistema Interbanking, conforme el detalle que se agrega a continuación marcado en amarillo.

fecha	Pagos día	tc	USD	Total Mes	Prom. Mes
Ago. 2019				456.005.234,28	22.800.261,71
Set. 2019				396.477.457,09	18.879.878,91
Oct. 2019				461.127.453,56	20.960.338,80
01/11/2019	809.048.332,20	59,67	13.558.711,78		
04/11/2019	834.234.939,35	59,75	13.962.091,04		
05/11/2019	902.465.466,45	59,70	15.116.674,48		
07/11/2019	2.712.029.238,50	59,65	45.465.703,91		
08/11/2019	1.176.482.044,05	59,60	19.739.631,61		
11/11/2019	1.644.745.878,89	59,50	27.642.787,88		
12/11/2019	527.544.563,68	59,95	8.799.742,51		
13/11/2019	940.206.569,18	59,70	15.748.853,76		
14/11/2019	1.234.160.330,33	59,72	20.665.779,14		
15/11/2019	1.559.384.806,10	59,72	26.111.600,91		
19/11/2019	975.454.289,68	59,67	16.347.482,65		
20/11/2019	1.238.429.944,55	59,69	20.747.695,50		
21/11/2019	1.265.762.217,00	59,73	21.191.398,24		
22/11/2019	949.246.586,88	59,80	15.873.688,74		
25/11/2019	986.807.566,80	59,77	16.510.081,43		
26/11/2019	955.813.718,12	59,71	16.007.598,70		
27/11/2019	914.255.504,93	59,94	15.252.844,59		
28/11/2019	1.163.498.798,69	59,77	19.466.267,34		
29/11/2019	1.723.148.314,52	59,85	28.791.116,37	376.999.750,58	19.842.092,14
02/12/2019	1.919.389.580,07	59,94	32.021.848,18		
03/12/2019	1.383.980.787,38	59,98	23.075.961,44		
04/12/2019	743.167.343,94	59,93	12.401.624,43		
05/12/2019	1.554.172.254,60	59,88	25.954.780,47		
06/12/2019	114.395.857,89	59,99	1.907.074,40		
09/12/2019	75.824.904,26	59,94	1.265.011,42	96.626.302,34	

Figure 7.4: VICENTÍN's statement.
Prepared by VICENTÍN S.A.I.C.

who those lucky "suppliers" were: namely, other companies of the VICENTIN group.

In business emptying maneuvers, it is common for a new company name to be created and the assets of the emptied company are transferred to it. In this case, VICENTIN S.A.I.C. used other companies of its group and of its associated company in RENOVA S.A., which is GLENCORE PLCembodied with financial interests in VITERRA SA and RENAISCO B.V.

Marina Marsili and Noelia Radyna maintain that the characteristic elements of the fraudulent use of the corporate form are:

1. *The shareholders of the companies are coincident;*
2. *Single administration centralized in a subject that does not present itself as a partner;*
3. *Coincidence of social or commercial addresses;*
4. *One company assumes the debt of another;*
5. *One company assumes services from another;*
6. *One company accounts for costs of others;*
7. *Invoicing for sales of doubtful verification for the items in question or the lack of essential documentation in them;*
8. *Unjustified equity increase accompanied by an absence of correlation between tax profiles and assets held* (Marsili, 2020:92).

The features described by the authors are recorded brilliantly in the matter addressed. The emptying occurred through the abusive use of the legal entities of the companies controlled by VICENTIN S.A.I.C.

The harmful action against the firm that they managed as members of the VICENTIN Board of Directors is our legal theory. Legal assets of the partners, creditors, and the community in general have been damaged.

The partners of VICENTIN S.A.I.C. hold shares that have lost all of their value. The firm has a negative equity of 368 million dollars.[23]

The creditors, especially the 1,200 grain originators that supported the firm's normal operations, already saw the value of their credits diluted by 50 percent, making it an unlikely event that they could collect their credits' nominal value.[24]

23 According to ANNUAL FINANCIAL STATEMENTS AS OF OCTOBER 31, 2020. "VICENTIN S.A.I.C." STATEMENT OF EQUITY NO. FROM THE INSPECTION OF LEGAL PERSONS OF SANTA FE: 330.

24 Own estimate made according to the variation in the price of a ton of soybeans from February 10, 2020 (VICENTÍN's submission to preventive bankruptcy) to March 23, 2021, taking as reference the price on the Rosario Stock Exchange. See the calculation at https://www.cac.bcr.com.ar/es/precios-de-pizarra/consultas?product=13&type=pizarra&date_start=2020-02-10&date_end=2021-03-23&year=&month=&period= day&op=Filter

The community of Avellaneda-Reconquista sees the survival and turnover of its main source of private employment and the driving force of the local economy threatened. Considering that VICENTIN S.A.I.C. was the fourth largest exporter of grains and derivatives in the country, capturing 10 percent of that market (Bartoli, 2020), and that agro-industrial exports are the main source of genuine foreign currency income for a country with structural problems of external constraint, it is clear that there are macro-social assets that have been impaired by the maneuvers and financial transactions of the board of directors of VICENTIN.

There is a quartet of potential legal assets impaired (i.e., members of the firm like shareholders; external agents to the firm such as creditors; groups in the firm itself such as workers; and groups of the community where the firm operates like Avellaneda city). The enterprise's actions herein are supportive of the legal theory of "emptying of company," a category of criminal law corresponding to the legal right to be protected. The quartet have been irreparably harmed by the wasting of corporate assets that formerly supported their well-being and development.

For Carlos Creus, the legal theory of the Emptying of Company as a criminal offense is intended to protect "property, understood as the right that creditors have to receive their legitimate creditsin the form of economic value"(Creus, 2007:570). Carlos Palacio Laje (2004) agrees with the position that what is protected is the tradition of a common pledge between debtors and creditors. Here, we have VICENTIN entering intoreceivership so its creditors cannot collect. Assuming the usual resolution of such insolvency proceedings, the unwinding of the debts will be characterized by administrative and other deductions, delays in distribution of assets, and dilution of the value of assets due to inflation and other factors (e.g., changes in foreign currency exchange rates, if applicable).

For other authors such as Diego Goldman, the protected asset is comprised of the totality of assets of the company itself.

> ...the object of criminal protection is none other than the assets of the company as such or, more precisely, the free availability of material and immaterial factors necessary for the development of business activity.(Goldman, 2020:125).

As stated, the company has negative equity, and given its cessation of payments, it has ceased to operate as a grain processor on its own account (its main corporate purpose by Statute), having to enter intofasón contracts and operate with third-party raw materials under another account holder's name(since no one trusts the firm) to deliver grain as originator.[25]

For our part, we agree with the typicity approach carried out by Jorge Marcelo Ilharrescondo, for whom the protected legal right is economic public order. This is on point to the criminal violations of the members of the board of directors of VICENTIN S.A.I.C. as we saw above.The professor at the Universidad Nacional de Rosario states:

> ...in addition to claiming that there is a specific impact on the company's assets, we are of the opinion that the figure requires that the action of the agent violates, disrupts, destroys, or transforms the so-called economic public order, understood as the violation of the economy national or regional, a circumstance that is clearly verified when an establishment of magnitude is attacked and the impairments toits normal functioning threatens the community as a whole(Ilhasrrecondo, 2008: 392)

The bankruptcy agent's actions caused the agricultural producers of the North of the province of Santa Fe; most of the time grouped in cooperatives, which are commercially referenced in VICENTIN S.A.I.C. given their geographical location, the loss of 50 percent of the value of credits as stated aboveunder the most favorable hypothesis. As a whole, and considering that the creditors of grain producers add up to 1,200 people, it implies a loss of more than 100 million dollars, something that has an impact on the economy of the region.[26] At the same time for the national economy,the impact was 450 million dollars less for the year 2020, serious for a country like Argentina that, due to its dependent economy, has recurring problems generating currency

25 See VICENTIN S.A.I.C. s/ insolvency proceedings, monthly reports of trustees.

26 See "Vicentin's creditors mobilize: they do not want to be pesified" in El Economista, website https://eleconomista.com.ar/2020-11-acreedores-vicentin-se-mobilizan, accessed March 3, 2021.

to balance its payments.[27] Similarly, the market shares operated by VICENTIN have been transferred to transnational companies such as GLENCORE, among others, which deepens the foreignization of the sector and the outflow of foreign currency (Longoni, 2020).

Hence, whatever the current doctrine to which we ascribe, or the legal right protected by the criminal type, the actions of the breakup agent in the case have already impaired the public economic order.

As far as the liability derived from the criminal category under consideration is concerned, those who formally integrate the administrative bodies of the company can be considered liable (Ilhasrrecondo, 2008).

7.5.9.1. Objective type

Says article 174 inc. 6 of the CP - *The one that maliciously affects the normal development of an establishment or commercial, industrial, agricultural, mining operation or intended for the provision of services; destroy, damage, make disappear, hide or fraudulently diminish the value of raw materials, products of any nature, machinery, equipment or other capital goods.*

The criminal type describes two typical actions. One, to affect the normal development of the company. The other, to destroy, disappear, hide, or reduce the value of raw materials, products, or capital goods. The actions of the VICENTÍN directorate perfectly cover the behavior required by the type, and in the two subtypes simultaneously. One would suffice, but here both are given.

This is because, by Jorge Ilharrescondo regarding violating the normal functioning of the firm:

> Who maliciously transfers part of the company's assets (real estate, furniture, vehicles, machinery, credits against third parties, etc.) to other natural or legal persons (national or foreign, in which they have participation or not), motivated by the intention of causing damage, without a doubt that it violates the regular operation of the establishment due to its impairment

27 The Olio Group occupied the market share that VICENTIN S.A.I.C. ceded due to its crisis, operating in harmony with some VICENTÍN S.A.I.C. facilities. In addition, the Olio group, which was not large enough to operate in the field. He did not liquidate the dollars he received for exports and, in turn, he also filed for bankruptcy protection. See: https://www.lanacion.com.ar/politica/ponen-lupa-grupo-olio-no-liquido-exportaciones-nid2614045/Accessed March 2, 2022.

of the necessary elements for the normal and expected development attributable from the activities carried out… has objectively impaired the public economic order.

*The absence of assets or the unjustified encumbrance of these (guaranteeing with them, for example, debts of third parties, owed to or for the benefit of non-existent companies) mortally wounds the solvency of the company and also prevents it from accessing credit "*normally*"; the latter, precisely because the heritage, goodwill, and reputation is adversely affected by those charges.* (Ilharrescondo, 2008:406)

The professor from Rosario seems to describe directly and not in the abstract what was the behavior displayed by the members of the board of directors of VICENTIN S.A.I.C.

The board of directors sold 16.67 percent of RENOVA, after which the board gave up his right to use 33.33 percent of RENOVA Timbúes plant, which provides it invaluable services as a grain processor. The RENOVA factory became totally removed from the VICENTIN method of production. Additionally, the board did not use the money obtained from the sale to improve company´s productivity or solvency, damaging partners and creditors. These actions harmed the ongoing operation of VICENTÍN. Such conduct fits exactly into the criminal type of 174 article,6 paragraph, first subtype.

With regard to the second subtype, reducing the value of the firm's assetsis also inherent in the conduct of the accused. By surreptitiously transferring part of the shareholding of its most valuable asset in exchange for 122.7 million dollars, and placingthis sum completely out of the reach of the mass of creditors and partners of VICENTIN, it resulted in an immediate decrease in the value of company assets. The debtor willfully decreased his assets so that the creditor is unable to collect.

The author of this crime, following Palacio Laje, could be any person who is related to the business of the company. As a passive subject (the injured party), he believes that special qualities are not needed to be so. De Luca maintains that the creditors and the affected company are passive subjects. Included also are the partners of the company (D'Alessio, 2004). In this case, the holders of the injured rights reach all of these subjects: the mass of creditors of VICENTIN S.A.I.C.; the community in general (grain producers, input suppliers, service providers, brokers, etc. of the agro-export activity); the firm's employees who see their job continuity in danger; and the partners of VICENTIN S.A.I.C. that are today shareholders of a company with negative net worth and subjected to the causes and results of the company´s dissolution per article 94, paragraph 5 of the LGS.

7.5.9.2. Subjective type: Intention to defraud

The malice in the conduct is registered in all of the mechanisms of abuse of the legal personality used to cover up the typical conduct. Such mechanisms, due to the thoughtful complexity of their implementation and their persistence over time, are not likely to occur by chance or by accident.

The fraud in the execution (which the type requires) is credited in the implementation of each one of the successive and concatenated acts, technically sophisticated, that make up the criminal conduct:in this case, the sequence of acts of transfer of 16.67 percent from VICENTÍN Paraguay, passing it to VICENTÍN, to reach RENAISCO, while at the same time, an agreement is made to change the Statute and ensure control of RENOVA to GLENCORE through its subsidiaries VITERRA and RENAISCO. Along the way, VICENTIN "disappears" the 122.7 million dollars collected in payments to companies of its own or associated group.

Such actions deployed are not susceptible to be the product of chance, incompetence, negligence, or imprudence. There is a complex planned machination behind them. Planned machination whose deployment extends to the present, as recorded in the preventive contest process by the rebellious conduct of the VICENTIN board of directors. The board's proposal in the preventive agreement to avoid the bankruptcyhas given privileges and advantages to GLENCORE to take over RENOVA to the detriment and exclusion of the remaining creditors, which may comprise aviolation of the governing principles of preventive contests,includingpars *condition creditorum* and universalism of debtor heritage.

The will to abuse of law is continuous. In its presentation to the legal process, and despite having specialized professional advice (it could not allege error or ignorance), the VICENTIN board of directors did not disavow any relationship to the some non-core entities, and it did not include these in its latest balance sheet, as required by subsection 3 and paragraph 4 of article 11 of the LCQ. Regarding the latter, after recurring insistence from the judge, the Control Committee and the creditors, the company be lately provide done in October 2020 (it should have done so in February of the same year) signed by a professional who was not the historical auditor of record of the company (which had been the global financial services firm KPMG). The professional could not declare with the required certainty that the data within the balance sheet report was truthful, accurate, and complete as the professional lacked the historical knowledge to do so. The signer himself avers that he is not convinced of the veracity of what he signed.

7.6. Conclusions

The arduous path traveled to determine that the actions of the directors of VICENTÍN were(helped by the necessary participation of GLENCORE), unlawful following our hypothesis. It has required going beyond those shadows projected in the cave that we know as fiction emanating from abuse of legal status. Fiction arguably created to boost trade and the economy, which we do not deny. If we reject the evidence that these fictions were used to isolate the assets of, in many cases, influential subjects from the potentially personally harmful consequences that their actions could have produced, we would ourselves be vulnerable to charges of delusion. If we also ignored the abuse of corporate mechanisms as a common means of committing complex property crimes, we would be further sunk in the deep, dark waters of unawareness of the nature and patterns of order in the political economy imposed by existing institutions arising from and within the hegemonic economic power.

There are other criminal actions that would protect the legal assets injured by the actions of VICENTÍN. We have mentioned scam, abuse of administration, and fraudulent bankruptcy, among others.

The problem posed by fraudulent bankruptcy is that you must wait for the bankruptcy to occur for that unlawful category to be registered, investigated, prosecuted, and punished. It is possible that this will never happen. The judges are afraid to proclaim (in front of society—in public) the company´s downfall and loss of jobs as something other than misfortune. As much as possible, VICENTÍN tries to keep the zombie alive. When bankruptcy is finally declared, many years will have passed and memories will have become vague and forgetful. By then, the proof has evaporated and the goods too. The judicial recovery of assets remains a potentiality and not an actuality. Even more so when we consider that the majority of bankruptcy proceedings in Argentina end in closure due to lack of assets (i.e., not reorganization but liquidation). This means that the process is closed because there is nothing left to distribute among the creditors.

A proper administration could try to protect those who have entrusted the management of their interests and assets to another person. Unfortunately, in the case we are studying, it would not ordinarily include the creditors or the economic order as victims due to the lack of general acceptance of the legal theory with which to remedy the public economic order.

That is why, faced with what we consider a crime of bad development, of macro-social consequences, of the menu of possibilities that the existing repressive legislation gives us, the misdeed that is best applied is that of emptying the company. It is the most encompassing for a network of behaviors that occur in corporate networks, where other companies are not usually victims of the acts, but rather are accomplices to them.

If we still have doubts that the emptying of the company is the appropriate norm, it is enough to refer to the year 2002, when the International Monetary Fund (IMF) pressured Argentina to repeal this legal action from its Penal Code. At that time, the type was typified by article 6 of Law 20,840 and concordant, called "Economic Subversion." The IMF argued that the article affected the "good business climate." We wonder if the IMF understands the meaning of good weather. We did not ask them. We know the meaning. Unfortunately, 6 Article of Law 20,840 was repealed (Página 12, 2002).

However, in an attenuated way and with a lesser scope, the criminal type of company emptying somehow managed to survive in the Argentine digest. Primary criminalization (creation of the punitive norm) has withstood the onslaught of power. But the most difficult remains—secondary criminalization; i.e., the law as applied.

What happens is that "emptying the company" is a behavior that today would serve to give repressive scope to the maneuvers in which GLENCORE was also the protagonist. It emerges as the strong candidate to be the big winner of this giga-scale fraud, acquiring RENOVA at an unfathomable bargain price. The necessary participation of the Anglo-Swiss (art. 45 CP) is undeniable if we analyze the conduct of VICENTÍN from the emptying of the company. Culpability that is diluted if only a simple fraud is charged (art. 172 CP).

Impairments of the public economic order (essentially, knowingly or recklessly causing bad development) need to be approached on a global comprehensive basis. The network of formally related or informally complicit corporate actors (puppets on a string) needed to create, transfer, conceal, and protect economic and financial resources would best be disabled through theorizing and conceiving of it as an international issue. As water may be diverted, financial interests and flows may be also. Sealing off one node / jurisdiction results in a deleterious overflow elsewhere. The remedy for the flight of capital obtained in a race to the bottom is to raise the floor and plug the holes.

The audacity in facing the investigation (being encouraged to put the bell on the GLENCORE cat) will define the scope that the State gives to the protection of the legal rights of its citizens: this is a solvable political issue.

References

ARGUMEDO, R. (Undated). "Naturaleza Jurídica del contrato de Joint Venture", file:///C:/Users/Lenovo/Downloads/Dialnet-NaturalezaJuridicaDelContratoDeJointVenture-5084956.pdf, Accessed May 24, 2021.

BARTOLI, M. (2020). "VICENTÍN: quién es quién en el ranking de los exportadores de granos, harinas y aceites", Clarín, June 6, 2020 https://www.clarin.com/rural/vicentin-ranking-exportadores-granos-harinas-aceites_0_XImK22k99.html, Accessed March 24, 2021.

BINSTEIN, G., et al. (1989). "Alguna notas sobre las Joint Ventures", Tomo La Ley 1989, Buenos Aires, La Ley.

BÖHM, M. (2019). "El delito del mal-desarrollo", Letra: Derecho Penal, N°8, pp 78–116.

CREUS, C. (2007). Derecho Penal Parte Especial (TII), Buenos Aires, Astrea.

D´ALESSIO, A-Director-,(2004).Código Penal: Comentado y Anotado, Buenos Aires, La Ley.

EL CRONISTA. (2012). "Glencore le ganó a Cargill y se quedó con la Canadiense Viterra", https://www.cronista.com/negocios/Glencore-le-gano-a-Cargill-y-se-quedo-con-la-canadiense-Viterra-20120321-0037.html, Accessed October 24, 2022.

GOLDMAN, E. (Undated). Breves notas en torno al delito de desbaratamiento de empresa del artículo 174, incíso 6 del Código Penal, http://www.saij.gob.ar/diego-hernan-goldman-breves-notas-torno-al-delito-desbaratamiento-empresa-articulo-174-inciso-6-codigo-penal-dacf130101/123456789-0abc-defg1010-31fcanirtcod, Accessed October 10, 2022.

HALPERÍN, I. (1998). Sociedades Anónimas, Buenos Aires, Depalma.

ILHARRESCONDO, J. (2008). Delitos Societarios, Buenos Aires, La Ley.

IRIBARNE, A., et al. (2021). "Informe final cuerpo de auditores forenses", VICENTÍN S.A.I.C. S/ Concurso Preventivo, Juzgado Civil y Comercial Segunda Nominación, Reconquista.

LONGONI, M. (2020). "Sin VICENTÍN en la cancha, las grandes cerealeras se repartieron sus negocios y creció la extranjerización", Bichos de Campo, August 12, 2020, https://bichosdecampo.com/sin-vicentin-en-la-cancha-las-grandes-cerealeras-se-repartieron-sus-negocios-y-crecio-la-extranjerizacion/, Accessed March 24, 2021.

MARSILI, M., et al. (2020). Crimen, Complejidad y Economía, Buenos Aires, Osmar Buyatti.

ORTEGA, J. (2021). "La dolarización del comercio granario y su administración en el concurso preventivo: cuando la productividad y el empleo pierden para que gane la especulación", Derechos en Acción, Autumn 2021 pp 115–147, La Plata, UNLP.

PÁGINA 12. (2002). "Dos que cayeron en la trampa conocida" https://www.pagina12.com.ar/diario/elpais/1-4381-2002-04-24.html, Accessed June 13, 2023.

PALACIO LAJE, C. (2004). Vaciamiento de empresas y el proyecto de modificar el artículo 301 del Código Penal, Buenos Aires, La Ley.

TAX JUSTICE NETWORK. (2021). "The state of tax justice 2021. "*Tax Justice Network*, November 16, 2021. https://taxjustice.net/reports/the-state-of-tax-justice-2021/, Accessed March 20, 2022.

TELAM. (2020). Boletín de Economía, June 17, 2020, https://www.telam.com.ar/notas/202006/478053-la-compania-vicentin-informo-sobre-el-destino-de-fondos-por-la-venta-de-parte-de-renova.html, Accessed September16, 2020.

VITERRA 2020 ANNUAL REPORT, https://www.viterra.com/dam/jcr:5e692425-6bda-4cbe-98bc-8d394e62750a/Annual-report-2020-.pdf, accessed October 24, 2022.

An epilogue that should be a prologue

On our tour, we have seen how the financial activities of man seem to unfold extraneous to the laws of economics and agricultural production. In fact, they evolve outside physics and logic. The notions of space-time and the principles of "identity," "non-contradiction," and "excluded third party" do not frame finance as it is conceived today. Presently, legal regulations are insufficient to provide control.

Finance articulates capital in its highest phase and controls relationships between people. It is not a material object; it is a set of institutions that condition and hold the behavior of a group of people. Those who are subjected serve for the benefit of another group of people who subject them. Capital, in other words, is nothing other than power today. It is not something that "you have." It is something that "is exercised."

Within this institutional plexus that is capital, corporations appear as a tool that concentrates, organizes, and shields it from the members of the community. Corporations are not an orthopedic of capital. Corporations are capital perched on a pinnacle unattainable for the rest of society.

The complex network of capital institutions can generate dynamics and channels through which the surpluses produced by the work of a community will flow to other latitudes. Thus, these riches will not take root in the territory and allow the quality of life of those who produced it to improve. On the contrary, they will migrate for the benefit of foreign minorities. Nothing guarantees the countries where these privileged minorities reside that such absorption of foreign surpluses will provide abundance to their population. This is because, at a higher level of capital institutions, tax evasions and asset flights continue to persist; the tax havens appear.

All these outlined elements conspire against the possibilities of territorial development with social and environmental equity of the society that suffers from them. Is this possibility of development, which is a holistic concept, a legal asset protected bylaw? Not in an integrated and comprehensive way. There are norms that protect the right to development, but they do so in an uncoordinated, subsidiary, accessory, and accidental way. Within this disorganized set, and in what corresponds to criminal law, conduct that threatens development is punished only in some of its aspects. The complexity of the same and the aspersion of the victims are obstacles for a rational and systematic process of which behaviors are punishable, assuming the dominant tools of liberal criminal law as implemented currently. Added to the phenomenon is the crystallizing and strengthening feature of the *status quo* functioning *as* protector of capitalized people under rules of law along with the conservative dogma of those who must interpret and apply it.

The conjunction of these extremes explains in a scientific and impersonal way what occurred in the consummation and impunity of the transnational fraud of the agro-export company VICENTÍN, a company that grew at the expense of State aid and later became a tool for discharging the surplus produced in the territory through dollarization and asset flight. It was achieved by making use (and abuse) of corporate instruments. The search for extraordinary and fast profitability led the firm to violate even the rules of the game that were clearly favorable to it, beginning to operate more as a capital manager than as an agribusiness company. Under that scenario, it fell into the orbit of transnational capital.

The gravitating GLENCORE became an unequal and absorbing ally of VICENTÍN. In this context of financial management that is separate from productivity, VICENTÍN indebtedness ceases to be a requirement for productive investment, transmuting into a means for speculative accumulation. To maintain this financialized and leveraged dynamic, the firm becomes a holding company with a rhizomatic structure. What follows is a Ponzi scheme that, like all of them, is short-lived. Analogous to a partner taking advantage of its partner's death, GLENCORE, which had already become a black hole, swallowed the most valuable assets of the disgraced VICENTÍN.

In VICENTÍN's history, we find elements that we mention in this work including autonomous finances of physics and logic and capital as a tool to control the conduct of others. Corporate vehicles are used as cover-ups to shield illegitimate appropriations. Migration of the surplus occurs from the territories that produce it. Moreover, there is insufficient legal and political protection of the right to development. These are the transversal stigmas to the VICENTÍN question.

Presently, the VICENTÍN case is open-ended. However, unless an event occurs that is expected only by those of us who believe that the rule of law is a constant and perpetual algorithmic process giving each his/her just deserts, everything seems to be moving toward a capture (at fire-sale auction price or free) of the most valuable assets of the Argentine agricultural exporter into the hands of transnational capital. The victims will be the creditors of VICENTÍN, the farmers who use its manufacturing capacity, and its workers and shareholders who contributed effort and capital in good faith. The economy of the area and that of the entire country will see its export apparatus more foreignized, increasing the problems of external restriction with which it is already familiar.

What would be a corrective proposal to avoid similar ravages in the future?

The creation of new rules does not seem to be the avenue forward. Argentina already has laws that are sufficient to avoid these damages. They were dispersed without an integrating behavioral thread, disjointed and lacking in cooperation and exchange of information with foreign states, and perhaps without a robust doctrinal and jurisprudential foundation for its application. We understand that the primary legal criminalization of behaviors (i.e., the rule of law as designed) was not enough to prevent plunder, though perhaps the legal apparatus could have been applied to mitigate the damage caused by them. Why didn't Argentina act quickly?

Perhaps, the problem is secondary criminalization (i.e., the rule of law as operationalized). This is the responsibility of state agencies that should impartially apply the law to effectuate the goals and objectives of the rule of law as designed. The ineffectiveness in the use of the norm for the protection of injured legal rights, in this instance, did not come from the lack of training of public officials. Nor of their scarcity in number. Nor of the notable deficiencies in infrastructure, facilities, materials, equipment, and technology.

The ineffectiveness of the State to tackle the issues is a question of managerialism within the public sphere. It would be useful to advance in a greater legal organization the doctrinal and jurisprudential development, as necessary, to promote the training of state personnel, provisioning them with adequate equipment to combat these predatory behaviors. We believe, however, that we would not attack the root of the problem with such a proposal and redevelopment of the criminal justice order. What to do?

In our experience, the damage that a case like VICENTÍN causes does not stop with its own implosion and reallocation of capital and assets. Moreover, it is not the scarce normative development or deficiencies in personnel and equipment of the state agencies; or of the judicial power; or of the public prosecutor's office; or even of executive power. The main factor in the failure to protect the assets of the majority is evidenced by an element that goes beyond ideology; there are cultural reasons and explanations:

1. Firstly, traceable to the government.
2. Secondly, traceable to career state officials.
3. Thirdly, traceable to hegemony or mimesis of a large part of the population.

Those who had the institutional responsibility of administering justice and even the very victims of these illegal and illegitimate actions, paradoxically sympathize with the privileges of the large private corporations. This goes beyond specific venalities, directed canonries, possible bribes, fear of reprisals, or hidden interests that are embedded in the matter. The root does not stop there: the problem is essentially cultural.

The Argentine State attempted an intervention through decree 522 of June 9, 2020, momentarily taking control of VICENTÍN, with the intention of preventing the continuation of the fraud and the blurring of its rights to specific assets. All in the safeguard of the creditors (among them the public banks); of the workers, and of the national economy. A media counterattack from the party of concentrated-extractive economic interests ensued, which provoked a collective proto-psychosis. The government was portrayed as a usurper, with the intention of violating all private property, however depleted the estate may be. Everything was under threat from their expropriating communism, which would not hesitate to confiscate even the two-room apartment of the poorest neighbor. This was conjugated with a judge of the preventive contest, friendly with the corporations like most of the commercial judges and condescending to the point of malfeasance with VICENTÍN. A precautionary measure ordered by the judge against the government and the deposing furies of some hegemonized (and partisan) middle-class groups were enough to break the will of the executive power. The government, on July 31, 2020, repealed the intervention; it withdrew from the matter: the Pied Piper of Hamelin heralded the march, demonstrating the resultant impotence of public power as the other state agencies and political leaders followed in flight.

We have talked to as many involved actors as possible from all levels of government. We have not collected any clues of an overwhelming, irresistible international corporate pressure that has achieved such a swift defection. Instead of this, we have perceived signs of lack of conviction to defend the general welfare. Also, we have witnessed extreme obsequiousness toward transnational capital, in no way reciprocated by any concession. Transversal and always present, we notice an inferiority complex, reverential fear, and a foolish admiration for the presumed power of the corporate world. This fact pattern reflects a cultural issue that, abandoning the ideological, is now directly introduced into the world of the mythological.

Max Weber considered that the substratum of Protestant religiosity, with its praise of hard work and ascetic savings to accumulate wealth (seeing in this something ethical and not greedy hoarding) was a platform of values on which capitalism perched for its expansion. Walter Benjamin disagrees. For him, capitalism does not use Protestantism. It directly replaces it as a religion. Capitalism has its own answers to satisfy the needs for rewards, torments, expiations, identities, guilt, and salvations that men and women previously sought in the religious story. Now they do it in capitalism. Thus, capitalism is essentially a religious phenomenon.

Religion is a cultural fact, with institutions as the superstructure of culture.

Our optimistic view is based on precisely that. We do not believe that there is an insurmountable question of the correlation of material forces where the dominant forces are inexorably impregnable. Their main asset is immaterial: culture. A study of history demonstrates how quickly cultures may change.

Feminist struggles have made advances in equality. The deconstruction of patriarchal cultural paradigms has been one of the tools through which important achievements have been achieved. This deconstruction has later been consolidated in the appearance of new institutions (laws, public agencies, private organizations, habits, customs, etc.) that have brought a little more justice to our society. There are still vast expanses to go. But the essence of the struggles is that they are never complete. The cooperative impulse and instinct motivating these struggles is inexhaustible.

The emancipating struggles (which include the struggle for an impartial and impersonal rule of law) must take place on all cultural fronts. In the macro and in the micro; in the collective; and in the personal: all simultaneously. To the extent that progress is made in such deconstruction, this will be reified in fairer, more protective institutions for men, women, and nature.

In the case of financial capitalism (institutional plexus with traits of patriarchal culture), it is a system rooted in beliefs and superstitions that legitimize the material exploitation of most of humanity to satisfy an incorporeal theory and concept known as profit or economic gain in terms of the monetary value of inputs—a practice creating a god-like objective and methodology almost as cruel as the blood-claimant Huitzilopochtli. Everything under the care and management of a priestly class, the speculative financiers—the experts and management consultants directing, managing, and influencing the operationalizing of profit contagion as a rule of action without alternative. It subsumes the individual; the entity; the enterprise; the government; even the nominally non-profit organizations under the same altar: inputs are to be sacrificed for monetary gain and profit for capital accumulation.

In fact, this professional managerial class (PMC) is comparatively as idle as the one that made up the one chosen by God to rule: Louis XVI. They supervise and control these corporeal inputs—agents and employees for disclosed and undisclosed principals seeking ever greater allocations to their stores of capital. It's, of course, no great mystery why the PMC and the well-capitalized enjoy their prerogative of making and enforcing policies and rules of law. The greater wonder is the subservience and belief systems of the governed. Recognizing that it is acceptable to obey one's betters goes a long way toward explaining the demonstrable willingness of the employees and agents to do as they're instructed to do. It's not shameful to be guided by such meritorious persons.

The PMC governs and guides in conformance with profit maximization. The theories and concepts underlying human conduct enthralled and entranced by the worshiping of increasing capital rest on an unproven, if not ridiculous as observed in practice, myth of meritocracy. As the king could do no wrong and the priests were infallible, the PMC as levers and instruments of the well-capitalized know best. Moreover, this best includes the best of all possible worlds for their subjects, who may toil lifelong without secure means of development.

However, we do not advocate beheading the king but for deconstruction of the cultural mythology.What happened with Huitzilopochtli and Louis XVI was not that long ago either. Just 500 and 300 years ago, respectively. Comparatively, little time since the 200,000 years that men and women have existed on this planet. We do not have much time to get rid of this other new superstition either, if we want to continue here a few more years.

Bibliography

AHMED NABIR, et al. (2022). "Las desigualdades matan", *OXFAM*, https://oxamilibrary.openrepository.com/bitstream/handle/10546/621341/bp-inequality-kills-170122-es.pdf;jsessionid=0DB2EE38FF5CC642C7493A0DB66F187C?sequence=5, Accessed January 1, 2022.

ALLEN-MILLS, T. (2008). "Congo sapped of riches as Denis menaces Boulevard Saint-Germain" *The Australian*, June 17 2008, https://web.archive.org/web/20091014162011/http://www.theaustralian.news.com.au/story/0,,23873480-643,00.html, Accessed June 14, 2021.

ALTHUSSER, L. (2003). Ideología y aparatos ideológicos del Estado. Freud y Lacan. Buenos Aires, Nueva Visión.

AMMANN, D. (2009). The King of oil, New York, St. Martin's Press.

ARELLANO, L. (2021). Argentina sangra por las barrancas del Paraná, Buenos Aires, Ágora.

ARELOVICH, S. (2020). "Informe individual de auditoría" en la causa *VICENTÍN S.A.I.C. S/ Concurso Preventivo.* Juzgado Civil y Comercial Segunda Nominación, Reconquista.

ARGUMEDO, R. (Undated). "Naturaleza Jurídica del contrato de *Joint Venture*", file:///C:/Users/Lenovo/Downloads/Dialnet-NaturalezaJuridicaDelContratoDeJointVenture-5084956.pdf, AccessedMay 24, 2021.

BARBERÍA, M. (2020). Los argentinos tienen USD 130.000 millones en el país: más de 4 veces el valor de todos los pesos que circulan en la economía, *Infobae*, March 15, 2020 https://www.infobae.com/economia/2020/03/15/los-argentinos-tienen-usd-130000-millones-en-el-pais-mas-de-4-veces-el-valor-de-todos-los-pesos-que-circulan-en-la-economia/, Accessed January 20, 2022.

BARNICHON, R., et al. (2018). The Financial Crisis at 10: Will We Ever Recover? *FRBSF Economic Letter*, August 13, 2018, https://www.frbsf.org/economic-research/publications/economic-letter/2018/august/financial-crisis-at-10-years-will-we-ever-recover/, Accessed January 11, 2022.

BARTOLI, M. (2020). "VICENTÍN: quién es quién en el ranking de los exportadores de granos, harinas y aceites", *Clarín*, June 6, 2020https://www.clarin.com/rural/vicentin-ranking-exportadores-granos-harinas-aceites_0_XImK22k99.html, Accessed March 24, 2021.

BASUALDO, E. and KHAVISE, M. (1994). "La Propiedad Rural en la Provincia de Buenos Aires"*en* Desarrollo Económico, 34–134.

BASUALDO, E. (2000). "Fuga de capitales y endeudamiento externo en la argentina", *Realidad Económica* N°173, Buenos Aires.

BASUALDO, E., et al. (2002). "Las transferencias de recursos a la cúpula económica durante la presidencia Duhalde" en *Revista Realidad Económica* Número 186 - 16 febrero al 31 de marzo de 2002, Buenos Aires.

BASUALDO, E. -Director- (2018). Endeudar y fugar, Buenos Aires, SXXI.

BASUALDO, E. (2021)."Análisis de los patrones de acumulación en Argentina" [Conference] *Maestría Economía Política Argentina*, FLACSO, Buenos Aires, August 17.

BENJAMÍN, W. (2016). "El capitalismo como religión", *Revista Katay*, http://sedici.unlp.edu.ar/handle/10915/127662, Accessed April 17, 2022.

BINSTEIN, G., et al. (1989). "Alguna notas sobre las *Joint Ventures*", *Tomo La Ley 1989*, Buenos Aires, La Ley.

BÖHM, M. (2019). "El delito del mal-desarrollo", *Letra: Derecho Penal*, N°8, pp 78–116.

BOURDIEU, P. (2008). El sentido práctico, Buenos Aires, Siglo XXI.

BOURDIEU, P., et al. (2018). La Reproducción. Elementos para una teoría del sistema educativo, Buenos Aires, Siglo XXI.

CAFIERO, M. and LLORENS, J. (2002). *La Argentina Robada*, Buenos Aires, Ediciones Macchi.

CALZADA, J., et al. (2018). "El 43% de las exportaciones fueron granos, harinas, aceites y otros subproductos", *Informativo semanal*– N° 1846 – February 9, 2018, Rosario, BCR.

CÁRCOVA, C., et al. (2012). "Análisis funcional del Derecho", *Las Teorías Jurídicas Post Positivistas*, Buenos Aires, Abeledo-Perrot.

CARDOSO, F., et al. (1999). Dependencia y Desarrollo en América Latina, Buenos Aires, Siglo XXI.

CASPARRINO, C., et al. (2007). La Fuga de Capitales, Historia, Presente y Perspectivas. CEFID-AR, Workingpaper N°14, Buenos Aires, CEFID-AR.

CHIRINO, J. (2020). "La ´Propiedad Privada` de VICENTÍN", *El Diario del Centro del País*, June 28, 2020, https://www.eldiariocba.com.ar/cultura/2020/6/28/la-propiedad-privada-de-vicentin-23570.html, Accessed August 1, 2021.

CHOMSKY, N., et al. (1988). Manufacturing Consent. The political Economy of The Mass Media, New York City, Pantheon Books.

COHEN, ADAM C. (2016). "Harvard'seugenics era."*Harvard Magazine*, March-April 2016. https://www.harvardmagazine.com/2016/03/harvards-eugenics-era,Accessed March 27, 2022.

CONSTITUTION ANNOTATED. (Undated). "Article I, Section 8, Clause 5."https://constitution.congress.gov/browse/essay/artI-S8-C5-1/ALDE_00001066/, Accessed March 26, 2022.

COX, B., et al. (2011). GLENCORE I.P.O Mimics Blacksonte an Draws Skeptics, The New York Times, May 3, 2011, https://www.nytimes.com/2011/05/04/business/04views.html, Accessed June 14, 2021.

CREUS, C. (2007). Derecho Penal Parte Especial (TII), Buenos Aires, Astrea.

D´ALESSIO, A-Director-,(2004). Código Penal: Comentado y Anotado, Buenos Aires, La Ley.

DAMHA NAJJAR, C. (2016). El levantamiento del velo corporativo en delitos ejecutados a través de la implementación de estructuras societarias complejas, *Tesis de Grado*, San José, Universidad de Costa Rica.

DELEUZE, G. y GUATTARI, F. (1998). El Anti Edipo, Barcelona, Paidós.

DI YENNO, F.,et al. (2021). "Ranking de exportación de empresas agroindustriales según ventas en la campaña 2020/21", *Informativo Semanal*, August27, BCR.

DOBB, M. (1938). Introducción a la Economía, México. FCE.

DOBSON, J. (1991). El abuso de la personalidad jurídica, Buenos Aires, De Palma.

DUNCKEL, M. (2013). Small, medium, large-Does farm size really matter?*Michigan State University Extension*, November14, 2013, https://www.canr.msu.edu/news/small_medium_large_does_farm_size_really_matter, Accessed April 11, 2021.

EL CRONISTA. (2012). "Glencore le ganó a Cargill y se quedó con la Canadiense Viterra", https://www.cronista.com/negocios/Glencore-le-gano-a-Cargill-y-se-quedo-con-la-canadiense-Viterra-20120321-0037.html, Accessed October 24, 2022.

ESCUDÉ, C. (2006). *Festival de Licuaciones*. Buenos Aires, Lumiere.

FAN, S., et al. (2018). "Quantifying the Cost and Benefits of Ending Hunger and Undernutrition", *IFPRI*, February, 2018, http://ebrary.ifpri.org/utils/getfile/collection/p15738coll2/id/132266/filename/132477.pdf,, Accessed January 11, 2022.

FELDMAN, G. (2021). Nunca fuimos Vicentín, Rosario, Editorial Fundación Ross.

FORBES. (2021). "Global 2000, World's Largest Public Companies"*Forbes*, May 13, 2021, https://www.forbes.com/lists/global2000/#1941e9b15ac0, Accessed June 14, 2021.

FORD, L. (2011). "Mining firm under fire over tax payments in Zambia", *The Guardian*, April 15, 2011, https://www.theguardian.com/global-development/2011/apr/15/mining-firm-tax-payments-zambia, Accessed June 14, 2021.

FOUCAULT, M. (1986). La verdad y las formas jurídicas, 1a conferencia, México, Gedisa.

FOUCAULT, M. (1991). Microfísica del poder, Madrid, Ediciones de La Piqueta.
FOUCAULT, M. (1996) .Vigilar y Castigar, Madrid, Siglo XXI.
FOUCAULT, M. (2013). El orden del discurso, México, Tusquets.
GAGGERO, A., et al. (2014). Restricción Eterna, Buenos Aires, Crisis.
GAGGERO, A., et al. (2020). "El Proceso de vaciamiento de VICENTÍN S.A.I.C., Un análisis reciente de las transformaciones de su estructura corporativa, la dinámica financiera y el intercambio comercial", *Informe final*, Buenos Aires, BNA.
GANOS, T. (2019). "World's best tax haven: the United States."*Forbes*, September 19, 2019. https://www.forbes.com/sites/toddganos/2019/09/19/worlds-best-tax-haven-the-united-states/?sh=55b7ceac4049, Accessed March 21, 2022.
GASPAR, V., et al. (2021). Global Debt Reaches a Record $226 Trillion, December 15, 2021, 15 https://blogs.imf.org/2021/12/15/global-debt-reaches-a-record-226-trillion/, Accessed January 5, 2020.
GLYN, A. (2006). "Marx's reserve army of labour is about to go global."*Guardian*, April 4, 2006. https://www.theguardian.com/commentisfree/2006/apr/05/comment.businesscomment, Accessed March 21, 2022.
GOLDMAN, E. (Undated).Breves notas en torno al delito de desbaratamiento de empresa del artículo 174, incíso 6 del Código Penal, http://www.saij.gob.ar/diego-hernan-goldman-breves-notas-torno-al-delito-desbaratamiento-empresa-articulo-174-inciso-6-codigo-penal-dacf130101/123456789-0abc-defg1010-31fcanirtcod, Accessed October 10, 2022.
GOLDSTEIN, M.andENRICH, D. (2022). "How one oligarch used shell companies and Wall Street ties to invest in the U.S."*New York Times*, March 21, 2022. https://www.nytimes.com/2022/03/21/business/russia-roman-abramovich-concord.html, Accessed March 22, 2022.
GOMEZ OLIVER, L. and GRANADOS SANCHEZ, R. (2016). "Las cuatro grandesempresas comercializadoras y los precios internacionales de losalimentos". *Economía Informa*. UNAM. México D.F, 400, 24–38.
GRAMSCI, A. (1981). Cuadernos de la Cárcel, México D F, Ediciones.
GRASMCI, A. (2003). Notas Sobre Maquiavelo: sobre la política y sobre el Estado moderno, Buenos Aires, Nueva Visión Argentina.
GRAÑA, J., et al. (2011). "Producción de la riqueza social y su distribución: productividad y salarios en Argentina. Medio siglo en perspectiva latinoamericana e internacional", Cuestiones de sociología, N°7, La Plata, UNLP.
GRONDONA, V. (2014). "Fuga de Capitales IV. Argentina, 2014. La Manipulación de los Precios de Transferencia".*Woorkingpaper*N°58. Buenos Aires, CEFID-AR.
GRONDONA, V.,et al. (2015). "Estimación de los precios de transferencia. El caso del complejo sojero". *Working paper*, N°71. Buenos Aires. CEFID-AR.
GRONDONA, V., et al. (2017). "Transfer Pricing in Argentina 1932–2015", *Working Paper*N°63, January 2017, London, ICTD.
HALPERÍN, I. (1998). Sociedades Anónimas, Buenos Aires, Depalma.
HAMILTON, A., et al. (2015). El Federalista, Madrid, Akal.

HARVARD UNIVERSITY. (2021a). "Financial report fiscal year 2021."https://finance.harvard.edu/files/fad/files/fy21_harvard_financial_report.pdf, Accessed March 15, 2022.

HARVARD UNIVERSITY. (2021b). "Tuition charges."https://registrar.gse.harvard.edu/files/gse-registrar/files/tuition_rates_2020-2021.pdf, Accessed March 15. 2022.

HARVEY, D. (2014). Seventeen contradictions and the end of capitalism. London: Profile Books.

HIDALGO, R. (2012). "Organización Mundial del Comercio: viejos dilemas y nuevos retos", *Revista Cubana de Economía Internacional*, CIEI, N° 1, February, 2012, http://www.rcei.uh.cu, Accessed April 19, 2022.

HILFERDING, R. (1963). El Capital Financiero, Madrid, Tecnos.

HOBBES, T. (2017). Leviatán, o la materia, forma y poder de una república eclesiástica y civil. México, FCE.

ICIJ-International Consortium of Investigative. (2017). "Paradise Papers", https://www.icij.org/investigations/paradise-papers/, Accessed June 14, 2021.

ICIJ-International Consortium of Investigative. (2020). "FinCen Files", https://www.icij.org/investigations/fincen-files/, Accessed June 14, 2021.

ICO SERVICES. (2017). "USA: the strongest tax haven in the world."*ICO Services*, July 11, 2017. https://medium.com/@icoservices/usa-the-strongest-tax-haven-in-the-world-6d7cef7ccedb, Accessed March 21, 2022.

ILHARRESCONDO, J. (2008). Delitos Societarios, Buenos Aires, La Ley.

INDEC-Instituto Nacional de Estadísticas y Censos. (2020). "Comercio Exterior", Vol. 5, N°4https://www.indec.gob.ar/uploads/informesdeprensa/complejos_03_21311B84F340.pdf, Accessed June 26, 2021.

INDEC-Instituto Nacional de Estadísticas y Censos. (2021). "Comercio Exterior", Vol.5, N°14, https://www.indec.gob.ar/uploads/informesdeprensa/ica_12_20B2C4146816.pdf, Accessed January 6, 2022.

INDEC -Instituto Nacional de Estadísticas y Censos. (2021). "Balanza de Pagos, posición de inversión internacional y deuda externa", *Informe Técnico*, Buenos Aires, INDEC.

IRIBARNE, A., et al. (2021). "Informe final cuerpo de auditores forenses", *VICENTÍN S.A.I.C. S/ Concurso Preventivo,* Juzgado Civil y Comercial Segunda Nominación, Reconquista.

JÄGER, H. (1989). Makrokriminalität: Studien zur Kriminalität kollektiver, Gewalt, Frankfurt, Suhrkamp.

JOHNSON, J. (2022). "'Their inflation strategy is working': corporate profits surged to record high in 2021."*Common Dreams,* March 31, 2022. https://www.commondreams.org/news/2022/03/31/their-inflation-strategy-working-corporate-profits-soared-record-high-2021, Accessed March 31, 2022.

JUNYENT BAS, F. and RICHARD, E. (2009). "Acerca de la Persona Jurídica a propósito de los debates sobre su conceptualización y otros aspectos derivados de ello". V Congreso de Derecho Civil, Córdoba (Argentina).

KALECKI, M. (1956). Teoría de la dinámica económica: ensayo sobre los movimientos cíclicos ya largo plazo de la economía capitalista, México DF, FCE.

KEYNES, J. (2001). Teoría general de la ocupación el interés y el dinero, Buenos Aires, FCE.

LACLAU, E. (2009). La razón populista, Buenos Aires, FCE.

LEGAL INFORMATION INSTITUTE. (Undated). "Article 1, Section 8, Clause 1."https://www.law.cornell.edu/constitution-conan/article-1/section-8/clause-1/spending-power, AccessedMarch 26, 2022.

LENIN, V. (2000). El Imperialismo, fase superior del capitalismo, Buenos Aires, Aguilar Taurus Alfaguara.

LONGONI, M. (2020). "Sin VICENTÍN en la cancha, las grandes cerealeras se repartieron sus negocios y creció la extranjerización", *Bichos de Campo*, August 12, 2020, https://bichosdecampo.com/sin-vicentin-en-la-cancha-las-grandes-cerealeras-se-repartieron-sus-negocios-y-crecio-la-extranjerizacion/, Accessed March 24, 2021.

MACÍAS, A. (2017). El colapso del capitalismo tecnológico, Madrid, Escolar y Mayo.

MARSILI, M., et al. (2020). Crimen, Complejidad y Economía, Buenos Aires, Osmar Buyatti.

MARTINEZ-GALIANA, X. (2019). "Una nueva investigación por sospechas de soborno hunde GLENCORE en la bolsa", *El Economista*, December 5, 2019,https://www.eleconomista.es/mercados-cotizaciones/noticias/10239990/12/19/Una-nueva-investigacion-por-sospechas-de-soborno-hunde-a-GLENCORE-en-bolsa.html, Accessed May 14, 2021.

MARX, C.and ENGELS, F. (2000). Manifiesto Comunista, Buenos Aires, El Aleph.com.

MARX, K. (2017). El Capital, Madrid, Siglo XXI.

MAXIMINO, M. (2014). "The influence of elites, interest groups and average voters on American politics."*Journalist's Resource*, November 14, 2014. https://journalistsresource.org/politics-and-government/the-influence-of-elites-interest-groups-and-average-voters-on-american-politics/, Accessed March 27, 2022.

MON, A., et al. (2020). "FinCEN Files: operaciones millonarias entre GLENCORE y VICENTÍN quedaron en la mira de Estados Unidos", *La Nación*, September 17, 2020, https://www.lanacion.com.ar/politica/fincen-files-operaciones-millonarias-GLENCORE-vicentin-quedaron-nid2453165/, Accessed May 17, 2021.

MONTESQUIEU, C. (1906). El Espíritu de las Leyes, Madrid, Victoriano Suarez.

MORGAN, D. (1983). *Los Traficantes de Granos*, Buenos Aires, Editorial Abril.

MOSHINSKY, B. (2015). "The four- decade story of GLENCORE´s rise and fall"*Insider*, October 7, 2015, https://www.businessinsider.com/glencores-history-and-what-happened-to-the-company-2015-10,Accessed May 28, 2021.

MUIÑO, G. (2022). "Mitos y verdades", El Cohete a la Luna, April 3, 2022, https://www.elcohetealaluna.com/mitos-y-verdades/, Accessed April8, 2022.

NEEM, JOHANN N. (2022). "The university in ruins."*Chronicle of Higher Education,* March 21, 2022. https://www.chronicle.com/article/the-university-in-ruins?utm_source=Iterable&utm_medium=email&utm_campaign=campaign_3932482_nl_Academe-Today_date_20220323&cid=at&source=ams&sourceid=&cid2=gen_login_refresh, AccessedMarch 23, 2022.

NIETZSCHE, F. (2006). Sobre la verdad y mentira en sentido extra moral. Madrid, Tecnos.

NISSEN, A. (2010). Ley de sociedades comerciales, Buenos Aires, Astrea.

OGLIETTI, G., et al. (2022). Argentina, tan rica afuera como pobre adentro, celag.org, April 7, 2022, https://www.celag.org/argentina-tan-rica-afuera-como-pobre-adentro/, Accessed April 11, 2022.

Organisation for Economic Co-operation and Development. (2001). "Behind the Corporate Veil: Using corporate entities for illicit purposes", Edited by OECD Publications Service, 2001, https://www.oecd.org/corporate/ca/43703185.pdf, Accessed October 21, 2022.

ORGANIZACIÓN MUNDIAL DEL COMERCIO. (2009). "Estadísticas del comercio internacional", https://www.wto.org/spanish/res_s/statis_s/its2009_s/its09_toc_s.htm, AccessedApril 8, 2017.

ORELLANO, L. (2020). Argentina sangra, Buenos Aires, Ágora.

ORTEGA, J. (2018). "Apropiación del excedente agroalimentario generado en el territorio: El caso Cargill en Argentina", *Tesis de Doctorado,* Madrid, Universidad Complutense de Madrid.

ORTEGA, J. (2021). "La dolarización del comercio granario y su administración en el concurso preventivo: cuando la productividad y el empleo pierden para que gane la especulación", *Derechos en Acción,* Autumn 2021 pp 115–147, La Plata, UNLP.

OSORIO, J. (2015). "Teoría de la Dependencia Hoy" [Conferencia], *Facultad de Ciencias Sociales, Universidad de Chile,* Santiago de Chile, September 2, 2015.

OTAEGUI, J. (1978). Invalidez de actos societarios, Buenos Aires, Depalma.

PÁGINA 12, (2002), "Dos que cayeron en la trampa conocida" https://www.pagina12.com.ar/diario/elpais/1-4381-2002-04-24.html, Accessed June 13, 2023.

PALACIOLAJE, C. (2004). Vaciamiento de empresas y el proyecto de modificar el artículo 301 del Código Penal, Buenos Aires, La Ley.

PANTLAND, W. (2018). "GLENCORE, enorme y despiadada empresa de explotación de materias primas".*Informe especial,* April 25, 2018, Industria ALL Global Unión, http://www.industriall-union.org/es/informe-especial-GLENCORE-enorme-y-despiadada-empresa-de-explotacion-de-materias-primas, Accessed June 14, 2021.

PARRAMORE, L. (2022). "Our economic system is making us mentally ill."*Institute for New Economic Thinking,* March 18, 2022. https://www.ineteconomics.org/perspectives/blog/our-economic-system-is-making-us-mentally-ill, Accessed March 19, 2022.

PAWLICZEK, A., et al. (2021). "A new take on voice: the influence of BlackRock's 'Dear CEO' letters". Rev Account Stud 26, 1088–1136. https://doi.org/10.1007/s11142-021-09603

PEIRANO, M. (14 de agosto 2019). Desarrollo industrial en argentina [Conference] Universidad Nacional de San Martín, San Martín, Argentina.

PIDD, H., et al. (2011). "The rise of GLENCORE, the biggest company you've never heard of",*The Guardian*, May 19, 2011. London.

PIKE, D. (2022). "At what point does a billionaire's greed hurt the rest of us?"*Institute for New Economic Thinking*, March 21, 2022. https://www.ineteconomics.org/perspectives/blog/at-what-point-does-a-billionaires-greed-hurt-the-rest-of-us, AccessedMarch 22, 2022.

PREBISCH, R. (1981). Capitalismo Periférico: Crisis y Transformación. México, FCE.

PRESS, A. (2019). "On the origins of the professional-managerial class: an interview with Barbara Ehrenreich."*Dissent*, October 22, 2019. https://www.dissentmagazine.org/online_articles/on-the-origins-of-the-professional-managerial-class-an-interview-with-barbara-ehrenreich/, Accessed March 27, 2022.

RANKIN, J. (2013). "Marc Rich: controversial commodities trader and former fugitive dies aged 78", *The Guardian*, June 26, 2013, London.

RODRÍGUEZ RODRÍGUEZ, J. (1977). Tratado de Sociedades Mercantiles, Ciudad de México, Editorial Porrúa.

ROSAS, J. (1972). Historia Argentina: Unitarios y federales (1826–1841), Buenos Aires, Editorial Oriente.

ROXIN, C. (1997). Derecho Penal Parte General, Civitas, Madrid.

RUIZ, A. (1986). "La Ilusión de lo Jurídico", Crítica Jurídica, N°4, May, 1986, México, UAP.

SANDEL, M. (2021). "Toppling the myth of meritocracy."*The Harvard Gazette*, January 5, 2021. https://news.harvard.edu/gazette/story/2021/01/the-myth-of-meritocracy-according-to-michael-sandel/, Accessed March 20, 2022.

SCALABRINI ORTIZ, R. (2014). Política Británica en el Rio de la Plata, Buenos Aires, Fabro.

SEGAL, P. (2016). The art of fact investigation.New York: Ignaz Press.

SHARFT, M., et al. (2010). "Is law fare worth defining?" in Report of The Cleveland Experts, Meeting, Cleveland.

SHAXSON, N. (2013). Las Islas del Tesoro, México DF, FCE.

SIGEN. (2020). "Auditoría de corte como consecuencia de la Intervención dispuesta por el DNU N° 522/20",*SIGEN*, June, 2020, Buenos Aires, Sindicatura General de la Nación.

SNEEP. (2020). "Informe Nacional 2020", https://www.argentina.gob.ar/justicia/politicacriminal/estadisticas-e-informes/sneep-2020, Accessed June 19, 2023.

SUTHERLAND, E. (1949). El delito de cuello blanco, Buenos Aires, Editorial B de F.

STANDING, G. (2017). The corruption of capitalism, Biteback Publishin, London.

STIGLITZ, J. (2002). El malestar en la globalización, Buenos Aires, Santillana-Taurus.

STRADA, J., et al. (Undated). "La producción de soja en Argentina: causas e impactos de su expansión", *Centro Cultural de la Cooperación Floreal Gorini*, https://www.centrocultural.coop/revista/23/la-produccion-de-soja-en-argentina-causas-e-impactos-de-su-expansion, Accessed June 27, 2021.

TALLEY, I. (2022). "Clandestine finance system helped Iran withstand sanctions crash, documents show."*Wall Street Journal*, March 18, 2022. https://www.wsj.com/articles/clandestine-finance-system-helped-iran-withstand-sanctions-crush-documents-show-11647609741?st=1mccxqpltgsplha&reflink=desktopwebshare_permalink, Accessed March 21, 2022.

TAX JUSTICE NETWORK. (2021). "The state of tax justice 2021."*Tax Justice Network*, November 16, 2021. https://taxjustice.net/reports/the-state-of-tax-justice-2021/, Accessed March 20, 2022.

TELAM. (2020). Boletín de Economía, June 17, 2020, https://www.telam.com.ar/notas/202006/478053-la-compania-vicentin-informo-sobre-el-destino-de-fondos-por-la-venta-de-parte-de-renova.html, Accessed September16, 2020.

TERRÉ, E. (2021). "Argentina embarcó granos por 56,5 millones de toneladas en el 2020, un 6% menos que el año anterior", BCR, https://www.bcr.com.ar/es/mercados/investigacion-y-desarrollo/informativo-semanal/noticias-informativo-semanal/argentina-17, Accessed January 23, 2022.

TOCQUEVILLE, A. (1985). La Democracia en América, México, FCE.

UNITED STATES GOVERNMENT. (2022). "Financial report of the United States government."https://fiscal.treasury.gov/reports-statements/financial-report/current-report.html, Accessed March 15, 2022.

U.S. DEPARTMENT OF THE TREASURY. (2022). "The state of labor market competition."*U.S. Department of the Treasury*, March 7, 2022. https://home.treasury.gov/system/files/136/State-of-Labor-Market-Competition-2022.pdf, AccessedMarch 26, 2022.

U.S. INTERNAL REVENUE SERVICE. (2022). "Donor-advised funds."*Internal Revenue Service*, January 21, 2022. https://www.irs.gov/charities-non-profits/charitable-organizations/donor-advised-funds, Accessed March 28, 2022.

VALLI, P. (2020). "Para la nueva gestión, hubo fraude en el crédito del Banco Nación a VICENTÍN", *Perfil*, January 25, 2020,https://www.perfil.com/noticias/politica/para-la-nueva-gestion-hubo-fraude-en-el-credito-del-banco-nacion-a-vicentin.phtml, Accessed August 1, 2021.

VERBITSKY, H. (2008). "Radiografía de la pampa", *Pagina 12*, June 15, 2008, https://www.pagina12.com.ar/diario/elpais/1-106061-2008-06-15.html, AccessedApril 5, 2021.

VON LISZT, F. (1999). Tratado de Derecho Penal, Madrid, Reus.

WEBER, M. (2002). Economía y Sociedad, Madrid, FCE.

WEBER, M. (2015). La ética protestante y el espíritu del capitalismo, Barcelona, Brontes.

ZAFFARONI, R., et al. (2000). Derecho Penal Parte General, Buenos Aires, Ediar.

ZUCMAN, G. (2015). La riqueza Escondida de las Naciones, Madrid, Siglo Veintiuno Editores.

Index